Contents

A GREAT RUSSIA

A GREAT RUSSIA

Russia and the Triple Entente, 1905 to 1914

Fiona K. Tomaszewski

Westport, Connecticut
London

Library of Congress Cataloging-in-Publication Data

Tomaszewski, Fiona K., 1963–
   A great Russia : Russia and the Triple Entente, 1905–1914 / Fiona K.
Tomaszewski.
     p. cm.
   Includes bibliographical references and index.
   ISBN 0–275–97366–2 (alk. paper)
   1. Russia—Politics and government—1894–1917. 2. Triple Entente, 1907.
I. Title.
DK262.T63   2002
327.47041′09′041—dc21   2001053083

British Library Cataloguing in Publication Data is available.

Library of Congress Catalog Card Number: 2001053083
ISBN: 0–275–97366–2

First published in 2002

Praeger Publishers, 88 Post Road West, Westport, CT 06881
An imprint of Greenwood Publishing Group, Inc.
www.praeger.com

Printed in the United States of America

The paper used in this book complies with the
Permanent Paper Standard issued by the National
Information Standards Organization (Z39.48–1984).

10 9 8 7 6 5 4 3 2

Copyright Acknowledgments

The author and publisher gratefully acknowledge permission for use of the following
material:

Chapter 2 originally appeared as "Pomp, Circumstance and Realpolitik: The Evolution of
the Triple Entente of Russia, Great Britain and France," in *Jahrbücher für Geschichte
Osteuropas* 47 (1999), pp. 362–80. Used by permission.

Chapter 6 originally appeared as "The Tsarist Regime's Manipulation of Public Opinion in
Great Britain and France, 1906–1914," in *Russian History/Histoire Russe* 24 no. 3 (fall
1997), pp. 279–300. Used by permission.

Introduction

In August 1914, less than a decade after the fiasco of the Russo-Japanese War and the ensuing revolutionary turmoil that threatened to topple the autocracy, tsarist Russia, together with two liberal constitutional states, France and Great Britain, went to war against the German and Austro-Hungarian empires. The epic conflict of the Great War, the first total war in history, destroyed the Romanov, the Hohenzollern, and the Habsburg empires and thereby the imperial order that had dominated east-central Europe for centuries. The Triple Entente of liberal Great Britain, republican France, and autocratic Russia, was an unusual diplomatic partnership, not only in light of recent Russo-German-Austrian cooperation in the form of the Dreikaiserbund, formed in 1873 under the auspices of Otto von Bismarck, but also given the lack of common European interests and competing Anglo-Russian and Anglo-French imperial claims. This book is an examination of the attitudes of the Russian government and bureaucracy toward France and Great Britain from 1905 to the outbreak of war in 1914. Many of the contradictions and tensions in late imperial Russian society, as it approached the abyss of World War I, are brought into focus; so also is the complex interplay between foreign and domestic policy. The book helps fill a gap in the study of imperial Russia by focusing on Nicholas II's embattled government and its attempts to survive, rather than the more frequently discussed revolutionary movements, opposition parties, and the press.[1]

Much has been written about the origins of World War I and the alliance system,[2] but comparatively little research has been done on the Russian perspective. This lacuna has, in large part, been caused by restricted access to Russian archives under the old Soviet regime but is also partly a result of a cold war vision of a divided Europe that has distorted recent scholarship. Our modern notion of a divided Europe is antithetical to the reality of pre-1914 Europe. Russia was an integral part of Europe and the European-state system prior to 1914. Russia viewed itself as a European great power, acted as such, and was regarded by the rest of Europe in a similar fashion. The recent opening of Russian archives to Western researchers has made it possible to examine the Triple Entente from the Russian perspective and thereby correct stereotypes that for too long have dominated our analysis of Russian foreign policy. An examination of official Russian attitudes toward Britain and France based largely on Russian archival sources will help correct the one-sided interpretation of the Triple Entente and the international scene in pre-1914 Europe that has dominated the debate until now. An understanding of Russian foreign policy is critical to an understanding of Russian history given the peculiar role of the Russian state and the fact that the imperial regime's raison d'être was a successful foreign policy. The history of Russia's foreign policy, moreover, needs to be reintegrated into our understanding of European history. This book helps redress the balance and fills in a serious gap in the understanding of both imperial Russian foreign policy on the eve of World War I and the nature of the Triple Entente.

D.C.B. Lieven has argued that in the prewar years the Russian imperial government system and other internal political factors influenced Russian foreign policy. He did not conclude, however, as did Fritz Fischer about Wilhelmine Germany, that the Russian elites sought war to consolidate their power and system of rule at home.[3] Nevertheless, the link between Russian *aussenpolitik* and *innenpolitik* existed. This book examines this relationship in some detail. Dietrich Geyer, in his important study of Russian imperialism, maintained that Russian expansion was an expression of economic weakness, not strength, and was caused in part by a compensatory psychological need at least to appear to be a great power.[4] He also argued that the Russian political elites had no reason to desire a European war in July 1914, and that they did not seek a preventive war.[5] The conclusions of this present study complement and help to expand the arguments of Lieven and Geyer.

It was not until the eighteenth century that there was a general turning by the Russian state and nobility toward Europe, when Peter I forced Russia on a path of Europeanization. Beginning with Peter the Great and ending with Witte and Stolypin, political leaders and high officials had attempted to use Western methods to adapt Russian society to the modern world. Many of the intelligentsia, although alienated from the regime and wielding no real power, also ardently desired that Russia should follow the Western political path.[6] In the Westerner/Slavophile debate, Russia was seen as either unique or as a backward section of Europe, in the latter case "a rung behind on a single evolutionary ladder."[7] In fact, at the turn of the century, Russia was a "developing society." Capitalism was taking root and the Silver Age of Russian literature was flourishing. In the decades before World War I, the debate about Russia's relation to the West appeared to be losing intensity, as Russia seemed to be catching up with the West.[8] A study, then, of what official Russia was actually thinking, on the eve of the First World War, about its Western diplomatic partners is an important part of the larger topic of Russia and the West.

The years covered in this study are 1905 to 1914. The 1905 revolution and the calamitous events of the Russo-Japanese War forced the government to rethink its approach to both its domestic and foreign policy. The result was a new era in Russian history. Two parallel experiments unprecedented in Russia—domestically, the inauguration of a constitutional regime[9] and, internationally, the movement toward the Triple Entente—signified a new westward orientation in Russian policy. P.A. Stolypin, the new chairman of the council of ministers, launched an ambitious program of domestic reforms that was designed to transform Russia. His domestic policy was linked inextricably to the emerging foreign policy of alignment with Great Britain and continued alliance with France. Russia now abandoned its Far Eastern adventures and refocused its attention on Europe. In its weakened condition, it was forced to accept a reduced status in the Franco-Russian alliance, which had been the cornerstone of Russian foreign policy since 1894, and to pursue for several years a low-key foreign policy whose main goal was peace.[10]

The consequences of Russian weakness were many, not least of which was its embrace of the Triple Entente, in what would prove to be a vain attempt to preserve the status quo in Europe. While never abandoning the goal of dominating the eastern Balkans and the straits, caution became the watchword of imperial foreign policy.[11] Among educated Russians, defeat in war had inspired contempt for the regime, whose primary historical role had been the expansion and preservation of a vast and powerful empire. Russia's lack of success in war and diplomacy in the six decades prior to 1914 sapped the country's moral strength. The Russian elite lacked the self-confident belief in their own society, values, and government, which was so pronounced at the time among the British and German middle and upper classes.[12]

After 1905 the constraints on Russian power continued for several years, despite the regime's valiant attempts to preserve Russia's status as a great power. The regime could not suppress easily the domestic troubles, and the fear of another revolution was a constant specter in government thinking. The basic inefficiencies and evils of Russian autocracy did not disappear with the celebrated October Manifesto. Even with Stolypin's counteroffensive against revolutionary terrorism, the government of Nicholas II was unable to suppress all dissent, and it was not willing to reform itself in a manner that might have satisfied substantial segments of the population.[13] Instead, the alienation between the official state and the wider society, which had long characterized Russia, became more pronounced.

The Russian government's perilous financial condition also acted as a brake on its exercise of power. By the end of 1905 the government faced imminent bankruptcy and narrowly avoided it by means of large international loans. Despite some industrialization, the country was still predominantly a peasant society with a literacy rate in 1913 of about 30 percent. The rapid economic development of Germany after 1870 increased the threat to Russia's relative standing among the European powers.[14] Russia had a per capita income of less than the equivalent of one hundred dollars. Foreign capital, moreover, played an integral part in Russia's economy.[15] A general lack of capital, low-consumer demand, a tiny middle class, vast distances, an extreme climate, and the heavy hand of autocracy all made the prospects for rapid industrialization in Russia bleaker than almost anywhere else in Europe.[16] Consequently its relative position vis-à-vis its much stronger neighbor, Germany, became untenable.

This book is concerned with Russian officialdom, both the government and the bureaucracy, especially the tsar and the Ministries of Foreign Affairs, Finance, and Trade and Commerce. Within each group, influential individuals have been singled out for close examination, with the intention of making clear the range of attitudes that were actually held toward Britain and France. Chapter 1 sets the diplomatic stage. Chapter 2, through the prism of various official visits, provides an overview of the subject. It is followed by examinations of the views of Nicholas II and the court (chapter 3), the Foreign Ministry (chapter 4) and other government ministries and the bureaucracy (chapter 5). The tsarist regime's concern with its image in France and Great Britain is discussed in chapter six. Special attention has been paid to how changing views of the Entente powers reflected Russia's domestic and international positions. The opinions of the intelligentsia, the press, and the new political parties are not part of this study in any major way. Despite the new constitutional order, these groups had little, if any, effect on foreign policy. Moreover, they were not part of official Russia, which is the main focus of this study. Also, the scholarly literature on them is vast and their pro-Western sympathies have already been established.[17] An understanding of official Russian attitudes towards Britain and France and the Triple Entente is critical to a better understanding of late imperial Russia and its position within Europe on the eve of the First World War and the 1917 revolutions.

Many people have helped me in numerous ways as I worked on this book. I would like to acknowledge the patient and well-informed counsel of Professor Robert H. Johnston, who played a crucial role in the project from the very beginning. Professors Alan Cassels, Wayne Thorpe, and Richard Rempel all contributed valuable advice at various stages. The Social Sciences and Humanities Research Council of Canada and McMaster University provided generous funding as did the Canadian Ministry of Foreign Affairs. The interlibrary loans departments at both McMaster University and Concordia University were helpful in locating various obscure works. I was lucky to be affiliated with the Moscow Historical-Archival Institute in Moscow while conducting my research. My father, Alvin Lee, has always provided an excellent example of a scholar to emulate, and he read various drafts of the manuscript along the way. My three sons—Marcel, Sebastian, and Alasdair—have inspired me with their curiosity about the world. My husband Mirek has always been patient, supportive, and understanding. He also provided indispensable computer support, whose contribution to this book should not be underestimated. And finally I wish to acknowledge my first teacher, my mother, Hope Arnott Lee, to whose memory this book is dedicated.

NOTES

1. The following works are some of those that deal with imperial Russia's governing classes: D.C.B. Lieven, *Russia's Rulers under the Old Regime* (New Haven, Conn., 1989); W.B. Lincoln, *In the Vanguard of Reform: Russia's Enlightened Bureaucrats, 1825–1861* (Dekalb, Ill., 1986); M. Raeff, *Understanding Imperial Russia* (New York, 1984); A. Sinel, *The Classroom and the Chancellery: State Educational Reform in Russia under Count Dmitry Tolstoi* (Cambridge, Mass., 1973); and A.M. Verner, *The Crisis of Russian Autocracy: Nicholas II and the 1905 Revolution* (Princeton, N.J., 1990).

2. The literature on the origins of the First World War is vast. Among the more influential studies are: L. Albertini, *The Origins of the War of 1914*, (London, 1965); S.B. Fay, *The Origins of the World War*, 2 vols. (New York, 1928); Fritz Fischer, *Germany's Aims in the First World War* (New York, 1967); James Joll, *The Unspoken Assumptions* (London, 1968); H.W. Koch, ed., *The Origins of the First World War* (London, 1984); A.J. Mayer, "Internal Causes and Purposes of War in Europe, 1870–1956," *Journal of Modern History* 41 (1969), pp. 291–303; J. Remak, ed., *The Origins of World War One, 1870–1914* (New York, 1967); and Marc Trachtenberg, "The Meaning of Mobilization in 1914," *International Security* 15 no. 3 (winter 1990/91), pp. 120–50.

3. D.C.B. Lieven, *Russia and the Origins of the First World War* (London, 1984), pp. 152–54. Fritz Fischer, *Germany's War Aims in the First World War* (New York, 1967).

4. Dietrich Geyer, *Russian Imperialism: The Interaction of Domestic and Foreign Policy, 1860–1914* (New Haven, Conn., 1987) p. 205.

5. Ibid., p. 314.

6. M. Raeff, "Russia's Perception of Her Relationship with the West," in D.W. Treadgold, *Development of the USSR* (Seattle, Wash., 1964), p. 373.

7. T. Shanin, *Russia, 1905–1907: Revolution as a Moment of Truth* (London, 1986), p. xi.

8. Ibid., p. 105. See also H.L. Roberts, "Russia and the West" in Treadgold, *Development of the USSR*, pp. 369–70.

9. There is disagreement among historians as to whether the October Manifesto and the introduction of an elected Duma and an appointed State Council constituted the beginning of a constitutional era for Russia. See in particular G.S. Doctorow, "The Fundamental State Laws of 23 April 1906," *Russian Review* 35 no. 1 (1976), pp. 33–52; Geoffrey Hosking, *The Russian Constitutional Experiment, Government, and Duma, 1907–1914* (Cambridge, 1973); and Theodore H. von Laue, "The Chances for Liberal Constitutionalism" *Slavic Review* no. 1 (1965), pp. 34–46. Jonathan Daly argues convincingly that after 1905 Russia was "no longer an absolute monarchy nor was it a 'police state.' . . . It was a regime in transition from absolutism to constitutionalism." See "On the Significance of Emergency Legislation in Late Imperial Russia," *Slavic Review* 54 (1995), p. 629.

10. J. Long, "Franco-Russian Relations during the Russo-Japanese War," *Slavonic and East European Review* 52 (1974) p. 213.

11. McGrew, "Some Imperatives of Russian Foreign Policy," in T.G. Stavrou, ed., *Russia under the Last Tsar* (Minneapolis, Minn., 1969), p. 227.

12. Lieven, *Russia and the Origins of the First World War*, p. 20.

13. For a good discussion of the limitations of Nicholas II's government, see A. Verner *The Crisis of Russian Autocracy*, passim.

14. Lieven, *Russia and the Origins of the First World War*, p. 8.

15. T. Shanin, *Russia as a Developing Society: The Roots of Otherness: Russia's Turn of the Century* (London, 1985), p. 186.

16. See P. Kennedy, *The Rise and Fall of the Great Powers* (London, 1988), pp. 232–41, for an assessment of Russian strengths and weaknesses.

17. Among others see: L.H. Haimson, *The Russian Marxists and the Origins of Bolshevism* (Cambridge, Mass., 1955); G.A. Hosking, *The Russian Constitutional Experiment, Government, and Duma, 1907–1914* (Cambridge, 1973); J.L.H. Keep, *The Rise of Social Democracy in Russia* (Oxford, 1963); A. Levin, *The Second Duma: A Study of the Social-Democratic Party and the Russian Constitutional Experiment* (New Haven, Conn., 1940); R. Pipes, ed., *Revolutionary Russia* (Cambridge, Mass., 1968); R. Pipes, ed., *The Russian Intelligentsia* (New York, 1961); N.V. Riasanovsky, *Russia and the West in the Teachings of the Slavophiles* (Cambridge, Mass., 1952); T. Riha, *A Russian European: Paul*

Miliukov in Russian Politics (Notre Dame, Ind., 1969); and A.B. Ulam, *In the Name of the People: Prophets and Conspirators in Prerevolutionary Russia* (New York, 1977).

Chapter 1

The Diplomatic Background

Late imperial Russia's geopolitical position was paradoxical. Regarded as one of the great powers of Europe since the beginning of the eighteenth century and the reign of Peter the Great, by the end of the nineteenth century the Russian empire suffered from imperial overreach. Yet, the regime still regarded the maintenance of the empire intact as absolutely essential. The imperial edifice rested on fragile foundations and defeat in war could result not just in the loss of territory but raised the specter of the dissolution of the state to the size of fifteenth-century Muscovy, as happened during the Time of Troubles, the early years of the Great Northern War and Napoleon's 1812 campaign.[1]

Despite the sheer size of Russia, which stretched from Poland to Vladivostok and from the Baltic to the Black Sea, a population nearly four times larger than Britain's, and possession of the largest standing army in Europe, by the beginning of the twentieth century Russia was falling behind its European rivals, as the Crimean War and the Russo-Turkish War had made clear. Russia lacked an adequate industrial base, an effective system of transportation and supply, and a viable political organization that was capable of mobilizing for war.[2] Moreover, Russia had the misfortune of bordering bellicose Germany, the strongest continental power, which believed its future lay in eastward expansion. Russia's geographical position, therefore, made it impossible for it to retire from power politics, even if the mentality of Russia's rulers would have allowed it, which was unlikely.[3]

In an era when wars were increasingly won by industrial strength, Russia was not industrializing quickly enough compared to its military rivals, particularly Germany. At the end of the nineteenth century, Russia was the most rural of the main European countries, with only 12.5 percent of the population living in the cities, compared to 40 percent in France and Germany and over 70 percent in England.[4] The export of agricultural products financed Russia's industrial development, and the peasantry bore the cost. Consequently, despite Russia's being an exporter of grain, the standard of living of Russia's peasantry was much below that of the farmers of countries to which Russia exported grain.[5] By 1914 Russia had become the fourth industrial power in the world, yet it was far behind the United States, Britain, and Germany. In 1913 Russia's per capita level of industrialization was less than one-quarter of Germany's and less than one-sixth of Britain's.[6]

The basic dilemma confronting Russia's rulers at the end of the nineteenth century was the conflict between the demands of external military security, particularly on the western frontier, and the demands of internal political security. Within this context Russia pursued a foreign policy of alliance with France, which led to the amorphous Triple Entente of Russia, France, and Great Britain. The Dual Alliance between Russia and France served as the cornerstone of Russian foreign policy for more than twenty years.[7] The formation of the Franco-Russian Alliance surprised many, including the new German emperor Wilhelm II, who had assumed that autocratic and Orthodox Russia would never ally with republican and secular France. When tsar Alexander III entertained the officers of a French squadron visiting Saint Petersburg in 1891 and bared his head during the playing of the "Marseillaise," a profound impression was made in Europe. The German ambassador to Saint Petersburg, General Lothar von Schweinitz, recognized the significance of the reorientation of Russian foreign policy in a letter to his wife:

I . . . now have the painful conviction that the dynastic policy—the solidarity of the monarchs against the Revolution—has definitely been laid to rest. In the thirty years that have passed since I was Military Attaché in Vienna . . . I have collaborated in the three-emperors policy; and today I shall ride in the parade . . . as a living anachronism. My political activity of thirty years thus ends in the breakdown of all the principles for which I have striven. It does not occur to me to regret what I have done, or to regard it as a mistake; but it is sad to end it all with a fiasco.[8]

France initiated the secret defensive alliance that began in 1891 with a modest political agreement between the two countries that they would consult each other on any matter that might jeopardize the general peace; this was followed by a military convention in 1894, which stipulated that if Germany, or Italy supported by Germany, attacked France, Russia would employ all its available forces for an attack on Germany. If Germany, or

Austria-Hungary aided by Germany, attacked Russia, France would employ all its available forces for an attack on Germany. The secret agreement called for immediate mobilization of Russian and French forces if one of the partners of the Triple Entente were to mobilize. The convention was to have the same duration as the Triple Alliance.[9]

In the 1890s the alliance with France enhanced Russia's position and caused both Germany and France to woo Russia. France was grateful to have escaped the international isolation it had endured since the Franco-Prussian War, and Wilhelm II regretted the lapse of the Reinsurance Treaty between Germany and Russia.[10] The Dual Alliance was in some respects the natural outcome of the Gorchakov formula. Prince A.M. Gorchakov was foreign minister from 1856 to 1866 and he believed "Il nous faut une France forte" while at the same time cultivating good relations with Germany. Russia recognized even in the 1890s that France could be a useful counterweight to an increasingly powerful and assertive Germany.[11]

Both Russia and France viewed the Triple Alliance of Germany, Austria-Hungary, and Italy as a threat. According to G. Kennan, with the lapse of the Reinsurance Treaty in 1890, "the Triplice became, for the Russians, a wholly hostile and menacing apparition on the international horizon."[12] Despite a common aversion for the Triple Alliance, important differences existed between the two new allies. Russia's military interests related primarily to Austria-Hungary and the Balkans. For France, it was Germany that posed the greater threat. This difference proved to be a continuing source of tension. As early as December 1895, during the Armenian conflict, Paris indicated clearly to Saint Petersburg that France did not intend to aid Russia in a Balkan conflict.[13]

The arrival of Théophile Delcassé as minister of foreign affairs in June 1898 led to a new stage in the life of the Alliance. In August 1899 the terms of the Dual Alliance were modified so that the duration of the military convention no longer depended on the Triple Alliance but was extended until either partner renounced it. The aims, now defined, were stated to be not merely the maintenance of the peace but also the preservation of the balance of power in Europe.[14] Imperial clashes between France and Britain and between Russia and Britain in the 1890s caused the Franco-Russian Alliance to take on an anti-British character. An April 1901 military protocol outlined the support that Russia and France would provide each other in case of a war against Britain. If Great Britain attacked France, Russia would mount a diversionary operation against India, and if an Anglo-Russian conflict erupted, France would assemble 150,000 men on the English Channel to invade the island. These provisions were not intended to go into effect automatically, but only if the two governments decided to give each other mutual support. The anti-English nature of this protocol became an embarrassment for the French as the Anglo-French rapprochement developed into the Entente Cordiale. In 1902 Nicholas II chaired a main staff conference, which decided on rapid military aid to France and committed Russia to an attack on Germany in the event of a European war. France exerted financial pressure on Russia to obtain this decision, which clearly served French strategic interests.[15]

The 1905 revolution and Russia's defeat in the Far East drastically altered the shape of the Dual Alliance. While Russian fortunes were at their lowest ebb, Nicholas II signed the Björko treaty with his cousin, Wilhelm II, during a courtesy visit on their yachts in July 1905. This abortive treaty provided for a Russo-German alliance against attack by any other power in Europe. The anti-French nature of the agreement was blatantly apparent to the Russian foreign minister, Count V.N. Lamsdorf, and he torpedoed the deal once he learned of it.

Dire financial circumstances forced Russia to conclude a large loan on the Paris and London markets; in return, Russia unequivocally supported France at the Algeciras conference, which resolved the first Moroccan crisis in France's favor.[16] At this conference, Britain, France, and Russia cooperated closely to thwart Germany, who had sought to isolate France and break up the newly formed Entente Cordiale of Britain and France. Consequently, the conference was an important stepping stone in the formation of the Triple Entente.[17] Russia agreed in April 1906 that the defeat of Germany would be the main aim of a European war. Moreover, the anti-British elements of previous military agreements were dropped.

Nonetheless, relations between the allies were cool until 1910. Franco-Russian collaboration was mediocre. France did not regard Russia as a militarily valuable ally, and Russia was stung by the lack of French support during its recent calamitous years. Beginning in 1910, however, Franco-Russian General Staff conversations were held annually in Paris and Saint Petersburg, alternately. In 1912, after having toyed with an eastward orientation in its military planning, Saint Petersburg signed the Franco-Russian naval convention. In November 1912 Poincaré promised French support to back Russian aims in the Balkans, a commitment that Russia had long desired and that rendered the Alliance much more valuable from the Russian perspective.

Russian military strength expanded considerably in 1913. The Duma allotted large sums of money to augment the artillery and reserve stores of munitions. French loans of four hundred to five hundred million francs a year were to be devoted to the development of strategic railroads in western Russia.[18] In August 1913 General Joseph Joffre, the French chief of staff, visited Russia and was pleased with the growing efficiency of the Russian army and the progress in railway construction.[19] In September 1913 the Franco-Russian military convention assumed its final form. Article 2 stipulated that in case of German mobilization or a German act of war, France and Russia would mobilize immediately without prior consultation. In the event of partial German mobilization or Austrian or Italian mobilization, consultation between the allies would be necessary before military measures would be undertaken. In Article 3, France undertook to concentrate virtually its entire army against Germany and to commence offensive operations on the eleventh day of mobilization. Russia promised that at least eight hundred thousand men would be deployed on the Russo-German frontier and offensive operations would begin on the thirteenth day of mobilization. This Russian commitment to its ally was to have significant repercussions on Russia's battlefield effectiveness. At the same time the convention was signed, the French government made another substantial loan to Russia for railway building and armaments. From 1894 to 1914 the Franco-Russian alliance had evolved from a secret limited defensive alliance to a tightly coordinated military alliance that was defensive in name only. As the Alliance evolved, so too did official Russian attitudes toward France.

In the years before World War I, in addition to the Dual Alliance, Russia entered into a friendly partnership with Great Britain. The 1904 Entente Cordiale had also tied Britain to France.[20] It was this loose grouping of powers that came to be known as the Triple Entente and that acted as a counterweight to the Triple Alliance.[21] Russia's new friendship with Britain ran contrary to the entire thrust of nineteenth-century Russian diplomacy. As late as the beginning of the twentieth century, Britain considered a war against Russia more probable than any other. As Russia's frontier in central Asia had moved southward in the late nineteenth century, protection of the Indian subcontinent had become a source of anxiety for the British.[22] Fear of a Russian invasion of India was real, but the main concern was the possibility that Russian activities on or beyond the Indian frontier would cause disaffection within India. Russia could not be allowed to establish itself along the Indian frontier without serious damage to British prestige.[23] In the last two decades of the nineteenth century, with the Russian occupation of Turkestan and the construction of the Transcaspian railway, many of the physical obstacles to a Russian invasion had been removed. As a result, the threat of such an occurrence came to dominate both British strategic discourse and the popular imagination.[24]

The intense Anglo-Russian rivalry of the nineteenth century continued unabated into the twentieth century. The accidental sinking of a British trawler off Dogger Bank on 21 October 1904, while the Russian Baltic fleet was on its way to the Far East during the Russo-Japanese War, brought the two countries to the brink of war. Anxious French diplomatic intervention averted a military conflict, but the incident was the nadir of Anglo-Russian relations, already strained by the Anglo-Japanese alliance and by the Russian conviction that Britain had incited Japan to war and provided it with the means to fight.[25] Russia's humiliating defeat at the hands of an Asiatic power in the Russo-Japanese War was Russia's third major military or diplomatic defeat since the Crimean War. The disaster in 1904–5 convinced Russia's rulers that, as the courtier and publicist General A.A. Kireyev said, Russia had "become a second-rate power."[26]

The consequences of the Russo-Japanese War, which was concluded with the Treaty of Portsmouth, were profound. Four hundred thousand Russian soldiers were killed or wounded during the conflict. A quarter billion rubles in naval assets were lost, and two and a half billion rubles were spent.[27] Russia's status in Europe was severely undermined and its political and economic position in the Far East jeopardized. Russia lost access to ice-free ports on the Pacific, and its means of exercising influence over Korea were significantly reduced. The war and the accompanying revolution, which had threatened to topple the imperial regime entirely, caused the balance of forces to change disadvantageously for Russia, whose prestige was tarnished in the eyes of small and great powers alike. Henceforth the specter of revolution arising from another military defeat haunted the imperial regime and colored all foreign policy decisions.[28] Under the circumstances, Saint Petersburg decided to conduct a foreign policy of understandings, to gain some much-needed respite in international affairs. The outcome of the war also reduced the Russian threat to Britain. In particular, the annihilation of the Russian Baltic fleet at Tsushima altered drastically the maritime balance, and the British navy was suddenly considerably larger than the next two ranking navies.[29] The military threat to India had been reduced, and diplomacy would be enough to protect it.[30] Moreover, Germany was now unequaled in Europe, both militarily and industrially.

This new constellation of forces caused both Russian and British statesmen to reconsider their old assumptions about each other. Sir Edward Grey, the British foreign secretary, began the Anglo-Russian talks in earnest after the Algeciras conference of 1906 and as a result of French encouragement. He regarded an entente with Russia as "the thing most desired in our foreign policy," since an agreement with Russia would eliminate the already reduced threat to India and provide protection against Germany.[31] The Russian government sought an agreement to protect its alliance with France, to mend its relationship with Tokyo, and to ensure peace and stability.[32]

Anglo-Russian negotiations had been attempted before, most notably with Lord Salisbury's abortive proposals in 1898, but succeeded in 1906–7 despite several obstacles including serious public opposition in Britain,[33] because Russia's changed circumstances forced Saint Petersburg to conclude an agreement. Since the establishment of the 1904 Entente Cordiale between Britain and France, Paris had been working hard to bring Russia and Britain together. The imperial government hoped an agreement with Britain might lead to a Russo-Japanese reconciliation, which would provide Russia's Far Eastern possessions with essential security. Moreover, Russia could no longer afford to compete with Britain. As V.N. Kokovtsov, minister of finance, said, "if in the past putting pressure on England was beyond our strength then at present it is completely impossible."[34] Russia believed that an agreement could be reached with Great Britain without alienating Germany.

The election of the Liberals in Great Britain and the selection of Sir Edward Grey as foreign minister also contributed to the rapprochement. Keith Wilson has argued convincingly that, contrary to the traditional interpretation of Britain's Entente policy, the agreement with Russia was concluded not to maintain the balance of power in Europe but to protect Britain's imperial interests. By concluding a limited colonial agreement with Russia, Britain sought to relieve India from the Russian threat, to avoid the necessity of becoming a continental state in central Asia with a common frontier with the Russian empire, and to stop the drain on British resources caused by the forward policies necessary to merely maintain the status quo in that region.[35]

After long and arduous negotiations, which had threatened to break down, Britain and Russia signed a convention in August 1907.[36] The agreement defined spheres of influence in Persia and the attitudes of the two countries to Tibet and Afghanistan. Ian Nish has described the 1907 convention as a "sensible compromise between two imperialist powers who had their Asian wings clipped, Britain for financial reasons, and Russia at the hands of Japan."[37] The ultimate result of the convention, however, was that Britain and Russia united to counter German efforts to dominate the European continent.[38] A "negative correspondence of interests," primarily a fear of Germany and a desire to maintain the balance of power in Europe, drew Russia, France, and Great Britain into the Triple Entente.[39] Anglo-Russian efforts to halt construction of the Berlin-Baghdad railway were a good example of this common distrust of Germany.[40] Although the 1907 accord did not mention European affairs, the British told the Russians that in the future Britain would no longer oppose Russian ambitions for passage through the straits, provided other powers agreed. But in general Britain and France were not particularly interested in helping Russia achieve its goals in the Balkans, a difference that would prove irksome to the Russians and cause them to question the utility of the Entente. Even after the formation of the Entente, then, problems in Anglo-Russian relations still persisted, but a new willingness to cooperate rendered most difficulties solvable or at least manageable.[41] Persia continued to be a *bête noire*, but Russia's revival and a growing fear of Germany prompted Britain to align itself more closely with Russia. Ultimately, in the spring of 1914, Britain agreed to begin naval conversations with Russia.[42]

From the formation of the Triple Entente in 1907 to July 1914, a series of diplomatic crises convulsed Europe. The overall impact of these events was to test and finally strengthen the Triple Entente. Since these diplomatic incidents were crucial in shaping official Russian attitudes to its Entente partners, they are outlined here to provide the necessary backdrop for the main body of this study.

The Bosnian annexation crisis of 1908–9 was the baptismal crisis of the newly formed Triple Entente.[43] This diplomatic fiasco, which unfolded disastrously for Russia, began with a seemingly successful meeting between A. Izvolsky, the Russian foreign minister, and his Austrian counterpart, Count A. Aehrenthal, on 16 September 1908 at Buchlau. From 1878 to 1908, Austro-Hungarian troops had occupied and administered the provinces of Bosnia-Herzegovina as though they were Austrian colonies, even though they were still nominally under Ottoman rule. Izvolsky agreed to Austrian annexation of this territory in return for the opening of the straits to Russian warships. Aehrenthal preempted Izvolsky, however, by unilaterally announcing shortly after their meeting the annexation of Bosnia-Herzegovina, before Izvolsky had had time to prepare the diplomatic groundwork with the other powers on the question of the straits. Stephen Pichon, the French foreign minister, made it clear to Russia that it could not depend on French support.[44] Grey also made it clear from the beginning of the crisis that Britain was unwilling to offer Russia anything more than diplomatic support.[45] In the end, in March 1909, Saint Petersburg was forced to accept a humiliating German ultimatum, which demanded immediate, unconditional, and unequivocal acceptance of Austrian terms. Russia, perforce, recognized the annexation and failed to receive compensation of any kind.

The ramifications of the crisis were many. It caused much bitterness within Russia, and the regime resolved to strengthen the Entente, which had failed it. In the short term, Russia felt little obligation to aid France in its struggles with Germany. Soon after the Bosnian imbroglio, Saint Petersburg concluded two agreements that caused Paris serious concern. In October 1909, at Racconigi, Russia signed, without informing France, a secret accord with Italy to preserve the status quo in the Balkans. In November 1910, Nicholas II, with his new foreign minister S.D. Sazonov (Izvolsky's tenure as foreign minister had been cut short as a result of his role in the crisis), visited Wilhelm II at Potsdam and signed an agreement on Persia and the Baghdad railway. The Bosnian annexation crisis was the nadir of Franco-Russian relations in the immediate prewar years.

As a result of the annexation, the Serbs within Bosnia, who saw their desire for a greater Serbia threatened, began an anti-Austrian terrorist campaign that would culminate ultimately in the assassination of the Archduke Franz-Ferdinand and his wife at Sarajevo on 28 June 1914, an event that would provide the pretext for the unleashing of the Great War. The Bosnian annexation crisis destroyed the balance that Russia and Austria-Hungary had maintained in the Balkans since 1897, when Nicholas II and Franz Josef agreed to put the Balkans "on ice." Bismarck's defensive arrangement with Austria-Hungary was transformed into a German obligation to bolster Austria-Hungary's deteriorating position in southeastern Europe. The crisis also demonstrated Austria-Hungary's dependence on Germany and, paradoxically, the extent to which the initiative within the alliance had passed to Vienna.

When the next major prewar crisis erupted in the summer of 1911, the Entente powers had taken the lessons of 1908–9 to heart. The second Moroccan crisis began on 1 July 1911, when the German gunboat, the *Panther*, was dispatched to Agadir on the coast of Morocco, allegedly to protect German commercial interests, which French expansion threatened in Morocco.[46] London, already concerned about German naval activity, thought that Germany wanted to establish a naval base at Agadir, which was close to Gibraltar and vital British trade routes. Consequently, on 21 July, David Lloyd George, chancellor of the Exchequer, gave a bellicose speech at the Mansion House, in which he warned:

If a situation were to be forced upon us, in which peace could only be preserved by the surrender of the great and beneficent position Britain has won by centuries of heroism and achievement, by allowing Britain to be treated, where her interests were vitally affected, as if she were of no account in the Cabinet of Nations, then I say emphatically that peace at that price would be a humiliation intolerable for a great country like ours to endure.[47]

France and Germany began direct negotiations, but in September the talks nearly broke down and war seemed imminent. In the end, Germany retreated, and in November an agreement recognized French rights in Morocco in return for the cession of territory in the French Congo.

In contrast to what happened in 1908–9, during the Bosnian crisis the members of the Triple Entente rallied together, as they had at Algeciras in 1906, and successfully contained German aspirations. Grey in particular was unwilling to let Germany intimidate France as it had Russia over Bosnia-Herzegovina.[48] London regarded the crisis as a test of the Entente.[49] Russia, on the other hand, chastened by its recent experiences, was reluctant to back France wholeheartedly. However, after an initial period of aloofness, which worried Paris, Russia let it be known that in case of war it would be true to the Alliance.[50]

The Anglo-French naval conversations begun in August 1912 were a direct result of the second Moroccan crisis. With its participation in these conversations, Britain incurred a serious moral obligation to aid France in the event of a conflict with Germany; it was agreed that France would concentrate its navy in the Mediterranean and that Britain would be responsible for the Channel and France's northern coasts. One of the most significant results of the Agadir crisis and the strengthened Anglo-French military and naval ties was to impart a more confident tone to French diplomacy. The victory of Raymond Poincaré as premier of France, an ardent nationalist and native Lorrainer, meant that, henceforth, a strong statesman, who hewed firmly to the Franco-Russian alliance and nursed a profound hostility toward Germany, would shape French policy. The second Moroccan crisis and its aftermath also revealed the deep divisions between Britain and Germany, and it seriously threatened the balance of power. The Triple Entente and the Triple Alliance both determined to swing the equilibrium in their favor and the buildup of armaments intensified.[51] It also became apparent that Germany's alliance with Austria-Hungary was not worth much unless Austria-Hungary's own interests were threatened as they had been during the Bosnian crisis. The second Moroccan crisis had much the same psychological impact on Germany as the events in 1908–9 had had on Russia.

After Agadir, the "struggle for mastery of Europe" returned to the Balkan peninsula. Russia's Balkan policy and pan-Slavism were crucial elements contributing to Balkan instability in the immediate prewar years.[52] The Balkan states exploited Austro-Russian rivalry for their own ends. The fear that their Balkan clients, unless humored, would join the enemy camp greatly weakened Saint Petersburg's and Vienna's ability to impose restraint. In the particular case of Russo-Serbian relations, Russia's failure to control Belgrade was exacerbated by the actions of N.G. Hartwig, Russia's Austrophobic minister to Belgrade from 1909 to 1914, who also had influential friends in Saint Petersburg. Hartwig successfully bound Serbia to Russia, but he could not be trusted to fulfill his instructions loyally, and his reports to Saint Petersburg were highly selective. He often acted without the direct authorization of his superiors, but his activities in Belgrade were "only the extreme manifestation of that general fear of Austrian ambitions which underlay Russian foreign policy in the years 1909–14."[53]

The Balkan wars of 1912–13 were the last dispute in that region of Europe that was kept localized.[54] Initially, Russia, through ambassador N.V. Charykov in Constantinople, had sought to achieve Russian aims in this arena by means of Russo-Turkish friendship and Turkish adherence to a Balkan League. But after Italy's annexation of Tripoli during the Libyan war, Said Pasha, the Turkish foreign minister, who had originally welcomed Charykov's overture, no longer had anything to gain by hinting at eventual Turkish adherence to the Triple Entente or the Triple Alliance.[55] Thus, the idea of a Russo-Turkish rapprochement foundered. Russia, and particularly Hartwig, then played a major role in organizing the Balkan League of Bulgaria, Serbia, Greece, and Montenegro, although Saint Petersburg seemed to intend that the Alliance play a defensive, not an aggressive, role against Austria-Hungary. The confidential talks Sazonov had with Grey and Poincaré in September and October 1912 to deal with the growing Balkan crisis greatly helped to reinforce Franco-Russian and Anglo-Russian friendship. For the first time, Russia could be reasonably certain that France would fight if a Russo-Austrian war arose out of a purely Balkan incident.[56]

Despite Sazonov's efforts to maintain the peace, the Ottoman empire's embarrassment at the hands of Italy provided the Balkan League with the opportunity to achieve their nationalistic aspirations. The First Balkan War began in October 1912 when the league attacked Turkey and won swift victories. During the war, the Foreign Office worried that Germany would persuade Russia to leave the Entente if Germany restrained Austria-Hungary. These British concerns were symptomatic of the larger British worry that their lack of firm commitment to Russia would ultimately prove insufficient for Saint Petersburg and would force Russia to cultivate more accommodating allies.[57] In contrast, Franco-Russian ties were strengthened by the appointment of Théophile Delcassé, a symbol of belligerent French nationalism, as ambassador to Saint Petersburg in February 1913. News of Delcassé's appointment caused the French and Russian press to rejoice and stocks to fall on the Berlin bourse. He would be a poor restraint on Sazonov's Balkan design as he was representative "of Poincaré's view that Franco-Russian solidarity was more important than peace."[58]

By May 1913 the great powers had secured a preliminary peace at the London Conference, under which Turkey surrendered most of its European territory on the understanding that the powers would create a new independent state of Albania. This arrangement displeased Serbia and Montenegro, as they wished to acquire the Albanian coastline. The former allies of the league quickly fell to squabbling over the division of territory. The Second Balkan War began on 29 June 1913, when Bulgaria launched a surprise attack on Serbia and Greece. Romania and Turkey invaded Bulgaria and it was quickly defeated. In August 1913 the Treaty of Bucharest divided most of Bulgaria's land claims in Macedonia and Thrace between Serbia and Greece. Bulgaria also ceded southern Dobrudja to Romania.

The effect of these wars was to limit Turkey's European possessions to the area around Constantinople and Adrianople. The ill-defined state of Albania was created. Serbia and Montenegro doubled in size, and Greece became the most important power on the Aegean Sea, possessing the port of Salonika. Bulgaria, one of the original members of the Balkan League, was left bitterly resentful and would join the Central Powers in World War I, as would Turkey.

The aftermath of the Balkan Wars left no one satisfied. Most significantly, Serbia, although victorious on the battlefield, had been thwarted in its main objective of obtaining the Albanian coastline through the peace settlement. Russia resolved not to let Serbia be trampled on again, a policy which was to have important ramifications during the July crisis of 1914. The wars also reinforced the Austrian conviction that Serbia was an extremely dangerous enemy that must be dealt with.[59] R. Langhorne has described the manner in which this conflict was handled as the last example of the European Concert in action. If a new crisis arose in which Austria and Russia were directly involved, they would not likely be able to resist their respective desires to destroy and defend Serbia. Nor was it clear that their allies would restrain them again or that the Concert of Europe would have the strength to endure.[60]

Shortly after the conclusion of the Treaty of Bucharest, another dispute threatened Russo-German relations and tested the strength of the Entente. In October 1913 it was announced that a German officer, General Liman von Sanders, was to be appointed to command the Turkish garrison at Constantinople.[61] His influence over promotions and appointments was likely to ensure a pro-German Turkish high command. Moreover, should the Ottoman empire collapse, the presence of German-commanded troops in Constantinople might seriously impede a Russian seizure of the straits. Saint Petersburg believed that this German action threatened fundamental Russian interests and therefore acted vigorously to overturn the appointment. Jules Cambon, the French ambassador to Berlin, believed that Russia used this incident to derail French negotiations with Germany on the Baghdad railway because it worried that such a transportation route would pose a threat to its Caucasian frontier. As international tension mounted, the negotiations with Germany were suspended. After the affair was resolved, however, by von Sanders relinquishing direct command of the Constantinople Corps but maintaining his rank of inspector-general of the Turkish army,

France and Germany reached an agreement on French participation in financing the Baghdad railway.

The compromise satisfied Russia, but the affair demonstrated how Russian relations with Germany had deteriorated. A newspaper war over the affair coincided with demands in the Russian press for a revision of the 1904 Russo-German commercial treaty (whose operations had been unfavorable to Russia) and in the German press for a preventive war against Russia.[62] Russian military intelligence emphasized German determination to control the straits should the Ottoman empire collapse, even at the cost of European war.[63] In February 1914 an extraordinary conference in Saint Petersburg made plans to enlarge the Baltic fleet in preparation for an offensive in the Near East. Russia also initiated, through France, naval conversations with Britain. On 14 May the British Cabinet sanctioned naval talks with Russia along the lines of the 1912 talks with France. Preliminary discussions were held, but the main negotiations were set for August.[64] In the spring of 1914, Saint Petersburg made overtures to London to enter into an actual alliance. The British response was ambivalent, but strong forces at the Foreign Office advocated closer ties with Russia.[65]

By the beginning of 1914 a signal change in attitude had taken place in the Russian government. For the first time since 1905, Russia's leaders began to entertain the idea that a military conflict was a possibility rather than a calamity to be avoided at all costs. For Nicholas II, Sazonov and Russian public opinion, growing anti-German and anti-Austrian sentiment crystallized over the Liman von Sanders affair. Anti-German sentiment, whose roots reached back to the Congress of Berlin in 1878, had grown more virulent, and concerns of prestige and national honor could be heard in official and unofficial Russia.[66]

In July 1914 Europe was a powder keg waiting to be ignited. From the first Moroccan crisis in 1906 to 1914 and the outbreak of general war, the stakes in the diplomatic game had been raised gradually. Each side suffered serious reverses, and consequently each side resolved not to back down again. The alliances stiffened and the margin to maneuver became narrower. The remainder of this study is a detailed, critical examination of how official Russian attitudes toward Britain and France changed as the international scene became more fraught and the Concert of Europe disintegrated, first into violent dissonance and then into outright destruction.

NOTES

1. Alfred J. Rieber, "Persistent Factors in Russian Foreign Policy: An Interpretative Essay," in Hugh Ragsdale and V.N. Ponomarev eds., *Imperial Russian Foreign Policy* (New York, 1993), pp. 315–59.

2. As Paul Kennedy has aptly pointed out, Russia "was simultaneously powerful and weak—depending, as ever, upon which end of the telescope one peered down." Paul Kennedy, *The Rise and Fall of the Great Powers* (London, 1988), p. 233.

3. J.H. von Laue, "The Chances for Liberal Constitutionalism," *Slavic Review* 24 no.1 (1965), p. 38.

4. A. Baykov, "The Economic Development of Russia," *Economic History Review* 7 (1954), p. 138.

5. Ibid., p. 144.

6. Kennedy, *The Rise and Fall of the Great Powers*, p. 234.

7. W.L. Langer's *The Franco-Russian Alliance 1890–1894* (London, 1929), now somewhat dated and written without access to Russian documents, is one of the standard works on the Dual Alliance. B.E. Nolde, *L'alliance franco-russe: les origines du systeme diplomatique d'avant-guerre* (Paris, 1936) challenges Langer's interpretation. More recently G. Kennan produced *The Fateful Alliance: France, Russia, and the Coming of the First World War* (New York, 1984). Kennan had access to Russian archives that makes his work more useful than Langer's. See also V.I. Bovykin, *Iz istorii vozniknoveniia pervoi mirovoi voiny: otnosheniia Rossi i Frantsii v 1912–1914gg.* (Moscow, 1961), Hogenhuis-Seliverstoff, *Une Alliance Franco-Russe: la France, la Russie et l'Europe au tournant du siècle dernier* (Brussels, 1997), and E.M. Rozental, *Diplomaticheskaia istoriia russko-frantsuzskogo soiuza v nachale xx veka* (Moscow, 1960).

8. Quoted in Kennan, *The Fateful Alliance*, p. 101.

9. The text of the military convention signed in August 1892 by General Nikolai Nikolayevich Obruchev and General Raoul le Mouton de Boisdeffre is reproduced in Kennan, *The Fateful Alliance*, pp. 271–72. The military alliance was ratified in January 1894.

10. D.C.B. Lieven, *Nicholas II: Twilight of the Empire* (New York, 1993), p. 93.

11. A.Z. Manfred, "Quelle fut la cause de l'alliance franco-russe?" *Cahiers du monde russe et soviétique* 1 (1959), p. 156. Manfred argues that the Alliance was the result of a common Franco-Russian fear of Germany and Great Britain, but the principle factor was the German threat.

12. Kennan, *The Fateful Alliance*, p. 120.

13. Pierre Renouvin, "Les rélations franco-russes à la fin du XIXe siècle et au début du XXe siècle. Bilan des recherches." *Cahiers du monde russe et soviétique* 1 (1959), p. 131.

14. For a discussion of the changing nature of the Franco-Russian Alliance see C. Andrew, "German World Policy and the Reshaping of the Dual Alliance," *Journal of Contemporary History*, 1, no. 3 (1966) pp. 137–51. Jacques Drimaracci, "La Politique de Delcassé et la Triple Entente" *Information Historique* 29, no. 4, (1967), pp. 181–89.

15. Lieven, *Russia and the Origins of the First World War*, pp. 103–4. Between 1889 and 1913, France extended fifteen important loans for a total of 9,800

million gold francs to Russia. In 1914, 80 percent of Russia's public debt under-written by foreigners was in French hands. Renouvin, "Les rélations franco-russes," p. 136.

16. See E.N. Anderson, *The First Moroccan Crisis, 1904–1906* (Chicago, 1930); F.V. Parsons, *The Origins of the Morocco Question, 1880–1900* (London, 1976).

17. For a discussion of the loan and the Algeciras conference see Olga Crisp, "The Russian Liberals and the 1906 Anglo-French Loan to Russia," *The Slavonic and East European Review* 39 (1961) pp. 497–511. R. Girault, *Emprunts russes et investissements français en Russie, 1887–1914* (Paris, 1973). P. Renouvin, "L'emprunt russe d'avril 1906 en France," *Etudes Suisses d'histoire générale* (1960/61), pp. 507–15.

18. L.C.F. Turner, "The Russian Mobilisation in 1914," *Journal of Contemporary History* 3 (1968), p. 257.

19. Ibid., p. 257.

20. For a standard work on the Entente Cordiale see P.J.V. Rolo, *Entente Cordiale: The Origins and Negotiation of the Anglo-French Agreements of 8 April 1904* (London, 1969). See also C. Andrew, *Théophile Delcassé and the Making of the Entente Cordiale, 1898–1905* (London, 1968).

21. B.E. Schmitt, *The Triple Alliance and the Triple Entente* (New York, 1947).

22. David Dilks, *Retreat from Power: Vol. One, 1906–1939* (London, 1981), p. 2. See also Z. Steiner, *Britain and the Origins of the First World War* (London, 1977), pp. 79–80; B.J. Williams, "The Strategic Background to the Anglo-Russian Entente of August 1907," *The Historical Journal* 9, no. 3 (1966), pp. 363–65; and B.J.C. McKercher, "Diplomatic Equipoise: The Lansdowne Foreign Office, the Russo-Japanese War of 1904–1905, and the Global Balance of Power," *Canadian Journal of History* 24, no. 3 (1989), pp. 299–339.

23. M.A. Yapp,"British Perceptions of the Russian Threat to India," *Modern Asian Studies* 21, no. 4 (1987), pp. 647–50.

24. Ibid., pp. 662–63.

25. Lieven, *Russia and the Origins of the First World War,* p. 28. See also Keith Neilson, "A Dangerous Game of American Poker: The Russo-Japanese War and British Policy," *Journal of Strategic Studies* 12, no. 1 (1989), pp. 63–87.

26. Quoted in Lieven, ibid., p. 21. For a history of the war, see J.A. White, *The Diplomacy of the Russo-Japanese War* (Princeton, 1974).

27. Fuller, *Strategy and Power in Russia,* p. 406.

28. D.M. McDonald has some interesting thoughts on the link between war and revolution. See "The Durnovo Memorandum in Context: Official Conservatism and the Crisis of Autocracy," *Jahrbücher für Geschichte Osteuropas* 44 (1996), pp. 481–502; and "A Lever without a Fulcrum: Domestic Factors and Russian Foreign Policy, 1905–1914," in Ragsdale and Ponomarev, eds., *Imperial Russian Foreign Policy*, pp. 268–311.

29. Paul Kennedy, *The Realities behind Diplomacy: Background Influences on British External Policy, 1865–1980* (Glasgow, 1981), p. 123.

30. K. Neilson, "A Dangerous Game of American Poker," p. 82.

31. Quoted in Keith Wilson, "British Power in the European Balance, 1906–1914," in David Dilks, *Retreat from Power*, pp. 34–36. See also P. Kennedy, *The Realities behind Diplomacy*, pp. 126–27. Z. Steiner, *Britain and the Origins of the First World War*, p. 83.

32. Lieven, *Russia and the Origins of the First World War*, pp. 30–31.

33. D.M. McLean, "English Radicals, Russia, and the Fate of Persia, 1907–1913," *English Historical Review* 93 (1978), p. 339. Beryl Williams, "Great Britain and Russia, 1905–1907," in F.H. Hinsley, ed., *British Foreign Policy under Sir Edward Grey* (Cambridge, 1977), p. 138.

34. Quoted in William C. Fuller, *Strategy and Power in Russia, 1600–1914* (New York, 1992), p. 416.

35. Keith Wilson, *The Policy of the Entente: Essays on the Determinants of British Foreign Policy, 1904–1914* (Cambridge, 1985), pp. 75–77. Wilson also argues that the agreement with Russia was based on two British assumptions that proved to be false: the Russian advance towards India would stop and that Russia would hold Germany in check in Europe, p. 82.

36. For a discussion of the difficulty of the negotiations see George Sanders, "Diplomacy and the Anglo-Russian Convention of 1907," *UCLA Historical Journal* 3 (1982), pp. 61–72.

37. Ian Nish, "Politics, Trade, and Communications in East Asia: Thoughts on Anglo-Russian Relations, 1861–1907," *Modern Asian Studies* 21, no. 4 (1987) p. 678.

38. McKercher, "Diplomatic Equipoise: The Lansdowne Foreign Office, the Russo-Japanese War of 1904–1905, and the Global Balance of Power," p. 32.

39. McGrew, "Some Imperatives of Russian Foreign Policy," p. 211.

40. For a discussion of this cooperation see Stuart A. Cohen, "Sir Arthur Nicolson: The Case of the Baghdad Railway," *The Historical Journal* 18, no. 4 (1975), pp. 863–872. On the issue of the Baghdad Railway, see also M.K. Chapman, *Great Britain and the Baghdad Railway, 1888–1914* (Northhampton, Mass., 1948) and John B. Wolf, "The Diplomatic History of the Baghdad Railway," *University of Missouri Studies* 2 (1936).

41. For a discussion of Anglo-Russian differences in central Asia see I. Klein, "The Anglo-Russian Convention and the Problem of Central Asia, 1907–1914," *Journal of British Studies* 11, no.1 (1971), pp. 126–147.

42. Steiner, *Britain and the Origins of the First World War*, pp. 114–15 and 121–23. On the question of Persia, see B.C. Busch, *Britain and the Persian Gulf, 1894–1914* (Berkeley, Calif., 1967); R.L. Greaves, "Some Aspects of the Anglo-Russian Convention and Its Workings in Persia, 1907–1914," *Bulletin of the School of Oriental Studies* 31 (1968); F. Kazemzadeh, *Russia and Great Britain in Persia, 1864–1914* (New Haven, Conn., 1968); and M. Kent, *Oil and Empire: British Policy and Mesopotamian Oil, 1900–1920* (London, 1976). D. M. McLean, "English Radicals, Russia, and the Fate of Persia, 1907–1913," *English Historical Review* 93 (1978), pp. 38–52.

43. See Francis Roy Bridge, "Izvolsky, Aehrenthal, and the End of the Austro-Russian Entente, 1906–1908," *Mitteilungen des osterreichischen Staatsarchivs* 29 (1976), pp. 315–62. A. Rossos, *Russia and the Balkans: Inter-Balkan Rivalries and Russian Foreign Policy, 1908–1914* (Toronto, 1981), and B.E. Schmitt, *The Annexation of Bosnia, 1908–1909* (Cambridge, 1937).

44. Renouvin, "Les rélations franco-russes," p. 134.

45. D.W. Sweet and R.T.B. Langhorne, "Great Britain and Russia, 1907–1914," in Hinsley, ed., *British Foreign Policy under Sir Edward Grey,* p. 246.

46. On the Agadir crisis see: J.C. Allain, *Agadir 1911, une crise Impérialiste en Europe pour la conquête du Maroc* (Paris, 1976); I.C. Barlow, *The Agadir Crisis* (Durham, N.C., 1940); G. Barraclough, *From Agadir to Armageddon: Anatomy of a Crisis* (London, 1982); J. Caillaux, *Agadir: ma politique extérieure* (Paris, 1919); R.A. Cosgrove, "A Note on Lloyd George's Speech at the Mansion House on 21 July 1911," *Historical Journal* 12 (1969); L.A. Neiman, "Frankorusskie otnosheniia vo vremia marokkanskogo krizisa 1911g," *Frantsuzskii Ezhegodnik* (1969) pp. 65–91; and K. Wilson, "The Agadir Crisis: The Mansion House Speech and the Double-Edgedness of Agreements," *Historical Journal* 15 (1972).

47. Quoted in James Joll, *The Origins of the First World War* (London, 1992), p. 58.

48. Nabil M. Kaylani, "Liberal Politics and the British Foreign Office, 1906–1912: An Overview," *International Review of History and Political Science* 12, no. 3 (1975), p. 38.

49. Steiner, *Britain and the Origins of the First World War,* p. 75.

50. Barlow, *The Agadir Crisis,* pp. 357–62.

51. Ibid., pp. 400–401.

52. For a general history of pan-Slavism see H. Kohn, *Panslavism* (New York, 1960). A recent work on Russia's Balkan policy is Barbara Jelavich, *Russia's Balkan Entanglements, 1806–1914* (New York, 1991). For a background study, see M.B. Petrovich, *The Emergence of Russian Panslavism, 1856–1870* (New York, 1956).

53. Lieven, *Russia and the Origins of the First World War,* p. 42. See also E.C. Thaden, *Russia and the Balkan Alliance of 1912* (University City, Pennsylvania, 1965) pp. 65–70.

54. For a history of these wars, see E.C. Helmreich, *The Diplomacy of the Balkan Wars* (Cambridge, Mass., 1938).

55. For a good account of Charykov's diplomacy in Constantinople, see Thaden, *Russia and the Balkan Alliance of 1912,* chapter 2, pp. 38–57.

56. Ibid., pp. 68, 79, 133, and 136. For an interesting discussion of the November 1912 crisis, see Turner, "The Russian Mobilisation in 1914," pp. 252–56.

57. Keith Wilson, "The British 'Démarche' of 3 and 4 December 1912: H.A. Gwynne's Note on Britain, Russia, and the First Balkan War," *Slavonic and East European Review* 62, no. 4 (1984), pp. 552–59.

58. Schuman, *War and Diplomacy in the French Republic,* p. 203.

59. Laurence Lafore, *The Long Fuse* (New York, 1971), pp. 178–79. See also R.J. Crampton, "The Decline of the Concert of Europe in the Balkans, 1913–1914," *Slavonic and East European Review* 52 (1974), pp. 393–419.

60. R. Langhorne, *The Collapse of the Concert of Europe* (London, 1981).

61. See U. Trumpener, "Liman von Sanders and the German-Ottoman Alliance," *Journal of Contemporary History* 1 (1966).

62. I.V. Bestuzhev, "Russian Foreign Policy February–June 1914," *Journal of Contemporary History* 1, no. 3 (1966), p. 97.

63. Lieven, *Russia and the Origins of the First World War*, p. 49.

64. Steiner, *Britain and the Origins of the First World War*, p. 121.

65. M.G. Ekstein, "Great Britain and the Triple Entente on the Eve of the Sarajevo Crisis," in Hinsley, ed., *British Foreign Policy under Sir Edward Grey*, p. 344.

66. D.M. McDonald, "A Lever without a Fulcrum," pp. 304–5.

Chapter 2

Pomp, Circumstance, and Realpolitik: The Evolution of the Triple Entente

From 1908 to 1914 Russia and its Triple Entente partners exchanged five state visits, as well as a 1912 visit by the French premier and a British naval visit. The style, timing, and substance of these occasions reflected the changing nature of the Triple Entente, a loose alignment of Russia, Great Britain, and France designed to counter Germany's growing power on the continent, and of official Russian attitudes toward the Entente in the immediate prewar years. These visits can be viewed as the external manifestation of the inner workings of the Entente. The first round of visits in 1908 and 1909—after the aborted 1906 one by the British fleet to Kronstadt—showed the ambivalent Russian attitudes to the Triple Entente and the precarious state of the diplomatic alignment. The second round of visits, from 1912 to 1914, reflected Russia's embrace of Britain and France and the growing solidarity among the Triple Entente powers. These latter visits projected an image of a united front among Britain, France, and Russia, which masked domestic tensions in each of the Entente countries and increasing international instability. By 1914, when the lavish visits of the British fleet and French President Raymond Poincaré occurred, most of the Russian elite had come to regard the Triple Entente as the best means of preserving both Russia's status as a great power and the imperial system. In 1914 Russia, outwardly confident, enthusiastically welcomed President Poincaré and the British fleet. This chapter will examine these state visits from the Russo-Japanese War to the outbreak of the Great War as a barometer of intergovernmental relationships to illustrate how imperial Russia came to embrace so warmly Britain, its traditional nineteenth-century foe, and republican France. The Triple Entente emerged only fitfully during these years and was not always cohesive. An analysis of the state visits among the Entente leaders shows the evolution of the Entente. It began as a shaky set of understandings, withstood various crises, and was transformed through mutual efforts into a robust league that became an alliance after the outbreak of the First World War.

The mood of the Russian government was somber in the spring of 1906, when London broached the idea of a naval visit. The humiliating Russo-Japanese War, which initially Saint Petersburg had thought would be easily won, and the revolutionary turmoil had shaken the imperial edifice to its foundation. Strategically, the Russo-Japanese War had seriously undermined Russia's political and economic position in the Far East. As a result, the balance of forces on the international stage changed disadvantageously for Russia, with Russian prestige diminished in the eyes of great and small powers alike. In these difficult international circumstances, aggravated by revolution at home and looming financial disaster, Russia was compelled to adopt a more conciliatory foreign policy.[1] The immediate result of Russia's changed circumstances was the 1907 Anglo-Russian Convention, which coupled with Russia's alliance with France, formed the beginning of the Triple Entente. This reorientation of Russian foreign policy coincided with the introduction of P.A. Stolypin's program of "pacification and reform," which assumed a relatively long period of quiet in international affairs. The connection between war and revolution became a persistent theme in public and official discussions of foreign policy from 1905 to 1914. Concerns about Russia's internal order colored all debates about Russia's foreign alignments, including the Triple Entente.[2] In the immediate aftermath of 1905, the main aim of Russian foreign policy was to remain on good terms with everyone. For a weak country in a Europe increasingly torn into two power blocs, this would prove to be an impossible task.[3] After a period of vacillation in which Russia tried to maintain good relations with all the European powers, Russia chose to side with Great Britain and France against the Central Powers of Germany and Austria-Hungary.

When Sir Arthur Nicolson, the British ambassador to Saint Petersburg, initially proposed a British naval visit to the Gulf of Finland, Nicholas II concurred with the idea: "My August Sovereign welcomed this news with a heartfelt satisfaction."[4] Perhaps he felt too weak to resist the British overture or he recognized the futility of continued animosity with Great Britain, a policy that had harmed Russia during the Russo-Japanese War and brought Britain and Russia to the brink of war when gunboats in the Russian fleet mistakenly sank several British trawlers at Dogger Bank in October 1904. In the end, however, justifiable fear about possible domestic upheaval prompted the Russian government tactfully to refuse the British request. In the spring of 1906, when Nicolson proposed the naval visit, although the urban revolution had been largely suppressed, the most serious peasant uprisings since the Pugachev revolt in the late eighteenth century were still convulsing the countryside. Only in the middle of 1906 were all the troops back from the Far East and order restored in the armed forces. Even in the winter of 1906–7, much of rural Russia was under martial law. Moreover, negotiations for the visit occurred simultaneously with the sitting and subsequent dissolution of the First Duma. In its reply to the British request, the Russian government cited the unruly nature of the opposition parties in both Britain and Russia as the main reason for refusing the visit, which earlier they had welcomed.[5] Nicholas II telegraphed Edward VII to suggest that it be delayed: "I can not but look upon the approaching visit of Your squadron with the greatest anxiety. To have to receive foreign guests when one's country is in a state of acute unrest is more than painful and inappropriate. You know how happy I should have been to receive the English fleet in normal times, but now I can only beg of You to postpone the squadron's arrival till another year.—Nicky."[6] The British government also worried about public disapproval of a visit which, according to Sir Edward Grey, had "aroused dislike and opposition among Liberals in the House of Commons, and caused great embarrassment at the Foreign Office." Not wishing to offend the tsar's government, the British government was relieved when "eventually the Russians themselves, with discretion and tact asked that the visit should not take place."[7] In this manner, the event was delayed with no offense taken on either side. The discussions concerning a British naval visit coincided with the first tentative negotiations for the Anglo-Russian Convention. The hesitant desire to improve Anglo-Russian relations that prevailed in 1906 and early 1907 can be seen in the anxious attempt to arrange a British naval visit to a Russian port and the visit's hasty cancellation. Both London and Saint Petersburg desired closer relations, but the reality of each country's domestic situation made this difficult to achieve.

Encouraged by France, however, Russia did conclude the Anglo-Russian Convention in August 1907, which settled outstanding colonial differences between Britain and Russia in Persia, Tibet, and Afghanistan. These negotiations succeeded where others had failed because the results of the Russo-Japanese War forced Russia to reassess its entire foreign policy. The election of the Liberals in Britain and the selection of Sir Edward Grey as foreign minister contributed to the talks' success. Limited as this agreement may have been, it was a startling reversal in Russian foreign policy: it ended Britain and Russia's long-standing animosity, led to the informal diplomatic alignment of the Triple Entente of Great Britain, France, and Russia, and opened the London money market to Russia, thereby assisting in its recovery from the events of 1904–6. Moreover, the agreement afforded Russia some breathing room as Russia could no longer afford to compete with Britain. The Anglo-Russian Convention also enhanced Russia's prestige with its French ally. Furthermore, Saint Petersburg believed it could make a deal with London without harming relations with Berlin.[8] Although the agreement did not eliminate all grounds for misunderstanding between Britain and Russia—Persia in particular remained a source of tension—it did allow for a limited collaboration on European questions from 1908 to 1914.

The first public affirmation of improved relations between Britain and Russia was the visit of Edward VII to the Baltic port of Reval in June 1908. By 1908 Russia was just beginning to recover from the twin blows of the humbling military defeat and revolution, which had been quelled by a mixture of repression and political concessions. In 1908, although the revolutionary disturbances had ceased, concern about the domestic impact of a British visit still lingered. Edward VII indicated he would not take the initiative and ask to touch Russian soil, since it would be better on such an occasion to avoid any event that could cause trouble and leave an unfortunate impression.[9] The visit was to be kept short and confined to the royal yachts to avoid possible domestic disturbances.[10]

The proposed visit, nonetheless, caused a sensation in Britain. Sir Charles Hardinge, permanent undersecretary at the Foreign Office, told Nicolson that Grey and Lord Henry Asquith were "both a little afraid of the extremists in their party and what they might say of the King's visit to Reval."[11] The Labour Party demanded that the Liberal government declare the visit to be of a purely personal nature. Labour member of Parliament Keir Hardy organized a motion of censure that had fifty-nine supporters.[12] Grey would not yield and his firm stand won him the Russian government's admiration. In a long speech to the House, Grey defended the upcoming visit, Anglo-Russian amity, the Russian emperor, and to a certain extent, the domestic policies of the Russian government. The foreign secretary refused to pass judgment on Russia's internal situation and even went so far as to prophesy a bright future for Russia.[13] Grey's speech pleased Saint Petersburg greatly.[14] The emperor told Hardinge he was very glad that the debate had taken place, as it showed the world that both the Conservatives and the Liberals shared the same warm feelings toward Russia.[15]

Despite the limited nature of the Reval visit, it was a personal and diplomatic success.[16] The presence of Russian and English royalty and important government officials from both countries made the occasion both a family affair and a working visit.[17] Nicholas and Alexandra had spent some of the happiest days of their youth and courtship at Queen Victoria's court, and they were delighted to be among family who brought back memories from less troubled times.[18] In his toast to his uncle, Nicholas wished that this royal meeting at Reval would have the result of drawing the two "countries closer together and of promoting the maintenance of the peace of the world."[19] Publicly the Russian government presented the visit as "the happy expression of very amicable relations which actually exist between Russia and England."[20] In private Nicholas II expressed his satisfaction with the visit to Hardinge, saying it "sealed and confirmed the intention and spirit of the Anglo-Russian Agreement."[21] Hardinge and the tsar discussed the warm coverage the king's visit to Reval received in the Russian press. The rapid spread of pro-British sentiment pleased Nicholas II, who thought that the idea of friendlier relations with Britain had firmly taken root and now only required "to be carefully fostered to bear fruit in the future."[22] The visit had been a convincing public affirmation of improved relations with Britain and Russia's prestige as a great power, a matter that had been in doubt as a result of the events of 1904–1906. The need to redeem Russia's international reputation and thereby justify the regime's raison d'être drove Russian foreign policy in these critical years.[23] In terms of Anglo-Russian relations, the visit was also a success. The original purpose of the meeting had been to cement the new Anglo-Russian relationship in general and to finalize the Anglo-Russian Macedonian reforms. Both purposes were well served by the conversations between Izvolsky and Hardinge, by the overall cordial air of the event, and by incidents such as the king's impulsive gesture of appointing the tsar Admiral of the Fleet. Although constitutionally improper, the king's act was highly effective.[24] Edward VII's 1908 visit to Reval illustrated the great improvement that had occurred in Anglo-Russian relations since the nadir of 1904, when the two powers were on the brink of war with each other.

Shortly after Edward VII's visit to Reval, the new French president, Armand Fallières, paid a state visit to Russia, as had been the practice of all new presidents since the formation of the Dual Alliance in 1894. Originally Russia entered into the alliance with France in reaction to Wilhelm II's abandonment of Bismarck's Reinsurance Treaty. Russia's goal had been to preserve France as an independent great power and to prevent Germany from amassing too much power. The Franco-Russian alliance had changed substantially since its inception as a primarily defensive alliance between two equal powers. Russia, as a result of its domestic upheavals and financial dependence on French loans, had become the subordinate partner in the alliance. Saint Petersburg resented this change, and was dissatisfied, moreover, with the French attitude during the Russo-Japanese War. The belief prevailed in Saint Petersburg, however, that little could be done to change the situation, and the alliance with France, now buttressed with the understanding with Britain, continued to serve as the cornerstone of Russian diplomacy.

Russian disenchantment with its French ally was apparent in the negotiations leading up to Fallières' visit. In the winter of 1906, the Russian ambassador in Paris, A.I. Nelidov, with some trepidation, had raised the question of a presidential visit to Russia with the foreign minister, V.N. Lamsdorf. Nelidov noted that such an event was expected and would have to take place but, in the light of domestic upheavals, the time was not propitious to have a head of state from a republic visit Russia. Nelidov noted that internal security left much to be desired, and demonstrations of every type were to be feared.[25] Similar concerns had been raised about the aborted British naval visit in 1906. The ambassador also indicated that Russia, as a result of France's Entente Cordiale with Britain, was no longer France's sole diplomatic friend and consequently they would have to proceed carefully in order not to offend France. In his reply, Lamsdorf concurred with Nelidov's assessment.[26]

This matter did not resurface, however, until the end of 1907. To Nelidov, A.P. Izvolsky, the new foreign minister, revealed that the idea of a state visit from Fallières "little appealed to the Emperor," who "was visibly annoyed by this project: a visit of this type demands, at maturity more or less brief, a visit in response which, in the actual circumstances presents serious difficulties."[27] Worried about the implications of a refusal of the French request, Izvolsky asked Nelidov to use his fertile mind "to find a way out."[28] Under renewed prodding from the new French ambassador to Saint Petersburg, Admiral Touchard, Izvolsky again broached the subject of the state visit with Nicholas II. The prospect of Fallières traveling to Russia had already been discussed in the European papers. If the president failed to visit Russia after his visit to the Scandinavian courts, Izvolsky worried that "one would not miss in Europe to deduce from this consequences which could have a great political significance."[29] Nonetheless, despite imperial recalcitrance, the imperative of maintaining good relations with France—Russia's ally and primary creditor—prevailed. In the end, Izvolsky won the emperor's reluctant consent, but the visit was to be kept as short as possible because of the empress's health. As for the return trip that protocol demanded, Izvolsky had to assure Nicholas that it would also be short and could occur in conjunction with a visit to Britain.[30] Nelidov was relieved to receive news of the emperor's change of heart.[31] He suggested to Izvolsky that the president should make a naval visit to one of the Baltic ports after he had been to the Scandinavian courts, to cause the imperial couple as little disruption as possible, and to avoid the necessity of visiting Paris in response.[32]

Matters, however, still did not proceed smoothly. An anti-French article in the influential conservative paper *Novoe Vremia* prompted a protest from

Touchard.[33] To complicate matters, a French socialist, Edouard Vaillant, insulted Nicholas II in the Chamber of Deputies. Vaillant protested strongly against the visit, referring to the emperor "in terms coarse and irreverent."[34] Nelidov sent Saint Petersburg the press account in *Le Matin* of the Vaillant incident, underlining twice in blue pencil and marking "NB" the passage describing Nicholas II as "the murderer of his best subjects."[35] Flesser, a senator, also opposed the French government's request for money to finance the trip to Scandinavia and Russia. Nelidov reported to Saint Petersburg that these protests had no effect on French public opinion, a matter of grave concern to the Russian government in light of their dependence on French loans, which were raised on the Paris bourse. The Russian ambassador accepted the French government's apology for the incident.[36] While satisfied with the official apology, Nelidov linked the French socialists, who protested the president's visit to Russia, with the Russian revolutionaries and with Jews in France: "These are the manifestations of hate of Messrs. Rubonovitch and Co., furious to have failed in their revolutionary attempts in Russia, seconded by some anarchists and encouraged by our refugees and by the Jews."[37]

After all the preliminary difficulties, president Fallières did visit Reval in July 1908, as had Edward VII in June. As the presidential visit began, the official newspaper *Journal de Saint Petersbourg*, published an editorial that sought to limit the damage caused by the *Novoe Vremia* article and the Vaillant incident by defending the alliance as "an essentially popular policy."[38] Nonetheless, the editorial still projected an image of an alliance under attack. The strongest praise the newspaper could summon was a nostalgic look back at the early days of the Dual Alliance: "Today the Franco-Russian alliance is a fact, and, the memories of its proud beginning have not more than the sweetness, a little melancholy, a little faded, of a diplomatic honeymoon."[39]

Although Nicholas II's government might resent its subordinate role in the alliance, it was well aware of the limitations within which its foreign policy had to operate. Consequently, care was taken during the visit not to offend or alienate Russia's main diplomatic partner. During their first meeting, the two heads of state had a conversation of "an unusual form and length,"[40] which lasted for three-quarters of an hour. The emperor told Stephen Pichon, the French foreign minister, that he was very satisfied with the pacific character given the alliance in France and Russia.[41] Pichon reported to the French Cabinet that his long interview with Izvolsky "had been more complete and more amicable than any of those that I had had previously in Paris with the Minister of Foreign Affairs of the Empire. I drew from it the impression that there was on the part of the Russian Government a desire, equal to ours, to maintain and practise the alliance."[42] Pichon also concluded that Russia was resolved to persevere with the policy of Entente with England. The Triple Entente had, to a large extent, been Izvolsky's creation. His reassuring words reflected his personal commitment to the Entente and the Russian government's realization both that it could not afford an adventuresome foreign policy and that its security lay in a policy of preserving the status quo in Europe, which meant containing Germany, the one great power which sought to disrupt the balance of power in Europe.

Russian coolness toward Fallières' visit, especially on the part of Nicholas II, reflected both a prevailing sentiment among the Russian elites that France had forsaken them during the Russo-Japanese War and a distaste for the left-wing character of the French government. Although the French were well pleased with the visit and publicly the Russians professed themselves to be so as well, the new president's trip to Russia did not completely alleviate the strains that stemmed from the war with Japan. Rather it served to mask them. In 1908 Britain was a newly acquired and cautiously praised friend, ideologically more acceptable than republican France, and with a monarch who was Nicholas II's uncle. France, however, was a somewhat worn and apparently not very useful old ally with a radical government. The two Reval visits of 1908 reflected these sentiments.

During the Bosnian annexation crisis of 1908–9, Russian sympathy for France and belief in its value as an ally reached its lowest ebb in the immediate prewar years. France failed, for the second time, to support its ally at a critical juncture and allowed Germany to dictate the terms by which Saint Petersburg had to accept Austria-Hungary's annexation of Bosnia and Herzegovina with no compensation. Already deeply shamed by the Russo-Japanese War, both the Russian government and public opinion were further infuriated by the Bosnian debacle. Hysteria reigned in much of the Russian press over the perfidy of Germany and Austria-Hungary.[43] Even at this moment of embarrassment for the Russian empire, however, it could not forsake its erstwhile ally because in truth it had nowhere else to turn. Although Britain cooperated closely with Russia during the crisis, Grey made it clear from the beginning that London was unprepared to offer more than diplomatic support.[44] The resentment in Russia over this affair led to a desire to avoid a similar humiliation, and this newly acquired resolve affected every aspect of Russia's foreign policy until 1914. Germany had attempted to use the crisis to split the Entente, but the Bosnian crisis served to strengthen the Entente as it convinced Russia of the need to tighten ties with Britain and France so Russia would not be left unsupported again. Moreover, the annexation crisis destroyed the basis of Austro-Russian collaboration in the region, which had functioned well for thirty years and caused

Russia to turn to the Balkan powers themselves. Ultimately this led in 1912 to the Balkan system of alliances and two Balkan wars, which would be a significant contributing factor in the outbreak of the First World War. At the time, criticism of Izvolsky's foreign policy was widespread. The critics condemned Saint Petersburg's policy of trying to have a foot in each camp and believed that for Russia to improve its situation and maintain some semblance of influence as a great power it was necessary to choose either the Triple Entente or the Triple Alliance.[45]

It was in such an atmosphere of international humiliation and virulent domestic criticism and bitterness toward France and Britain that, in 1909, Nicholas II and his wife, as required by protocol, returned the visits made in 1908 by Edward VII and President Fallières. In keeping with imperial wishes, the visits were brief and made at the same time. The imperial yacht *Standart* visited the French port of Cherbourg for two days, from 31 July to 1 August 1909. The Russian emperor reviewed the French fleet and in his toast to the French president paid "homage to the superb fleet" which had "vigorously impressed" him.[46] Nicholas once again expressed his firm conviction that the Dual Alliance constituted "a precious guarantee for the general peace." Russian rage at French behavior during the Bosnian annexation crisis was carefully concealed during Nicholas's visit to Cherbourg because Russian vulnerability forced them to accept the unsatisfactory state of Franco-Russian relations.

After his perfunctory visit to France, Nicholas proceeded to Cowes. The Foreign Office was enthusiastic about the imperial visit because they believed it would help to cement the bonds of the Anglo-Russian Convention and the meeting would strengthen liberal forces in Russia. The Foreign Office even went so far as to monitor the reaction of Russian liberals to the visit.[47] Before the emperor's arrival, Sir Edward Grey referred in the House of Commons to the upcoming visit as official.[48] Also, in the House, William Thorne, a Labour member of Parliament, attacked the upcoming Russian imperial visit and described the tsar as "an inhuman brute."[49] Thorne's behavior appalled Count Benckendorf, the Russian ambassador to Great Britain, and prompted an official protest to Grey, whose own outrage mollified Benckendorf.[50] *The Times* was vehement in its denunciation of Thorne's behavior and "the disgraceful scene which was got up in the House of Commons" and strong in its praise of Nicholas II:

Mr. Thorne and his friends no more represent English opinion on this subject than the Extremist members of the First Duma represented Russian opinion. The great body of the English people have a sincere regard and admiration for Nicholas II. They know the great services which, on his own initiative and by his own exertions, he has rendered to the cause of international peace. . . .

They know something, too, of what Nicholas II has done for his own people.[51]

The response of "the great papers, with *The Times* at the head," pleased Benckendorf.[52]

A campaign against the emperor's visit was led by the Society of Friends of Russian Freedom and the *Daily News.* On 25 July 1909 a demonstration was held at Trafalgar Square, during which one of the speakers urged the crowd to spit in the tsar's face.[53] The Labour Party also issued a manifesto protesting the imperial visit.[54] A Russian delegation of Duma members that was visiting Britain issued a statement rejecting the contrast made in the Labour Manifesto between the delegates as representatives of the Russian people and the tsar, who by implication was not: "As commissioned by my colleagues I think it my duty to protest resolutely against the insult to ourselves conveyed in this contrast. We are happy to feel that the cordial welcome which we are receiving everywhere entitles us to be sure that the manifesto of the Labour party does not express the opinion of the English people."[55] The British press hailed the protest as "stamped with dignity and appropriate."[56] Furthermore, V.A. Maklakov, a Kadet member of the delegation, in a *Morning Post* interview, said that all Russia regarded the emperor as the representative of the nation and consequently any insult to the tsar was an insult to Russia. Benckendorf viewed these initiatives as "very useful."[57] They also pleased Grey, who told Benckendorf that "for the English Government this Russian display was so useful and opportune that he had avoided speaking to me of it until now fearing to appear to have suggested it."[58] In the end what had begun as an insult to imperial dignity became a minor public relations triumph for the Russian government with the Duma apparently rallying behind the tsar and the British government and the leading British paper supporting Nicholas II.

The Russian imperial visit to English waters proceeded harmoniously because Russia was cowed and prepared to accept the Anglo-Russian relationship on British terms, which meant the entente remained informal and would not develop into anything more binding.[59] At Cowes neither the tsar nor Izvolsky pressed for any closer definition of the entente; rather they expressed their keen appreciation of the common point of view which the two governments enjoyed.[60] Edward VII and Queen Alexandra were present, as were the king and queen of Spain, the prince and princess of Wales, and other members of English royalty.[61] In his toast to his uncle, Nicholas II referred to the 1908 Reval visit and the Anglo-Russian Convention as having "fully answered its purpose." He said, "Never have the relations between England and Russia been more cordial; it is My warmest desire that these relations founded on common interests and mutual esteem, should remain as perfect in the future, for the general cause of peace and the benefit of mankind."[62] This almost effusive imperial toast, composed by Nicholas himself, signified the growing official Russian commitment to Britain as an important diplomatic friend, also Russian awareness of its tenuous international position after the Bosnian failure. Nicholas II's sincerity contrasted with the lukewarm toast he had proposed at Cherbourg to the French president only a few days previously. Despite the Labour Party protests, the Russian emperor was clearly pleased to be in English waters, among friends and family, furthering a policy of rapprochement with England, which was personally dear to him and ideologically acceptable as another monarchy.

When Premier Raymond Poincaré visited Russia in August 1912, Russian attitudes toward its ally were distinctly warmer than hitherto, despite the Russian celebrations of the centenary of the battle of Borodino. The cordial reception accorded the French premier illustrated the significant changes that had transformed the Franco-Russian relationship, the re-emergence of Russian strength and confidence after 1905, and the growing rigidification of the alliance system in the years immediately prior to World War I. Poincaré visited Kronstadt, Peterhof, Saint Petersburg, and Moscow. Fallières had not even touched Russian soil. No unpleasant controversy, like the Vaillant incident, preceded the 1912 visit. The Russian government and society welcomed Poincaré as a strong, respected leader with whom it was possible to agree and work as equals. Russian timidity and caution, while not completely exorcised, had receded into the background.

By 1912 most European statesmen were discussing the inevitability of a war between the Triple Alliance of Germany, Austria-Hungary, and Italy, and the Triple Entente.[63] Consequently the powers began to plan accordingly and tried to strengthen their diplomatic arrangements. In this sense, and as Poincaré's 1912 visit to Russia showed, 1912 marked a significant turning point in the evolution of the Franco-Russian alliance. From 1894 to 1911, the alliance had a primarily defensive character, but the Agadir crisis of 1911, the strengthening military and naval bonds between France and Great Britain (most notably the Grey-Cambon letters of 1912), and the accession of Poincaré to power gave French diplomacy a new and more confident tone.[64] Russian restraint and German tactics during the Agadir crisis made the French government determined not to submit to German pressure and prepared to give far greater support to Russia's Balkan policies than in the past.

Unlike most French politicians, Poincaré, the Lorrainer, was highly regarded in official Russian circles. His accession to power had been a victory for the French nationalists. French policy was now directed by a strong statesman (Poincaré took the portfolio of Foreign Affairs himself) who combined a passionate hostility toward Germany with a strong belief in the Franco-Russian alliance.[65] His conservatism and unconditional support for the Triple Entente won him praise and respect from the Russian government, which had been frustrated by the absence of strong French support for Russian concerns.[66] Poincaré appealed to the Saint Petersburg establishment in a way no French leader in recent memory had done. His steadfast loyalty to Russia helped to reinforce both the Dual Alliance and the growing belief among the Russian elites that Russia's survival depended on a foreign policy of close cooperation with both France and Great Britain.

Nicholas II received the French premier at Peterhof, where they discussed various questions including the military and national awakening of France, which pleased the emperor. He "was delighted with the state of mind he saw existent in France; he congratulated the French Government on cherishing and developing it." The emperor's remarks left Poincaré "convinced of his absolute loyalty to the alliance."[67] A statement written by Poincaré and Sazonov publicly confirmed the cordial and mutually satisfying nature of Poincaré's Russian visit.[68] The communiqué stressed the "spirit of absolute confidence and sincere friendship" with which the leaders dealt with all questions. The discussions were "not only to exchange views, but to plan practically their action. The two Governments noted that the accord is complete between them and that the ties which unite the two nations have never been more solid."[69] The language of the communiqué was strong and clear. After the doubts and misgivings following the Russo-Japanese War, the humiliation of the Bosnian annexation crisis, Saint Petersburg's flirtation with Berlin at Potsdam in 1910, and Russia's lukewarm support for the French position during the Agadir crisis, the alliance was publicly reaffirmed as a result of Poincaré's successful visit.

From aboard the *Condé* Poincaré telegraphed Sazonov to thank him for his "friendly welcome."[70] Sazonov replied that the premier's visit had given them great pleasure: "Permit me to say that you carry from here unanimous sympathy. I am particularly happy to have been able to develop a personal rapport with you which I will hold to my heart and cultivate."[71] In his report to the tsar, Sazonov indicated that the two foreign ministers had discussed the Franco-Russian naval conversations and the circumstances in which the allies would support one another in a war, among other matters. Sazonov concluded his report by saying that, in Poincaré, "Russia possesses a sure and faithful friend, endowed with a political spirit above the line and an inflexible will."[72] Poincaré so impressed the Russian foreign minister that he believed it would be most desirable for Russia to have Poincaré or someone of similar character at the head of France in the case of a crisis.[73] Poincaré's 1912 visit left Sazonov confident that French support could be counted upon in any eventuality.[74] The July 1912 Franco-Russian Naval Convention and the secret Izvolsky-Poincaré talks on the Balkans in October—during which Poincaré assured Izvolsky that if a Balkan crisis brought on a war between Russia and the Central Powers, France would recognize this in advance as a *casus foederis* and would not waver in fulfilling its obligations to Russia—served to bind Russia and France even more closely together.[75] Such a promise was a significant gain from the Russians' perspective and confirmed their belief that Poincaré was an invaluable friend.

The Russian press also was "practically unanimous in extending a warm welcome to M. Poincaré," displaying an attitude of "sincere and hearty cordiality," according to Buchanan.[76] *Novoe Vremia,* so cold to France in 1908, now praised Poincaré most warmly: "For the first time M. Poincaré comes to Russia. Russian public opinion had already appreciated him for a long time: consummate orator, brillant lawyer, financier of the first order, worker such as one rarely sees, . . . this man so interesting for his simplicity and his personal charm . . . we welcome him who has always been one of the protagonists of the Franco-Russian alliance."[77] This conservative newspaper, perhaps naively, rejected the supposition that the raison d'être of the Franco-Russian alliance was the recovery of Alsace-Lorraine and the Russian plundering of French savings. Rather, *Novoe Vremia* maintained that the Dual Alliance had been created to restore the balance of power in Europe which had been destroyed by Bismarck.[78] This passionate defense of the Franco-Russian alliance was symptomatic of a fundamental shift in Russian public opinion from what it had been in 1908: questioning the partnership rather than defending it had been the fashion. Fear of Germany appeared to motivate *Novoe Vremia*'s change of heart and in general was an important reason for the increased Russian support for the alliance. Both *Vechernoe Vremia* and *Rossiia* endorsed the Dual Alliance as the cornerstone of Russian foreign policy. *Vechernoe Vremia* pointed out that the premier's visit came at an important moment, as Austria-Hungary had just passed a law increasing its army and its fleet; Germany had recently increased its army by a whole corps, and its navy was a cause of deep anxiety for Great Britain.[79]

The zenith of these official visits between the Entente powers came in the early summer of 1914. In June and July respectively, Russia played host to a squadron of the British fleet and to the new French president, Raymond Poincaré. On these two occasions an outwardly confident Russia lavishly entertained its valued Triple Entente partners in a fashion markedly different from that of the subdued visits of 1908. Yet behind the façade of toasts, banquets, and military and naval reviews, domestic troubles plagued all the Entente powers.[80] The Caillaux scandal in France, the fear in Great Britain of civil war over Ireland, and worker unrest in Russia provided troubled domestic backgrounds, as the unfolding Sarajevo crisis threatened, and finally broke, the uneasy international peace. Russia, in particular, faced a difficult task in its struggle to maintain order at home while at the same time maintaining its place among the great powers.[81]

When 1914 began, however, Russia outwardly seemed fully recovered from its previous troubles. The Balkan Wars had ended in 1913. Nineteen fourteen appeared likely to be a year of calm. The British Foreign Office observed and exaggerated Russia's revival. The prevailing belief among British diplomats was that Russia would soon overtake Germany as Europe's leading military power.[82] Meriel Buchanan, the daughter of the British ambassador to Saint Petersburg, described in her memoirs the mood in Saint Petersburg high society: "People were full of confidence and hope that winter, the memory of the Japanese War was fading, an era of new prosperity was dawning, there were rumours of possible Court balls, of a revival of the old brilliance of the Russian Court."[83] Such was the atmosphere when the first British battle-cruiser squadron came to Saint Petersburg in June 1914. During this British visit, fears of domestic disturbances did not hamper the ceremonies as they had in 1908. Two of the smaller light cruisers even came up the Neva and anchored at the Nicholas bridge, while the rest of the fleet anchored at Kronstadt.[84] At a garden party given by the Grand Dukes Cyril and Boris, Nicholas II wore the uniform of a British admiral, the rank Edward VII had bestowed upon the tsar at Reval in 1908. George Buchanan, the British ambassador to Saint Petersburg, was told that this was a compliment "quite unprecedented . . . equivalent to treating the Squadron with Sovereign honours."[85] The officers of the squadron described the reception accorded them by naval officials and the inhabitants of Reval "as being nothing less than affectionate. . . . [It] well accorded with the best traditions of Russian warm heartedness and hospitality."[86] Great distance had been traveled in relations between the two countries since the aborted 1906 naval visit, which had so frightened both the British and the Russian governments. The June 1914 visit was a festive occasion of genuine warmth, a "further proof of the real friendship" which Russia felt for Britain.[87]

Beneath the surface display of friendship and bonhomie, however, dissension simmered. The appointment of a German officer to command the garrison at Constantinople in October 1913 and Britain and France's reluctance to back Russia's opposition to the appointment persuaded Sazonov that Russia must take a stronger stand than it had in 1912–13 or its vital interests would be ignored by Britain and France and trampled upon by the Central Powers. Sazonov had been prepared to block Liman von Sanders' appointment, which Saint Petersburg viewed as extremely harmful to its determination to seize the straits, by occupying selected Ottoman ports had British support been available.[88] Anti-German sentiment—whose roots extended back through the Balkan Wars and the Bosnian annexation crisis to the Congress of Berlin—hardened with the Liman von Sanders affair. By 1914 there was a significant change in Russian attitudes. Concerns of national prestige and honor were expressed in official and unofficial Russia, and the idea of avoiding a military conflict at all costs no longer prevailed.

Difficulties threatened the Anglo-Russian relationship in the spring of 1914, especially concerning Persia and the question of a naval agreement, which the Russian government earnestly desired and from which the British government shied away as an unnecessary entanglement.[89] Nicholas II worried that Britain's preoccupation with the Irish question might prevent London from acting vigorously in foreign affairs. The emperor believed this would be very dangerous as it would cause the old Concert of great powers, which had previously managed past crises, to break down.[90] In fact, British foreign policy was bedeviled by the central dilemma of how to maintain its understandings with Russia and France without upsetting Germany.[91] This would prove to be an impossible balancing act as the events of July and August 1914 showed. Despite these serious problems, however, Russia was firmly committed to Britain, even going so far as to propose an alliance in February 1914 similar to Russia's alliance with France, clearly indicating the Russian government's desire not just to adhere to the Triple Entente but to strengthen it.[92] The failure to transform the Entente into an alliance, despite support in the Foreign Office, stemmed from the British government's reluctance to conclude an alliance that could have split the Liberal Cabinet and raised the question of the future of the Liberal Party.[93] Domestic British concerns thwarted the Russian government's desire to transform Anglo-Russian relations into a stronger, more useful coalition.

Shortly after the departure of the gratified first battle-cruiser squadron of the British Royal Navy, Raymond Poincaré and his foreign minister, Réné Viviani, made their celebrated visit to Saint Petersburg, on the eve of a war that would destroy the balance of power in Europe, which the Dual Alliance had been originally designed to preserve. In retrospect, the irony of this visit was great. Official Russia, glittering in imperial splendor, welcomed its ally with all the pomp and circumstance an ancien régime could muster. In 1914 Russian commitment to the Dual Alliance appeared absolute, and the state visit of the French president was an opportunity to publicize this solidarity. In one sense, however, this visit too was an illusion, which masked tensions in the Alliance and in Russian society. Russia had sufficiently recovered from 1905–6 to mount an impressive display for a state visit but not sufficiently to endure the coming war. In fact, when Poincaré visited Saint Petersburg more than 110,000 workers were on strike in the capital. Almost all the factories and commercial establishments in the working-class districts of Saint Petersburg were closed, and thousands of workers were engaged in fierce battles with Cossacks and police detachments.[94]

Prior to the visit, the Caillaux scandal (with the attendant rumors of the French minister of finance's secret negotiations with Germany during the Agadir crisis) and the fall of the Ribot Ministry and its potential impact on French military laws, had troubled many within Russia.[95] The French ambassador to Saint Petersburg, Maurice Paléologue, nervously monitored the situation for Gaston Doumergue, the minister of foreign affairs. The German newspapers, which had a large readership in Moscow and Saint Petersburg, used the French scandals as an argument against the Franco-Russian alliance. According to Paléologue, the efforts of the German papers were "not in vain" and found sympathy in the emperor's entourage and even in liberal Duma circles.[96] *Birzhevie Vedomosti* published an anonymous article entitled "Russia Is Ready: France Must Be as Well," which was said to have been inspired by the Russian minister of war, General Sukhomlinov, whose dislike of the French was well known.[97] The article dealt with the military preparedness of the two allies and indicated that Russia "cannot with sang-froid contemplate the French ministerial crisis." The author hoped that the French government would be able to maintain the law of three years' military obligation,[98] which had been passed in August 1912 in response to the reorganization of the German army after the Balkan Wars. Poincaré succeeded in spearheading the bill through the Chamber against heated opposition from the Socialists and many Radicals, but the measure proved to be intensely unpopular with the people.

Developments leading up to Poincaré's July 1914 visit, then, were not entirely propitious. On the surface, the visit was a proud display of allied unity and imperial might, quite unlike the hurried visit of President Fallières in 1908. Despite Russian concern about domestic problems in France, however, the Alliance was closer than it had been since the Russo-Japanese War. This mutual commitment to the Alliance was apparent in the length, the style, and the substance of Poincaré's visit. In "faultless French" Nicholas II told Poincaré "how happy a recollection" he had of Poincaré's last visit in 1912, stressing his loyalty to the Alliance. During the president's audience with the tsar, Poincaré and Nicholas II discussed at length the difficulties between Britain and Russia.[99] The emperor was adamant that "no problem should present itself which might jeopardise good relations between England and Russia." The tsar was committed to the proposed Naval Convention with Britain, about which he had just written to King George begging him to speed things up. Nicholas expressed his gratitude to the French for their aid in advancing this matter with the British. According to Pierre Gilliard, the tsare-vich's tutor, the president "made an excellent impression upon the Czar," who warmly praised Poincaré: "He is a remarkable man, with a splendid intellect, and a brilliant talker. That's always useful: but what I like most is that there is nothing of the diplomat about him. He is not reticent, but plain-spoken and frank and wins one's confidence at once."[100] Poincaré promised Russia France's full support in the developing international crisis, arising from the assassination of Arch-Duke Franz Ferdinand, the heir to the Austrian throne, in Sarajevo by a Serbian terrorist. Buchanan reported to Grey that France and Russia were in full agreement and had decided to take action in Vienna to pre-vent any intervention in Serbian internal affairs.[101] Sazonov's 1912 assess-ment of Poincaré as a "sure and faithful friend" who would be useful in a crisis appears to have been vindicated.[102] During the July crisis of 1914 Rus-sia finally received firm French support of Russia's position in the Balkans, its elusive goal for almost a decade. Austria-Hungary delayed presenting its ultimatum to Belgrade until 23 July, when Poincaré and his party left Saint Petersburg to avoid close cooperation between the allies.[103]

The visit gave the impression of cordial cooperation between Russia and France. Cheering crowds, organized by the police, hailed Poincaré on his way to the Peter and Paul Fortress.[104] The Grand Duke Nicholas held a ban-quet in Poincaré's honor after a military review at Krasnoe-Selo. The grand duke's wife, the Montenegrin Princess Anastasia, showed Paléologue a box filled with soil from Lorraine. The banquet tables were decorated with Lorraine thistle.[105] Poincaré hosted a dinner at the French Embassy for the Russian ministers, important generals, admirals, and civil servants during which he conversed with the new Russian prime minister, I.L. Goremykin, who seemed "very friendly to France where he has spent a great deal of his time."[106] The nobility of Saint Petersburg formed a delegation to greet the French president and pay its respects. Their address illustrated their com-mitment to the Dual Alliance and faith in Poincaré as a friend of Russia. They stressed friendship with France, "indissoluable ties" between the two countries and the heartfelt support of all classes of Russian society for the Alliance.[107] The nobility's welcome to the president of a republic betrayed no hint of ambivalence or doubt.

In the same warm vein of appreciation, Sergei Pavlovich Ispolatov, bu-reau chief of the General Staff, wrote a poem, entitled "Greetings to the High Guest" and dedicated it to the French president. The poem welcomed the president to the great capital of tsarism. Ispolatov referred to Poincaré with the familiar "tyi," expressing the hope that once he has been shown the "peaceful north... that love this north will YOU." He beseeched Poincaré to accept "our greeting . . . from love." The last stanza says that the author alone did not shape these words "BUT ALL THE RUSSIAN PEOPLE."[108] Such a flight of fancy from an officer of the General Staff for President Fallières in 1908 would have been difficult to imagine.

Nicholas II's final toast to Poincaré was as profuse as Ispolatov's poem, but somewhat more dignified. The emperor requested the president to return to his beautiful country with "the expression of the faithful friendship and the cordial sympathy of all of Russia."[109] The last state visit between imperial Russia and the Third Republic of France thus ended on "a truly cordial note."[110] President Poincaré and his foreign minister Viviani sailed away aboard the cruiser *La France.*

The presentation of the Austro-Hungarian ultimatum in Belgrade a few hours earlier plunged Europe into a crisis. The harshness of the ultimatum and its forty-eight-hour deadline was a shock. Sazonov is said to have remarked, "C'est la guerre européene."[111] In seven days the allies were at war with the Central Powers, and the words of solidarity and trust spoken over good wine during peacetime were put to the ultimate test. In the final analysis, Russia's commitment to France and Great Britain endured longer than might have been reasonably expected, given the disastrous way in which the war unfolded and the strain it inflicted on the imperial regime. Russian loyalty during the war was testament to Russian commitment to the policy of the Triple Entente.

In slightly less than a decade since the end of the Russo-Japanese War, official Russia, after a period of deep ambivalence toward France and Great Britain, came down firmly on the side of the Triple Entente as the visits of June and July 1914 illustrated. The experience of 1905 had made tsarist officials more cautious in their foreign policy.[112] But while cognizant of the risks a European war would present to the very survival of the regime, Nicholas II's government, nevertheless, pursued a policy of closer ties with Britain and France, which fanned inadvertently the flames of Berlin's phobia about encirclement. In June and July 1914, official Russia publicly embraced and reaffirmed its commitment to the Triple Entente as the cornerstone of Russian foreign policy. The "Fateful Alliance"[113] was celebrated in Saint Petersburg as the clouds of the war that would destroy imperial Russia gathered over Europe. The support and firm belief in their longtime ally, France, and in their new friend, Great Britain, that Russia's rulers and educated society expressed during the visits of June and July 1914 survived three bloody years of war and ended only with the Bolshevik seizure of power in October 1917.

NOTES

1. For a good discussion of Russian foreign policy in the Far East see A.V. Ignatiev, "The Foreign Policy of Russia in the Far East at the Turn of the Nine-

teenth and Twentieth Centuries," in H. Ragsdale and V.W. Ponomarev, eds., *Imperial Russian Foreign Policy* (New York, 1993), pp. 247–267.

2. D.M. McDonald, "A Lever without a Fulcrum," ibid., p. 282.

3. D.C.B. Lieven, *Nicholas II: Twilight of the Empire* (New York, 1993), pp. 190–191.

4. AVPR, f. 133, op. 470, 1906g., d. 83, l. 130, 24 May/6 June 1906.

5. Ibid., l. 131, 28 June 1906.

6. AVPR, f. 133, op. 470, 1906g., d. 97, part II, l.80, secret telegram from Benckendorf, 28 June 1906.

7. Viscount Grey of Fallodon, *Twenty-Five Years, 1892–1916* (Toronto, 1925), p. 150. Grey had defended the proposed naval visit in the House of Commons. He argued that Great Britain was not taking sides in Russia's internal problems: "The Fleet goes without reference to the internal affairs of Russia. It goes to pay its compliment to the Tsar, the head of the great Russian nation. . . . [T]he visit is also intended for the Russian people." *Parliamentary Debates*, 4th series, vol. 160, 5 July 1906, p. 329.

8. W.C. Fuller, *Strategy and Power in Russia, 1600–1914* (New York, 1992), pp. 416–417. Resistance to the accord did exist in official quarters, most notably from General F.F. Palitsyn, chief of the General Staff. He objected to the generous concessions to Britain, particularly in Persia and was loathe to surrender Russia's position because of temporary weakness. Furthermore, he was worried about alienating Germany. See I.V. Ignat'ev, *Russko-angliiskie otnoshenie nakunune pervoi mirovoi voiny* (Moscow, 1962), pp. 59–63.

9. AVPR, f. 133, op. 470, 1908g., d. 60, l. 106, 9/22 May 1908, Benckendorf to Izvolsky.

10. Ibid., l. 69, 18/31 May 1908, letter to O'Beirne, British chargé d'affaires.

11. *BD*, vol. 5, doc. 194, Sir Charles Hardinge to Sir Arthur Nicolson, 13 April 1908, p. 236.

12. D. McLean, "English Radicals, Russia, and the Fate of Persia, 1907–1913," *English Historical Review* 93 (1978), p. 339. The English radicals had been vehemently opposed to the Anglo-Russian Convention since the beginning and had protested Edward VII's visit to Reval, although, as McLean points out, their ability to change Grey's policy was quite limited.

13. *Parliamentary Debates*, 4th series, 4 June 1908, col. 246.

14. AVPR, f. 133, op. 470, 1908g., d. 60, ll. 227–28, 28 May/10 June 1908, Poklevskii-Kozell to Izvolsky. Grey, *Twenty-Five Years, 1892–1916*, pp. 150 and 203, appendix to chapter 12, "Report of Sir Charles Hardinge to Sir Edward Grey on the Visit of King Edward to the Tsar at Reval in June 1908," 12 June 1908.

15. Ibid., p. 207.

16. Harold Nicolson, First Lord Carnock, *A Study in the Old Diplomacy* (London, 1930), p. 271. See also BD, vol. 5, doc. 195, 12 June 1908, pp. 237–45.

17. Present at Reval, among others, were Nicholas II and the Empress Alexandra, Edward VII, Queen Alexandra, Princess Victoria, the Russian Premier P.A. Stolypin, the Russian Foreign Minister A.P. Izvolsky, Russian Ambas-

sador to the Court of St. James Count Benckendorf, Sir Charles Hardinge, the British First Sea Lord Admiral Fisher, and Sir Arthur Nicolson, the British ambassador to Saint Petersburg. AVPR, f. 133, op. 470, 1908g., d. 60, ll. 69 and 132.

18   A.A. Mossolov, *At the Court of the Last Tsar* (London, 1935) p. 212.

19.   AVPR, f. 133, op. 470, 1908g., d. 60, l. 192.

20.   Ibid., l. 219.

21.   BD, vol. 5, doc. 195, Hardinge's Report on the King's Visit to Reval, 12 June 1908, p. 243.

22.   Ibid., p. 244.

23.   D. Geyer, *Russian Imperialism* (New Haven, Conn., 1987), passim. See also D.C.B. Lieven, *Russia and the Origins of the First World War* (London, 1983), p. 153.

24.   D.W. Sweet and R.T.B. Langhorne, "Great Britain and Russia, 1907–1914," in F.H. Hinsley, *British Foreign Policy under Sir Edward Grey* (Cambridge, 1977), p. 244.

25.   AVPR, f. 133, op. 470, 1906g., d. 107, part 1. ll. 192–95.

26.   AVPR, f. 133, op. 470, 1908g., d. 108, l. 564, 2/15 May 1906.

27.   AVPR, f. 133, op. 470, 1908g., d. 69, ll. 183–84, 8/21 December 1907; private and confidential letter, Izvolsky to Nelidov.

28.   Ibid.

29.   AVPR, f. 133, op. 470, 1908g., d. 69, ll. 183–184, 8/21 December 1907; private and confidential letter, Izvolsky to Nelidov.

30.   Ibid.

31.   AVPR, f. 133, op. 470, 1908g., d. 69, ll. 187–88, 16/29 April 1908; personal letter, Nelidov to Izvolsky.

32.   Ibid.

33.   DDF Second Series, vol. 11, no. 392, Touchard to Pichon (29 June 1908), p. 678.

34.   AVPR, f. 133, op. 470, 1908g., d. 69, l. 34, 17/30 June 1908; secret telegram from Nelidov.

35.   Ibid., l. 36, article from *Le Matin*.

36.   AVPR, f. 133, op. 470, 1908g., d. 69, ll. 41–43, 26 June/9 July 1908; personal and confidential letter, Nelidov to Izvolsky.

37.   Ibid., l. 40, 30 June/13 July 1908; dispatch from Nelidov.

38.   France et Russie, in *Journal de Saint Pétersbourg*, 15/28 July 1908, p. 1.

39.   Ibid.

40.   DDF, Second Series, vol. 11, no. 421, Note du Ministre (5 August 1908) p. 724.

41.   Ibid., p. 727.

42.   Ibid., p. 730.

43.   Lieven, *Nicholas II*, p. 193.

44.   Sweet and Langhorne, "Great Britain and Russia, 1907–1914," p. 240.

45.   Ibid., p. 9.

46. AVPR, f. 133, op. 470, 1909g., d. 196, l. 160.

47. K. Neilson, "Wishful Thinking: The Foreign Office and Russia, 1907–1917," in B.J. McKercher, ed., *Shadow and Substance in British Foreign Policy, 1895–1939* (Edmonton, Alberta, 1984) p. 157. Grey also requested an official dispatch from Nicolson on whether there had been an improvement in Russia concerning executions for political crimes and a general cessation of martial law to counter hostile British public opinion about the emperor's visit to Cowes. K. Neilson, *Britain and the Last Tsar* (Oxford, 1995), p. 14.

48. AVPR, f. 133, op. 470, 1909g., d. 197, l. 2, 3/16 June 1909; secret telegram from Benckendorf.

49. Parliamentary Debates vol. 6, 15 June 1909, col. 806.

50. AVPR, f. 133, op. 470, 1909g., d. 197, l. 4, 3/16 June 1909; secret telegram from Benckendorf.

51. *The Times*, 16 June 1909, p. 11.

52. AVPR, f. 133, op. 470, 1909g., d. 197, l. 3, 3/16 June 1909; secret telegram from Benckendorf.

53. Barry Hollingsworth, "The Society of Friends of Russian Freedom: English Liberals and Russian Socialists, 1890–1917," *Oxford Slavonic Papers* 3 (1970), p. 62. The society had also protested against the 1907 Anglo-Russian Convention.

54. Ibid., l. 6, 13/26 June 1909; secret telegram from Benckendorf.

55. *The Times*, 29 June 1909, p. 5. A.S. Khomiakov issued the statement for the delegation.

56. AVPR, f. 133, op. 470, 1909g., d. 197, l. 7, 16/29 June 1909; secret telegram from Benckendorf.

57. Ibid.

58. Ibid.

59. An April 1909 memorandum by Sir Charles Hardinge on the possibility of war shows clearly British unwillingness to promise Russia material aid in the event of war with Germany and Austria. "It would be imprudent to give a pledge of this kind to a reactionary Gov[ernment] whose sympathies are with Germany and it w[oul]d be an alliance wh[ich] w[oul]d be a sham and in opposition to England the repres[entati]ve of liberal and const[itutio]n[al] Gov[ernmen]t." BD, vol. 5, appendix 3, p. 825.

60. Sweet and Langhorne, "Great Britain and Russia, 1907–1914," p. 247.

61. AVPR, f. 133, op. 470, 1909g., d. 197, l. 29, 25 June/8 July 1909; secret telegram from Benckendorf.

62. Ibid., l. 127.

63. Fuller, *Strategy and Power in Russia, 1600–1914*, p. 439.

64. L.C.F. Turner, "The Russian Mobilization in 1914," in P.M. Kennedy, ed., *The War Plans of the Great Powers, 1880–1914* (London, 1979), p. 251.

65. Ibid., p. 252.

66. For example, LN vol. 1, Izvolsky to Sazonov (16/29 February 1912), pp. 203–4.

67. Raymond Poincaré, *The Memoirs of Raymond Poincaré, 1912* (London, 1926), Poincaré's notes from his audience with Nicholas II, 11 August 1912, p. 226. Russian high society lionized Poincaré during his stay. The premier had tea with the Grand Duchess Maria Pavlovna, Nicholas II's aunt; visited V.N. Kokovtsov, chairman of the Council of Ministers at his home; and the Russian Imperial Academy of Science held a luncheon in Poincaré's honor. See Poincaré, *Memoirs, 1912*, p. 221 and AVPR, f. 133, op. 470, 1912g., d. 201, ll. 23–24 and 69.

68. Poincaré, *Memoirs, 1912*, p. 235.

69. AVPR, f. 133, op. 470, 1912g., d. 201, l. 95.

70. Ibid., 4 August 1912; telegram from Poincaré to Sazonov.

71. Ibid., l. 82, 4 August 1912; telegram from Sazonov to Poincaré.

72. LN, vol. 2, Sazonov's report to Nicholas II (4 August 1912), p. 345.

73. Ibid., p. 345. See also BD/CP, vol. 6, no. 113, Buchanan to Grey (18 August 1912), p. 260.

74. F.L. Schuman, *War and Diplomacy in the French Republic* (New York, 1969), p. 169.

75. The Anglo-Russian relationship was also tightening at this time. Despite British annoyance over Russian behavior in Persia, Grey wrote in 1912 that he "staked everything upon pulling the Agreement through all difficulties." Quoted in Rose L. Greaves, "Themes in British Policy towards Persia in Its Relation to Indian Frontier Defence, 1798–1914," *Asian Affairs* 22, no. 1 (1991), p. 43. See also K. Wilson, *The Policy of the Entente* (Cambridge, UK, 1985), in which he argues that Britain was more dependent on good relations with Russia than vice versa.

76. BD/CP, vol. 6, no. 112, Buchanan to Grey (11 August 1912), pp. 257–58.

77. Ibid., p. 258.

78. Ibid., p. 259.

79. Ibid., p. 258.

80. Volker Berghahn has written of the so-called golden age of pre-1914 Europe that "it is probably more accurate to say that behind a splendid façade there existed an international community convulsed by growing conflict." V. Berghahn, *Germany and the Approach of War in 1914* (London, 1973), p. 211.

81. Theodore von Laue, "The Chances for Liberal Constitutionalism," *Slavic Review*, 24, no. 1 (1965), pp. 34–46. Von Laue argues convincingly that the rapidity of Russian industrialization threatened Russia's political and social stability but it did not come "fast enough to secure Russia's sovereignty in the competition of the Great Powers." See p. 45.

82. M.G. Eksteins, "Great Britain and the Triple Entente on the Eve of the Sarajevo Crisis," in Hinsley, ed., *British Foreign Policy under Sir Edward Grey*, pp. 342–343.

83. Meriel Buchanan, *Russia Observed: The Dissolution of an Empire* (New York, 1971), p. 71.

84. AVPR, f. 133, op. 470, 1914g., d. 197, l. 10, 18 June/1 July 1914; Buchanan to Sazonov.

85. BD, vol. 10, Part 2, no. 555, Buchanan to Grey (25 June 1914), pp. 810–11.

86. Ibid., p. 810.

87. Ibid., p. 811.

88. Lieven, *Russia and the Origins of the First World War*, p. 47.

89. I.Klein, "The Anglo-Russian Convention and the Problem of Central Asia," *Journal of British Studies* 11, no. 1, (1971), pp. 126–47 argues that the Anglo-Russian Convention caused the British serious dissatisfaction and it failed to achieve Britain's aim of halting Russian expansion in areas deemed crucial to the defense of India and in central Asia; after 1912, the Anglo-Russian Convention hindered Britain's quest for security. In the spring and early summer of 1914, sharp Anglo-Russian bargaining over Britain's new policy in Tibet threatened to break down the Anglo-Russian accord altogether. John A. Murray discusses British public outrage over Russia's aggressive policy in Persia in "Foreign Policy Debated: Sir Edward Grey and his Critics, 1911–1912," in: W.C. Askrew and L.P. Wallace, eds., *Power, Public Opinion, and Diplomacy: Essays in Honour of E.M. Carroll* (Durham, N.C., 1959), pp. 140–71.

90. Lieven, *Nicholas II*, p. 197.

91. Eksteins, "Great Britain and the Triple Entente," p. 342.

92. D.W. Spring, "The Trans-Persian Project and Anglo-Russian Relations, 1909–1914," *Slavonic and East European Review* 54 (1976), p. 78. Keith Neilson argues in *Britain and the Last Tsar* that Anglo-Russian relations were strained from the November 1910 Potsdam conference to the outbreak of war in 1914 and that the working of the convention in Persia was the most obvious difficulty between the two powers but only a symptom of deeper problems. In Neilson's opinion, Britain had two concerns about Russia. London worried that as Russia recovered from 1905, it would grow more aggressive in central Asia and Russia would disassociate itself from Britain and France and conclude an understanding with Germany, p. 317. Yet in the spring of 1914, the main thrust of Russian diplomacy was to tie Britain more firmly to Russia.

93. See Wilson, *The Policy of the Entente*, pp. 45–53, for a discussion of the constraints on British foreign policy.

94. Leopold Haimson, "The Problem of Social Stability in Urban Russia, 1905–1917 (Part One)," *Slavic Review* 23, no. 4 (1964), pp. 619–642. Haimson shows that in 1914 Russia experienced the greatest number of strikes, economic and political, since 1905, p. 628. He argues in the second part of his influential essay that 1914 was "approximately, a half-way station between 1905 and 1917. What the war years would do was not to conceive, but to accelerate substantially, the two broad processes of polarization that had already been at work in Russian national life during the immediate prewar period." See Haimson, "The Problem of Social Stability in Urban Russia, 1905–1917 (Part Two)," *Slavic Review* 24, no. 1 (1965), p. 17. In a recent article Haimson has moderated somewhat his earlier views. See Haimson, "The Problem of Political and Social Mobility in Urban Russia on the Eve of War and Revolution Revisited," *Slavic Review* 59, no. 4 (2000), pp. 848–75.

95. J.F.V. Keiger, *France and the Origins of the First World War* (London, 1983), p. 139. DDF, 3rd Series, vol. 10, no. 404, Doulcet to Viviani (18 June 1914), pp. 579–80.

96. Ibid., no. 95, Paléologue to Doumergue (10 April 1914), p. 159.

97. Ibid., no. 404, Doulcet to Viviani (18 June 1914), pp. 579–80.

98. Ibid., no. 369, Doulcet to Bourgeois (13 June 1914), pp. 542–43.

99. Raymond Poincaré, *The Memoirs of Raymond Poincaré, 1913–1914* (London, 1928), p. 165.

100. Pierre Gilliard, *Thirteen Years at the Russian Court* (London, 1921) pp. 98–99.

101. Turner, "Russia's Mobilization in 1914," p. 260. F.L. Schuman also makes the point that the most significant result of this last state visit by a president of the French republic to tsarist Russia was to impress upon Nicholas II and Sazonov French willingness to follow Russia in any course chosen by them and to strengthen their determination to resist Austrian demands on Serbia. Schuman, *War and Diplomacy in the French Republic*, p. 215.

102. LN, vol. 2, Sazonov's report to Nicholas II, 4 August 1912, p. 345.

103. James Joll, *The Origins of the First World War* (London, 1968), p. 14.

104. Poincaré, *Memoirs, 1913–1914*, pp. 169–70. H. Rogger, "Russia in 1914," *Journal of Contemporary History* 1, no. 3 (1966), p. 107.

105. Schuman, *War and Diplomacy in the French Republic*, p. 214.

106. Poincaré, *Memoirs, 1913–1914*, p. 172.

107. AVPR, f. 130, op. 470, 1914g., d. 330, l. 18.

108. AVPR, f. 133, op. 470, 1914g., d. 329, l. 4.

109. AVPR, f. 133, op. 470, 1914g., d. 330, l. 89.

110. Poincaré, *Memoirs, 1913–1914*, p. 181.

111. Quoted in Joll, *The Origins of the First World War*, p. 14.

112. A.V. Ignatiev, "The Foreign Policy of Russia in the Far East at the Turn of the Nineteenth and Twentieth Centuries," in H. Ragsdale and V.W. Ponomarev, eds., *Imperial Russian Foreign Policy* (New York, 1993), p. 266.

113. George Kennan, *The Fateful Alliance: France, Russia, and the Coming of the First World War* (Princeton, 1979).

Chapter 3

A Marriage of Convenience: Nicholas II and the Triple Entente

Despite his reputation as a reactionary and weak-willed ruler, Nicholas II was consistent in his post-1905 foreign policy. He regarded the Dual Alliance, formed by his revered father, as the base of Russian foreign policy and never seriously considered abandoning it. Moreover, once the last Romanov emperor embraced the Entente with Great Britain, he remained faithful to it and even sought to transform it into a defensive alliance. Nicholas II might have been an initially reluctant partner to the Triple Entente, but once he had entered into it he was faithful to it to the end. In the second half of his reign, Nicholas II's primary goal was the preservation of imperial Russia and the Romanov dynasty. For this the overriding imperative was peace. The tsar and his foreign ministers concluded that the Triple Entente was the best means to this end. Thus reasons of realpolitik, not ideology, motivated the tsar's Triple Entente policy.

The tsar played a central role in the formation and execution of Russian foreign policy. Scholars and memoirists have often cast aspersions on Nicholas II's strength of character and consistency of purpose, but his power as the sole arbiter of foreign policy, as outlined in article 12 of the Fundamental Laws, has not been challenged.[1] Nicholas II was a ruler who maintained a close watch on foreign policy events, read "conscientiously the despatches and telegrams which were submitted to him every day and, blessed by an excellent memory, was exceptionally well-informed on questions of international relations."[2] The new Duma did exercise a limited power over foreign policy because of its restricted role in budgetary matters, including increases in defense expenditures, and a relatively free and increasingly vocal press blossomed after 1905. Nonetheless, those who wished to alter the course of Russian foreign policy had to catch the ear and influence the views of Nicholas II.[3]

The view of the centrality of the tsar to the formulation and execution of Russian foreign policy has been challenged recently but not essentially altered. D.M. McDonald has argued that, as a result of the 1905 revolution, the council of ministers and particularly its chairman began to play an important role in foreign policy and thereby diminished the emperor's hitherto preeminent role.[4] According to McDonald, Witte, Stolypin, and Kokovtsov all aimed for "United Government." McDonald admits that after Stolypin's death Nicholas reemerged as an important political player.[5] Moreover, the question of the emperor's "confidence" (*doverie*) was always critical to the effectiveness of the council chairman.[6] While not primarily concerned with foreign policy, Andrew Verner characterizes the last emperor as a man psychologically alienated by temperament and circumstances from the role forced on him, and thereby distant and remote from matters of vital concern.[7] Neither McDonald nor Verner denies that Nicholas II continued to play a key role in the functioning of the Russian state and the conduct of Russia's foreign policy.

Despite the undisputed importance of Nicholas II to foreign policy, certain problems do exist that complicate any discussion about him. Although an articulate man, fluent in several languages, the main sources in the emperor's voice are terse and often unrevealing of any opinion he might have had. His famous diary is the classic case in point. The paucity of first-hand sources, however, does not necessarily mean the emperor held no opinions but rather that he was reserved in voicing them, but not necessarily from acting on them. This facet of Nicholas's character has often led memoirists and historians to make derogatory judgments about his character, the most frequent of which were and are that the last emperor was a dull, unimaginative prisoner of his court circle and easily swayed.[8] But, in reality, despite his gentle and impressionable manner, when his convictions were at stake he could be quite stubborn.[9] Coming to the throne of a vast and disparate empire at such a young age in a period of rapid societal change would prove to be a formidable assignment. Nonetheless, intellectually Nicholas II would prove quite able and he believed in his role and was determined to fulfill the responsibilities that he believed God had placed upon him.[10]

A final problem is the nature of the man himself. He never embraced his role as autocrat with any enthusiasm, and he ruled in extraordinarily troubled circumstances. In a certain sense the character of Nicholas II was both anachronistic and paradoxical. He was the supreme ruler of a vast, rapidly industrializing empire as it entered the twentieth century. Yet his outlook and values were in many ways a throwback to the distant Russian past, which he so admired. Nicholas's view of the good society was entirely rural and out of touch with the twentieth century. In 1902 he said, "I conceive of Russia as a landed estate of which the proprietor is the tsar, the administrator is the nobility, the steward is the zemstvo, and workers are the peasantry."[11]

Always aware that he had been born on the nameday of Job the Sufferer, Nicholas II was almost medieval in his acceptance of God and fate. Once when asked how he could keep his composure when in the background the guns suppressing the mutiny at Kronstadt could be heard, the emperor replied: "It is because I have a firm, an absolute conviction that the fate of Russia—that my own fate and that of my family—is in the hands of God who has placed me where I am. Whatever may happen to me I shall bow to his will with the consciousness of never having had any thought other than that of serving the country which he has entrusted to me."[12] Nicholas never deviated from this faith and in fact it enabled him to accept stoically his abdication, imprisonment, and execution. Nicholas II also maintained a belief in the medieval notion of the union between tsar and people. In 1903 the emperor spent four days at Sarov, where Saint Seraphim was buried. On this occasion Nicholas II was nearly mobbed by enthusiastic crowds, an event which deeply moved him and confirmed "his own self-image of a noble and benign monarch, and he believed that in their mutual devotion to Saint Seraphim, tsar and people were as one."[13] The birth of the heir a little more than a year later confirmed Nicholas II's belief in his faith. He said, "As for Saint Seraphim's holiness and the authenticity of his miracle, I am so fully convinced of them that no one will ever shake my belief."[14]

Nicholas's dual role as both the father of the Russian tribe and the head of the imperial government greatly limited his effectiveness.[15] In his role as father of his people, Nicholas was engulfed with personal petitions from his subjects, many of them concerned with trivial matters. Yet, at the same time he was expected to preside over a government that had evolved into a complex state apparatus. Nicholas II, however, performed this function with the offices of an eighteenth-century household. The emperor of all Russia had no personal secretariat, let alone a private secretary. No one stemmed the flow of material that flooded his desk, and the last tsar even stamped his own envelopes.

There were also serious problems with the post-1905 system, which Nicholas had adopted under duress. The main failing of autocratic government was a lack of coordination between ministries and the absence of coherent policies that took into consideration all the state's interests. Ultimately such coordination was the emperor's responsibility, and consequently he was widely blamed for its absence. The ministers blamed the tsar, but the tsar himself became increasingly suspicious of his bureaucracy. Such a situation of mutual blame and distrust between the autocrat and his ministers was not conducive to effective governance. There quickly developed a rivalry between the autocrat and the chairman of the council of ministers, who needed the tsar's full support to function effectively, but such support was usually not forthcoming, as Nicholas II was not prepared to accept a reduced role. There was also a conflict between the legislative and executive with the ministers caught in the middle without the full support of either the tsar or the Duma. Finally there existed a conflict between the State Council and the Duma. The State Council members were appointed and were largely former ministers and senior officials, most of them elderly, conservative landowners. Yet, the State Council, like the tsar, had an absolute veto over legislation. Such a system was a recipe for stalemate, which is exactly what transpired.[16]

No clear ideological motivation for foreign policy was evident during the reign of Nicholas II. Prior to 1904 he believed that Russia had a unique Eurasian destiny; consequently, his main foreign policy goal was to develop Russia's position in Siberia and the Far East. The Russo-Japanese War curtailed the emperor's eastern ambition and turned his attention back to Europe. Although he did not subscribe to the popular pan-Slavism of the period, he was determined that should the Ottoman empire collapse, no other power should seize Constantinople and block Russia's access route out of the Black Sea. The realities of Russia's international position after the crippling 1905 revolution and the humiliating military defeat at the hands of an Asiatic power forced Nicholas to adopt an unassertive foreign policy. A policy of "attentisme" became essential to preserve the empire and thereby the regime's raison d'être.[17] In the second decade of his rule, this absence of ideological motivation for foreign policy became even more apparent as the Triple Entente, an alignment which some regarded as contrary to traditional Russian interests, emerged. In part this new direction in Russian foreign policy was a desperate bid to preserve peace, to gain time and breathing space to ensure the survival of the ancien regime.

Throughout his reign, Nicholas remained faithful to his father's alliance with France, although occasionally French republicanism exasperated him and he never sympathized with the political traditions of the country of the Revolution. In the first years of his reign, the young emperor and his wife exchanged a series of visits with the French president. Nicholas's first visit to France in 1896 was a huge success. The people of Paris were unrestrained in their enthusiastic welcome. Nicholas wrote his mother and told her that "The reception in Paris was tremendous, as you probably know from the papers. I repeat I can only compare it to my entry into Moscow!"[18] The young tsar never forgot this overwhelming display of emotion and "in the future, this favourable impression in the mind and the heart of the young Tsar was to serve France well."[19] The popular image of the emperor in France was extremely positive. He was regarded as the father of his people, "the unshakeable guarantee of the Franco-Russian alliance."[20]

Aside from the 1905 Björkoe aberration, Nicholas never took any action to indicate that he wished to abandon France as an ally. Even with the abortive Björkoe treaty, the emperor believed, mistakenly, as his foreign minister later took great pains to point out, that an agreement with Germany could be reconciled to the alliance with France. Izvolsky in his memoirs described the emperor as a true friend of Britain and France.[21] In a December 1906 audience, Nicholas told Maurice Bompard, the French ambassador, that the alliance was "the base of my foreign policy, the foundation on which it rests entirely," and the emperor emphasized his statement by putting two vigorous fists on the writing table.[22]

Part of this strong commitment no doubt derived from Russia's financial dependence on French loans to see the empire through a period of reconstruction and repression of the revolutionary threat. When the Russian finance minister, Kokovtsov, visited Paris in 1906 to arrange a critically important loan, the tsar clearly understood the significance of the trip and the necessity of a quid pro quo between allies. Nicholas told Kokovtsov to apprise the French government of the "particular importance" he attached to the undertaking and the tsar was prepared "to support the French government in whatever form it most desired at the present time." He made clear that he meant strong Russian support for France at the Algeciras conference, which he felt the French could find quite useful.[23] Several years later, in 1913, when Kokovtsov, then chairman of the council of ministers, was on a similar mission to obtain loans for the construction of Russian railways, Nicholas sent a message of strong solidarity to Poincaré.[24] Nicholas was well aware of the material benefits for Russia's development to be derived from the Alliance and he was shrewd enough to cultivate good relations with French leaders.

Nicholas also appreciated French military strength and the importance of maintaining and strengthening military ties in the event of a war. He took an especial interest in high-level French participation in Russian military maneuvers in 1911.[25] In February 1912 Nicholas approved the notion of closer connections between the two countries' Naval General Staffs.[26] In 1913 Nicholas told Poincaré that he entirely shared his opinion about "the importance of correlated measures to be adopted in view to reinforce our two armies." He praised the new French military effort and assured the French president that Russia would not lag behind.[27] French financial assistance to Russia and the strength of the French army were two important factors that helped to ensure Nicholas II's continued devotion to the Dual Alliance, especially as the threat from Austria-Hungary and Germany seemed to be increasing, not decreasing.

Although the tsar was a faithful ally, French domestic politics often annoyed him, as they did many in the Russian government. In a masterpiece of British understatement, Nicolson described "the union between Socialistic freethinking France and Orthodox Russia" as "not a sympathetic one."[28] In October 1903 Nicholas commented to the kaiser that the French domestic situation disturbed him and French irreligiosity repulsed him. He attributed the problem to the Freemasons who, he believed, were influential everywhere. Nevertheless, he told Wilhelm that he had to maintain the alliance to ensure that France did not defect to the English camp.[29] In a similar vein Nicholas remarked to his mother years later about disturbances in Berlin and railway strikes in France: "There is a foul odour of revolution in all of this."[30]

Given his distaste for secular republicanism, it is not surprising that Nicholas disliked the left-wing French president Armand Fallières, as demonstrated during his 1907 visit to Russia. In a letter to the German emperor, Nicholas apparently made a slighting reference to "the woodcutters [sic] von Fallières," which caused Wilhelm "unlimited amusement."[31] In contrast, Nicholas admired the successor to Fallières, Raymond Poincaré, a man whose world view and attitudes were much closer to those of Nicholas II. When the emperor met Poincaré in 1912 for the first time, he told his mother that he "liked him very much; he is a calm and clever man of small build."[32] When Poincaré was elected president, Nicholas sent him an effusive telegram of congratulations.[33] In a sign of his pleasure, Nicholas awarded Poincaré the Order of Saint Andrew, Russia's highest order, citing the tsar's "sincere attachment to France as well as MY esteem and MY personal friendship for you."[34] The emperor's letter deeply touched the French president, who requested permission to publish it, which the Russian ambassador to Paris authorized.[35] The published letter created a sensation in France with the entire press, regardless of *parti pris,* remarking on the letter's cordial tone and the importance of such friendly sentiments when Germany was beginning new armament projects.[36]

With a French president he liked personally and agreed with on matters of foreign policy, Nicholas felt more at ease with his French ally than he had in a long time. Although Nicholas had always regarded the Dual Alliance as the base of his foreign policy, he had also taken it for granted. The original enthusiasm he had felt when he visited France as a young tsar in 1896 resurfaced only when Poincaré assumed the leadership and began to represent French interests more vigorously on the international stage.

This pattern of detached loyalty to France contrasts sharply with the real affection Nicholas held for the British royal family and British aristocratic life. Great Britain had been the traditional foe for the Russian empire throughout much of the nineteenth century, but this did not prevent Nicholas from developing a deep attachment to Britain, perhaps partly because Britain was the land of his courtship and the childhood home of his beloved wife. In his youth Nicholas had had an English tutor, a Mr. Charles Heath, whom the emperor always remembered fondly.[37] The emperor spoke English fluently and idiomatically and had a thorough knowledge of English literature.[38] The imperial couple always spoke to one another and corresponded in English. According to an intimate of the empress, the emperor "merely wished to live the quiet life of a well-bred gentleman: chivalrous by nature, he . . . came nearer the British public school idea than any other."[39] Nicholas was passionately fond of tennis, hunting, and walking and had a kennel of English collies in which he took great pride.[40] Moreover his extremely well-honed manners and his emphasis on duty and service were primarily Victorian attributes.

An important factor in Nicholas's regard for Britain was the close and warm family ties that bound the House of Windsor and the Romanovs. As tsarevich, Nicholas had attended the wedding of his English cousin George, who was to become George V. The young tsarevich's letter home reveals his sheer pleasure at his first visit to London and the ease he felt with the British royal family: "How nice it is to feel as if one were among family. I immediately felt quite at home. . . . I am delighted with London, I never thought I would like it so much."[41] Nicholas thoroughly enjoyed himself visiting Westminster Abbey, Saint Paul's, and the Tower. He also attended a ball at Buckingham Palace but, as he wrote his mother, he "didn't see many beautiful ladies. It's really much more fun to go to Rotten Row in the morning, where the whole of Society goes riding: what a pity we have nothing of the kind!"[42] Nicholas also spent a pleasant idyll in Britain with his fiancée in 1894 just prior to his father's death: "And so we spent three ideal days in their cosy cottage on the Thames quite quietly, not seeing anybody. We were out all day long in beautiful summer weather, boating up and down the river, picnicking on shore for tea. 'A veritable idyll.' I'm delighted by this only too short stay at Walton."[43] It was probably the last carefree interlude the young man had before he assumed the onerous duties of emperor, which must have rendered his memories all the more poignant.

After Nicholas ascended the throne, he maintained a close relationship with his English cousin George. The two first cousins resembled each other so much that they could have passed for identical twins and even members of their family would sometimes confuse them. Their similarities went beyond the physical. At heart they were both country gentlemen who loved their wives, preferred family life to the social whirl, and had inherited a simple Christian faith from their mothers. Both monarchs had absorbed a military code of command and obedience, and neither was particularly adept at the subtleties of politics.[44] The cousins corresponded regularly and quite cordially. In one letter Prince George assured Nicholas of his constancy: "What a long time it is since we met, you are often in our thoughts dear Nicky, I am sure you know that I never change and always remain the same to my old friends."[45] George gratefully acknowledged the role Nicholas played in the improvement of relations between their two countries: "I am so happy to think that the relations between our two countries are so good now, they never ought to be otherwise and I know how much you have done to bring this about, but then you have always been a friend of England's."[46]

The death of Edward VII in 1910 shook Nicholas II, who felt great sympathy for what his cousin now had to endure. Nicholas himself had sobbed "I am not ready to be Tsar" when his father died.[47] To his mother, who attended the funeral, he commented: "It is with great pleasure to read and hear how well, with what composure and intelligence, Georgie has begun to attend to his difficult work. May God help him to go on with it and to follow in dear Uncle Bertie's footsteps."[48] The official condolences referred to the deceased king as "a sincere friend of Russia," an opinion shared by Nicholas II.[49] Although unable to attend the funeral, the emperor and empress attended the memorial service held at the Anglican church in Saint Petersburg[50] and "the Emperor went far beyond the conventional to mark his feelings."[51]

The sympathy and support that his Russian cousin expressed touched the new English king deeply: "I thank you from the bottom of my heart for your dear letter and am deeply touched by the sympathy which you have shown me at the irreparable loss which I have sustained in the death of dearest Papa. . . . I saw Sir Arthur Nicolson today and he told me of all your kindness and sympathy which has touched me deeply and all the sorrow which has been expressed in Russia."[52] This heartfelt letter stressed the king's desire for good relations with Russia and his conviction that his Russian cousin shared his opinion completely on this matter. George emphasized the value he placed on their old friendship. Moreover, he stated his belief that "if only England, Russia, and France stick together then peace in Europe is assured. I believe these are also your sentiments."[53] On this matter George V was right. As the Central Powers became more aggressive, Nicholas II became convinced of the need to strengthen the Entente. A close and easy relationship with George V, which contrasted sharply with the strained relations between Nicholas and his German cousin, facilitated this process and made Nicholas perhaps more amenable to it than he might have been.

Nicholas followed the details of his cousin's coronation, which the dowager empress Marie attended, with great interest.[54] The correspondence between Nicholas and George became more frequent and substantive after George became king. The affable tone remained, and the two monarchs seemed able to discuss important matters frankly and without rancor. The theme of the letters concerned their common conviction that good relations between England and Russia be maintained and even strengthened. In this vein in March 1911 George V wrote: "It is my great object, as I know it is yours, that the friendly relations between Russia and England should not only be maintained but become more intimate than they are now. I feel convinced that if Russia, England and France have mutual understandings that the Peace of Europe will not be disturbed. . . . I know you don't mind me writing quite frankly what I think, as we have always been such good friends, I like to tell you everything."[55]

In the summer of 1913 the two cousins met in Berlin and had a chance to say in person what they had been communicating through letters and their ambassadors. Apparently the meeting, although short, went off smoothly, and no difference of opinion marred the event. Rather, it seemed to have reinforced their desire to work together for "the peace of Europe."[56] Just prior to the outbreak of World War I, George V sent his cousin a private letter outlining his concerns about Persia, the one matter which he believed caused tensions between the two countries. He called upon Nicholas's "friendship of so many years" to do what he could to clear up any misunderstandings.[57] This last peacetime letter from King George reveals plainly the close working relationship between the two cousins and monarchs, which both used to further cooperation and goodwill between their two countries.

Nicholas II felt more affection toward Britain than is sometimes acknowledged. Although he did have major reservations about the British political system and, as his attitude toward the Duma indicated, he certainly never considered emulating it in Russia, he did regard himself as a friend of Britain and was consistent in that friendship. In 1905 Nicholas expressed his pleasure to an English journalist at the large number of sympathetic letters he had received from England in the past year. He called them "nice letters, such nice, sympathising, kind letters."[58]

At Sir Arthur Nicolson's first audience as British ambassador, the emperor made a dignified impression and convinced Nicolson of his sincere desire to secure a mutually beneficial agreement between Russia and Great Britain.[59] Interestingly, given Nicholas's known conservatism, he also told Nicolson that he thought that the matter would be facilitated by the Liberal government in England. Nicolson had been appointed British ambassador to negotiate an agreement with Russia. The Anglo-Russian Convention, concluded in August 1907, marked the beginning of substantially improved relations between the two empires. Stolypin informed Nicolson that the emperor "was equally pleased" that the convention had been signed.[60] The British Foreign Office generally regarded Nicholas II as pro-Entente, although the British diplomatic establishment was aware that the emperor often found Britain too radical politically.[61]

By 1909 Nicolson could report that the emperor was "cordially in favour of maintaining close relations with England."[62] When Sir George Buchanan became British ambassador in 1910, Nicholas had fully convinced the British of his friendship. Buchanan admired the tsar and in his memoirs wrote that "there was, if I may say so without presumption, what amounted to a feeling of mutual sympathy between us."[63] Buchanan regarded Nicholas II as "a true and loyal ally."[64] In the spring of 1914 the actions of some Russian consuls in Persia marred what otherwise were smooth relations with Britain. But, in an audience with Buchanan, the emperor said, "I can only tell you, as I have so often told you before, that my one desire is to remain firm friends with England and, if I can prevent it, nothing shall stand in the way of the closest possible understanding between our two countries."[65]

At this point the tsar even advocated a defensive alliance between Russia and Great Britain. He believed that the absence of such an alliance meant that Great Britain could not give Russia "the same effective support as France."[66] The question of an alliance with Britain occupied entirely the last meeting the tsar had with Sazonov in April 1914 before he went to the Crimea.[67] Upon his return from Livadia, the emperor pushed the issue forcibly with the British ambassador. Nicholas commented on the division of Europe into two camps and the disquieting international situation, observing that, "What I should like to see is a closer bond of union between England and Russia, such as an alliance of a purely defensive character."[68] The emperor's main concern was that the present Anglo-Russian agreement be extended either in some fashion like the one he had suggested or "by some written formula which would record the fact of Anglo-Russian co-operation in Europe."[69] While advocating a defensive alliance with Britain, Nicholas II worried that the Irish problem might impede the Foreign Office from acting in foreign affairs.[70]

By the spring of 1914, therefore, Nicholas II had moved from passive acceptance of the need for an Entente with Britain to settle colonial differences to active advocacy of an alliance guaranteeing Anglo-Russian cooperation in Europe. The changing nature of international relations and the heightened threat that all participants had begun to see in European affairs wrought this change in Nicholas's thinking. Germany was the power disturbing the European equilibrium. Russia and Great Britain were, by the beginning of the twentieth century, status quo powers that could not afford major changes in the European balance of power. As such it was natural that they should seek each other out to balance what they perceived to be the growing German threat. Seen in this light, Nicholas II's desire to embrace Great Britain as an ally was the logical act of a ruler who sought above all else to maintain his empire and his dynasty, both fast becoming anachronisms in the modern world.

Given the pragmatic reasons which governed Nicholas's attitude toward Anglo-Russian relations, it is not contradictory that he also held serious reservations about Britain. Part of the tsar's resentment sprang from the Anglo-Japanese Treaty of 1902, which he thought had encouraged the Japanese to believe they could wage war successfully against Russia. In 1905 he described this treaty as "a moral backing that encouraged her [Japan] to attack us."[71]

The English press often irritated the tsar when it portrayed events in a light unflattering to the Russian state. In October 1905 he complained to his mother about the English press's reporting of recent pogroms, which he regarded as the spontaneous anger of the people against the revolutionaries. Because "nine tenths of the trouble-makers are Jews, the People's whole anger turned against them." He lamented that "In England, of course, the press says that these disorders were organised by the police; they still go on repeating this worn-out fable."[72] To the English journalist W.T. Stead, the tsar bemoaned "these stupid lies published in some books in England."[73]

The liberal nature of the British political system, which provided asylum for Russian radicals and revolutionaries, also offended Nicholas. To his German cousin Wilhelm II, Nicholas complained about anarchists who could live freely in certain countries, particularly Britain, and plot to assassinate people.[74] Nicholas viewed the impetuous comments of the British prime minister, Sir Henry Campbell-Bannerman, after the dissolution of the First Duma as insulting and inappropriate. Campbell-Bannerman had declared to a visiting Duma delegation in London that "the Duma is dead: long live the Duma!" Izvolsky recorded that Russian government circles perceived the exclamation as a challenge and an impertinence to the emperor. Izvolsky "had the greatest trouble to explain to my colleagues and to convince the Emperor himself that Mr. Campbell-Bannerman had only paraphrased, in applying it to the Duma, the time-honoured announcement which expressed in ante-revolutionary France the idea of the continuity of the monarchical principle: 'le Roi est mort: vive le Roi.' "[75]

A later incident enraged the emperor even more. The news that "a grotesque deputation is coming from England with an address to Mouromtseff [president of the First Duma] and his friends" infuriated Nicholas. He complained to his mother about the English government's inability to prevent the visit: "Uncle Bertie informed us that they were very sorry, but were unable to take any action to stop their coming. Their famous 'liberty,' of course! How angry they would be if a deputation went from us to the Irish to wish them success in their struggle against their government!"[76] In 1914 when the Irish question was at the forefront of British domestic politics, although Nicholas admitted he did not understand it, he did fear that the crisis might deprive Britain of its international standing.[77] Such incidents appear, however, to have strengthened Nicholas's belief that the English maintained a double standard in their judgment of Russia and that they should view Russia on Russian, not English, terms. As Izvolsky explained to Sir Edward Grey, the tsar was "by training and education not on the Liberal side," and it was possible to keep him on the side of the Entente with Britain only by proving that such a policy benefited Russia.[78]

In general Nicholas II disliked foreign things and regarded himself as a true Russian patriot. In a telling letter to Stolypin about the Naval General Staff, Nicholas wrote after his instructions: "Such is My will. Remember that we live in Russia and not abroad."[79] Frequently Nicholas would refer disparagingly to "the Jews abroad," revealing an anti-Semitic view of the world, typical of Russian conservatives.[80] Nicholas had little affection for his ancestor Peter the Great, the Romanov who had forced Russia to Westernize and become a European power for the first time. On the bicentenary of the foundation of Saint Petersburg, Nicholas commented to A.A. Mossolov, the head of the Court Chancellery, that Peter I was "the ancestor who appeals to me least of all. He had too much admiration for European 'culture.' . . . He stamped out Russian habits, the good customs of his sires, the usages bequeathed by the nation, on too many occasions."[81] In contrast, Nicholas's favorite ancestor was Alexei the Mild, Peter's father and the last of the Muscovite tsars.[82] Nicholas even named his long-awaited heir Alexei when he was born on 12 August 1904.

For similar reasons Nicholas II disliked words of foreign origin which had infiltrated the Russian language. On one occasion he said: "The Russian language is of such wealth that it is possible to give Russian equivalents for every expression in any foreign language; no word of non-Slav origin should be allowed to disfigure our speech."[83] To that end Nicholas would underline in red any word of foreign extraction he found in his ministers' reports. When he discovered incidentally that Izvolsky and his political assistant, N.V. Tcharykov, corresponded in Russian, not French, as had their predecessors, the emperor was "pleasurably surprised."[84]

Any discussion of Nicholas II's attitudes toward foreign policy must at least briefly consider the views of the imperial family and the court. Although in general the tsar did not discuss foreign policy questions with his suite or his family, there were a few major exceptions, notably his mother and his wife.[85] It is worth noting that most of those closest to the tsar in his small circle of intimates were anti-German and pro-Entente, which contradicts the traditionally accepted view that the emperor was surrounded by a circle of pro-Germans who exercised considerable influence on the execution of foreign policy.[86] Moreover, the Russian court was not monolithic in its views. The grand dukes tended to quarrel among themselves, dispelling the notion that there was a Grand Ducal party. There was even an "English" faction at the court centered around such prominent families as the Benckendorfs, the Dolgorukovs, and the Naryshkins.[87]

Maria Feodorovna, the Danish-born wife of Alexander III, exercised considerable influence over her son, Nicholas II, especially in the early years of his reign. Although her ascendancy over her son declined as he matured and his wife began to play a more dominant role, Nicholas II continued to correspond regularly with his mother and valued her opinions. The dowager empress was vehemently anti-German because of the Prussian invasion of her native Denmark in 1864 and the incorporation of Schleswig into the German empire. She regarded herself as a Westerner[88] and held the English royal family in high affection as her sister was married to Edward VII, for whom she had "the greatest regard."[89] Like her son, the empress Marie was hostile toward the foreign press, including the English. She told W.T. Stead, the English journalist who interviewed her in 1905, of her distaste for freedom of the press: "Yes, but if you only saw the horrid things they publish in the papers. They print all manner of horrid lies and then the foreign press reprint all these lies. If that is freedom of the press, you cannot wonder that we don't like it much."[90] She also received anonymous, abusive letters from Britain which she resented.[91]

Despite her dislike of certain British institutions such as a free press, the dowager empress spent much of her time during this period in Britain with her sister. She made her first visit in thirty-four years to Britain in February 1907 and was thrilled to be back. She had nothing but praise for the British royal family, Windsor Castle, and Buckingham Palace: "Everything is so tastefully and artistically arranged—it makes one's mouth water to see all their magnificence! . . . Everyone is so kind and friendly to me. It is most touching."[92] From 1907 to 1914 the dowager empress Marie made almost annual visits to her sister in Britain. All the visits were pleasant affairs, which reinforced her affection for the English royal family, Britain, and the Entente. While in Britain she would write to her son so he was well aware of his mother's feelings. On these visits to England she often dined with influential Englishmen, including Lord Rosebery, the former foreign secretary and prime minister, and Sir Edward Grey.[93] At home she did what she could to promote better relations between Great Britain and Russia. She favored strongly Izvolsky's appointment as foreign minister because he was a keen proponent of improved relations with Britain. She also frequently invited the British ambassador, Sir George Buchanan, to her informal luncheon parties, a privilege he considered to be a great honor.[94]

As the dowager empress's influence over her son waned, that of empress Alexandra waxed. She had throughout her married life an extremely intimate and caring relationship with her husband—an unusual circumstance for a royal marriage. Although Alexandra was a German princess, her mother had been Queen Victoria's daughter. Consequently, Alexandra was as English as she was German. Alexandra's mother died when her daughter was seven. After her mother's death, the young princess became very close to her maternal grandmother.[95] The young "Alix" became Queen Victoria's favorite granddaughter and was largely brought up at the English court.[96]

When Alexandra became empress of Russia, her grandmother's early influence did not disappear. A large portrait of Queen Victoria hung in one of the chief living rooms at Tsarskoe Selo.[97] As empress, the only time Alexandra wept in public was at the memorial service of Queen Victoria at the English church in Saint Petersburg.[98] According to a friend of the empress she was "a typical Victorian; she shared her grandmother's love of law and order, her faithful adherence to family duty, her dislike of modernity."[99] Alexandra's "conception of the bedroom was 'à-la-mode de' Windsor and Buckingham Palace in 1840."[100] Although she eventually spoke Russian fluently, for more than ten years after her arrival in Russia the empress retained an English accent.[101] She and her family always conversed together in English. Her command of French was comparatively poor, a distinct disadvantage as French was often spoken at court. Such attitudes and habits did not blend in well with the cosmopolitan Russian court and helped to contribute to the empress's alienation from Russian high society, a problem that worsened the longer she lived in Russia. The Russo-Japanese War, the 1905 revolution, the constant worry about the tsarvich's health, and the collapse of the empress's own health brought an end to the great court balls and spectacles. The reasons for the imperial couple's withdrawal from the high society of Saint Petersburg were not well understood, and the isolation of Nicholas and Alexandra in the latter half of his reign contributed to the weakening of the bonds of loyalty between the Russian elite and the crown.[102]

The empress's passionate embrace of Russian mysticism and a fervent belief in the bond between the tsar and his people contributed to her estrangement from the Westernized elite of Saint Petersburg. She was friendly with General A.A. Kireev, the pan-Slav publicist, whose views on Orthodoxy, Russian nationhood, and the union between tsar and people endeared him to the empress. Although not as zealous as his wife, Nicholas II shared her views about Russian piety and the unique bond between him and his people. The imperial couple's belief in the mystic purity of the Russian people led them ultimately to their notorious relationship with Rasputin, which did so much to discredit Nicholas and Alexandra, especially during the war years.

Despite the reputation she gained during the war as a German sympathizer and even spy, the empress in fact preferred Britain over Germany and was loyal to the Dual Alliance.[103] When the imperial couple visited Cowes in 1907, the empress was overjoyed to be back where she had spent the happiest days of her childhood. She wrote of the hospitality shown them by Edward VII that "dear Uncle Bertie has been most kind and attentive."[104] She raised her family in the English manner, and the private life of the last tsar was English in its customs and activities. For example, the sitting room of the empress at the gloomy hunting lodge at Spala in Poland was decorated in bright English chintzes.[105] Tea was always served in the English fashion.[106] The children slept on camp beds and had a cold bath every day.[107] When it came time for the eldest grand duchess, Olga, to marry, a match with Edward, the prince of Wales, was mentioned, but nothing came of it.[108]

The grand dukes were a varied lot spanning the spectrum in terms of political sympathies. They were a cosmopolitan group and traveled frequently abroad, particularly in western Europe. When forced to leave Russia because of his morganatic marriage, the grand duke Mikhail Mikhailovich chose to spend the rest of his life in London.[109] Of his many uncles, the one to whom the tsar paid the most attention was the grand duke Nicholas Nikolaievich, the inspector-general of cavalry and commanding officer of the Petersburg Military District. The grand duke was suspicious of Germany and regarded Austrian ambitions with grave misgivings. The grand duke's 1895 visit to French maneuvers pleased him. According to the emperor, his uncle had been "delighted with his long and interesting stay in France."[110] He telegraphed Saint Petersburg after the 1912 maneuvers in France and stressed "the gratifying impression" they had made on him.[111] His attachment to the Dual Alliance was clearly a long-term and constant one. In fact, after the 1917 Revolution, the grand duke chose to spend his exile in France.

The grand duke Sergei Mikhailovich, the inspector-general of artillery and an influential Romanov, admired the French artillery and the French armed forces. His attitude helped to develop trust and cooperation between the allied armies.[112] The political opinions of the grand duke Nicholas Mikhailovich, a historian, contrasted sharply with those of his military brother Sergei Mikhailovich. Nicholas Mikhailovich had Frenchified political views, so much so that his nickname in the Chevalier Guards was "Philippe Egalité." He wrote a monumental biography of Alexander I. The French Academy elected him a member, and he was often invited to lecture before French historical societies. According to his brother he was "an enthusiastic admirer of the parliamentary regime and an inveterate follower of the Clemenceau-Jaurès duels. . . . My brother had all the necessary qualifications of a loyal president of a civilized republic, which led him often to mistake the Nevsky Prospect for the Avenue des Champs-Elysées."[113] Not surprisingly, given his liberal sympathies, the Grand Duke became good friends with the British ambassador, Sir George Buchanan, who admired him as "a liberal-minded and a cultured man."[114]

The liberal historian's brother, the grand duke Alexander Mikhailovich, in hindsight, described the Triple Entente as "nonsensical and eventually fatal."[115] The original alliance with France he viewed as a "perilous pact," and he could not imagine how a sensible man like Alexander III had approved of it.[116] This grand duke categorically rejected the European way for Russia. He strongly disapproved of the 1905 constitution. In his opinion, the tsar of Russia had become "a mere parody on the King of England in a country that was kneeling before the Tartars in the days of the Magna Carta."[117] Alexander regarded Sazonov as a mere puppet of the English and the French who followed policies that could only lead to trouble with the Central Powers.[118] The extended Romanov family thus was not uniformly pro-German, and in reality those closest to Nicholas II—his mother, wife and uncle, the grand duke Nicholas Nikolaievich—were strong supporters of the Dual Alliance and the Entente with Britain.

The court was no more homogeneous in its attitudes toward Britain and France than was the imperial family. An anti-Entente faction did exist,[119] but its limited influence declined as the years passed and German and Austro-Hungarian behavior toward Russia became more threatening. During negotiations for the Anglo-Russian Convention, British diplomats regularly reported to London about the "temporary ascendancy of the reactionary party around the Tsar," which they found troubling and obstructive to their efforts to reach an agreement.[120] An influential Russian at the ministry of foreign affairs informed Nicolson that the emperor favored "a complete understanding with Great Britain, but that it must be borne in mind that there were several influences at work in favour of the Russian Court and government receiving advice and guidance from Berlin."[121]

Nicolson identified General Trepov, the commander of the Winter Palace, and Baron Frederiks, the minister of the court, as pro-Germans at court.[122] By all accounts Frederiks was the official closest to the imperial couple. He lunched often with the intimate imperial family circle, participated in all court ceremonies, hunted frequently with the tsar, and attended family occasions such as birthdays and Christmas.[123] Frederiks regarded Germany as the last bastion of the monarchical principle and believed that "Britain would never be a loyal ally, and he predicted the worst perils" for Russia.[124]

The pro-Germans believed that no essential interests divided Saint Petersburg and Berlin. They also feared, almost prophetically as it transpired, that war with Germany would cause a socialist revolution in Russia. Their connections with the emperor, the court, and high officialdom, and not public support, gave the pro-Germans their strength.[125] By 1914, however, the pro-Germans were no longer in the ascendant. Almost all the well-known pro-Germans in the foreign ministry were either retired or in secondary posts. They could draw Nicholas's attention to individual memoranda, as P.N. Durnovo did in February 1914, but they had no constant influence of the sort available to Sazonov or Izvolsky.[126] The events of 1909 to 1914 had weakened the German faction and "by 1914 the pro-Germans were in a small minority in Petersburg high society, the press, the officer corps and educated society as a whole."[127]

Pro-Entente sentiments also existed at court, and everything English became fashionable in the years preceding the war. To a large extent, the court thus reflected the tastes of the imperial family. By the beginning of the twentieth century, English had supplanted French among the Russian aristocracy as the stylish language of choice. According to a court intimate, Lili Dehn, English

was invariably spoken at Court, and, although [it was] once more fashionable to have German nurses, the fashion in 1907 was to have only English ones, and many Russians who could not speak English spoke French with an English accent! The great shopping centre was "Druce's" where one met one's friends and bought English soaps, perfumery and dresses. The "Druce habit" primarily emanated from the Court where everything English was in special favour.[128]

It had also become something of a fashion for Russian noblemen to study in England as did Prince Felix Yusopov, the future assassin of Rasputin, at Oxford.[129]

After the 1905 revolution it became common among some monarchists to look to the French Revolution as an ominous example and to compare Nicholas II to Louis XVI.[130] The Countess Kleinmichel wrote in her memoirs that in the sons of the local agents and managers she saw "a little Marat of fourteen and a Thèroigne de Méricourt of thirteen."[131] She also perceptively observed that Nicholas II resembled Louis XVI in that neither of them "knew how to grant at the right moment what they had not the power to refuse."[132] The Countess Kleinmichel occupied a prominent position at the Russian court and in Saint Petersburg society. She was an ardent Anglophile and Francophile. Her aunt married Honoré de Balzac, and the countess herself spent a winter in Paris when she was young as part of her training as a lady.[133] In her youth she knew and was charmed by Edward, the prince of Wales, whom she met at Cannes. When he became king he sent her a diamond brooch representing Diamond Jubilee, his horse.[134] The countess professed herself to be an admirer of England and retained an English companion for sixteen years.[135] The countess exemplified the growing favor with which all things British were viewed at the Russian court. The views of the people surrounding the last emperor, therefore, were varied, ranging from wholehearted sympathy for the Triple Entente to strong support for a closer relationship with Germany based on shared monarchical principles.

In the first decade of Nicholas II's reign, Asian questions had been at the fore; in the second decade Russian diplomacy became preoccupied with the developing European crisis. In 1906 Nicholas and his statesmen struggled to salvage something from the wreckage of the Russo-Japanese War and the 1905 revolution. A reconsideration of Russia's limited options forced a reorientation of Russia's foreign policy. Although initially a somewhat reluctant adherent to the Triple Entente, Russian resentment at the country's humiliation during the Bosnian annexation crisis and the growing aggressiveness of the Central Powers prompted the emperor to increase his commitment to the Dual Alliance and to advocate closer ties with Great Britain.[136] From 1905 to 1914, the emperor's views evolved and hardened to reflect the changing reality of a Europe dividing into two armed camps.

A strong Russian patriot whom the West often exasperated, Nicholas II pursued a foreign policy designed, he believed, to strengthen Russia and ensure the survival of the Romanov dynasty. To that end the Triple Entente was a pragmatic arrangement, and the emperor did not allow his personal feelings of distaste for Western liberal traditions to affect his loyalty to the Entente. He viewed the Triple Entente as the best means to preserve the existing state of affairs both at home and abroad. The "revolutionary" implications of the alignment of tsarist, autocratic Russia with the democratic West escaped Nicholas II or were ignored by him. The alignment between Russia, France, and Great Britain was a marriage of convenience between the status quo powers designed to bolster Russia's sagging prestige and world position in return for support against German ambitions. Nevertheless, once the emperor had entered into the marriage, he was loyal to it to the bitter end. It proved to be a match that extracted a heavy toll for loyalty—war, revolution, abdication, and execution. Ironically, the diplomatic policy designed to ensure the security of imperial Russia became one of the instruments of the empire's destruction. Nicholas II and those closest to him failed to recognize that the survival of autocracy in Russia required far more than a utilitarian diplomatic arrangement designed to maintain the balance of power in Europe.

NOTES

1. Constantin de Grunwald, *Le Tsar Nicholas II* (Paris, 1965), p. 278. E. de Schelking, *Recollections of a Russian Diplomat, the Suicide of Monarchies* (New York, 1918), see chapters 5 and 6.

2. D.C.B. Lieven, *Russia and the Origins of the First World War* (London, 1983), p. 57.

3. Ibid., p. 40. B.J. Williams and G. Katkov share Lieven's interpretation. B.J. Williams, "The Revolution of 1905 and Russian Foreign Policy," in *Essays in Honour of E.H. Carr* (London, 1974), p. 105 and George Katkov, "Russian Foreign Policy, 1880–1914," in *Russia Enters the Twentieth Century, 1894–1914* (New York, 1971), p. 10.

4. D.M. McDonald, *United Government and Foreign Policy in Russia, 1900–1914* (Cambridge, Mass., 1992), pp. 1–4 and 217.

5. Ibid., pp. 161–4, 187–190.

6. Ibid., pp. 6–7. Lieven argues in his biography of Nicholas II that "the Emperor could not coordinate and manage his government effectively but was in a position to stop anyone else from attempting to do the job for him." D.C.B. Lieven, *Nicholas II* (New York, 1993), p. 260.

7. Andrew Verner, *The Crisis of Russian Autocracy: Nicholas II and the 1905 Revolution* (Princeton, 1990), pp. 319–20, 330, and 333.

8. For example, Paul Kennedy, *The Rise and Fall of the Great Powers* (London, 1988), p. 240. See also S.D. Sazonov, *Les Années Fatales* (Paris, 1927), p. 61.

9. Lieven, *Russia and the Origins of the First World War*, p. 57

10. Lieven, *Nicholas II*, p. 43.

11. Quoted in R.W. Thurston, "New Thoughts on the Old Regime and the Revolution of 1917 in Russia: A Review of Recent Western Literature," in E.H. Judge and J.Y. Simons, eds., *Modernization and Revolution: Dilemmas of Progress in Late Imperial Russia* (New York, 1992), p. 138.

12. Quoted in Noble Frankland, *Crown of Tragedy: Nicholas II* (London, 1960), p. 38.

13. D.C. Warth, "Before Rasputin: Piety and the Occult at the Court of Nicholas II," *Historian* 47 (1985), p. 334.

14. Ibid., p. 334.

15. Lieven, *Nicholas II*, pp. 113–14.

16. Ibid., pp. 170–171.

17. D. Geyer, *Russian Imperialism* (New Haven, Conn., 1987), pp. 273–74.

18. Edward J. Bing, ed., *Letters of Tsar Nicholas and the Empress Marie* (London, 1937), 2 October 1896, p. 121.

19. Robert K. Massie, *Nicholas and Alexandra* (New York, 1967), p. 61.

20. Paul Gerbod, "Image de la Russie en France de 1890 à 1917," *Information historique* (May-June 1979), p. 116.

21. A.P. Izvolsky, *Recollections of a Foreign Minister: Memoirs of Alexander Iswolsky* (Toronto, 1921), p. 289.

22. Maurice Bompard, *Mon Ambassade en Russie, 1903–1908* (Paris, 1937), p. 250.

23. V.N. Kokovtsov, *Out of My Past* (Stanford, 1935), p. 90.

24. Ibid., pp. 377–78.

25. AVPR, f. 133, op. 470, 1911g., d. 204, ll. 3, 8, 9.

26. *LN*, vol. 1, Izvolsky to Sazonov, 16/29 February 1912, p. 202.

27. *LN*, vol. 2, Nicholas to Poincaré, 17 March 1913(os), p. 54.

28. *BD/CP*, vol. 4, doc. 187, Nicolson to Grey, 2 January 1907, p. 282.

29. S.S. Oldenburg, *Last Tsar Nicholas II: His Reign and His Russia*, vol. 2 (Gulf Breeze, Fla., 1975), p. 61.

30. Bing, *Letters of the Tsar Nicholas and the Empress Marie*, 21 October 1910, p. 258.

31. N.F. Grant, ed., *The Kaiser's Letters to the Tsar* (London, 1920), pp. 223–24.

32. Bing, *Letters of the Tsar Nicholas and the Empress Marie*, 8 August 1912, p. 271.

33. AVPR, f. 133, 1913g., op. 470, d. 118, l. 11, Nicholas to Poincaré, 1 February 1913.

34. Ibid., d. 124, l. 11, 5 February 1913.

35. *LN*, vol. 2, secret telegram from Izvolsky, 12/25 February 1913.

36. *LN*, vol. 2, Izvolsky to Sazonov, 14/27 February 1913, p. 31.

37. N.V. Tcharykov, "Reminiscences of Nicholas II," *Contemporary Review* 134 (1928), p. 449. According to Lieven, Nicholas was closest to Heath of all his tutors. *Nicholas II*, p. 34.

38. R.J. Barrett, *Russia's New Era* (London, 1908), p. 14.

39. Lili Dehn, *The Real Tsaritsa* (Boston, 1922), p. 89.

40. Anna Viroubova, *Memories of the Russian Court* (New York, 1923), p. 17.

41. Bing, *Letters of the Tsar Nicholas and Empress Marie*, 24 June 1893, p. 71.

42. Ibid.,p. 72.

43. Ibid.,p. 82.

44. Lieven, *Nicholas II*, pp. 28–29.

45. GARF, f. 601, op. 1, d. 1219, no. 9, Prince George to Nicholas II, 28 December 1907.

46. Ibid., no. 10, Prince George to Nicholas II, 29 December 1908.

47. Marc Ferro, *Nicholas II* (London, 1991), p. 1.

48. Bing, *Letters of the Tsar Nicholas and the Empress Marie*, 8 June 1910, p. 255.

49. AVPR, f. 133, 1910g., op. 470, d. 186, l. 12, 24 April 1910.

50. Ibid., l. 46, A. Nicolson to Izvolsky, 30 April/13 May 1910.

51. *BD/CP*, vol. 6, doc. 21, newsletter dated 28 May (Communicated to Foreign Office by Professor Pares June 1, 1910), p. 35.

52. GARF, f. 601, op. 1, d. 1219, no. 13, George V to Nicholas II, 27 May 1910.

53. Ibid.

54. Bing, *Letters of the Tsar Nicholas and the Empress Marie*, 18 June 1911, p. 261.

55. GARF, f. 601, op. 1, d. 1219, no. 18, George V to Nicholas II, 15 March 1911.

56. Ibid., no. 22, George V to Nicholas II, 30 December 1913.

57. Ibid., no.23, George V to Nicholas II, 16 June 1914.

58. Joseph Baylen, "The Tsar's 'Lecturer-General': W.T. Stead and the Russian Revolution of 1905 with Two Unpublished Memoranda of Audiences with the Dowager Empress Maria Fedorovna and Nicholas II," *Georgia State College School of Arts and Science Research Papers*, no. 23 (July 1969), p. 52.

59. AVPR, f. 133, 1906g., op. 470, d. 66, l. 71, Nicolson to Grey, 4 June 1906.

60. *BD/CP*, vol. 5, doc. 9, Nicolson to Grey, 18 October 1907, p. 36.

61. K. Neilson, "Wishful Thinking: Foreign Office and Russia," in B.J.C. McKercher and D.J. Moss, eds., *Shadow and Substance in British Foreign Policy, 1895–1939* (Edmonton, Alberta, 1984), p. 156.

62. Ibid., doc. 74, Nicolson to Grey, 16 May 1909, p. 284.

63. George Buchanan, *My Mission to Russia* (Boston, 1923), p. 170. See also *BD/CP*, vol. 6, doc. 62, Annual Report on Russia for 1910, p. 105.

64. G. Buchanan, *My Mission to Russia*, p. x.

65. Ibid., p. 117.

66. Ibid., pp. 138–39.

67. *LN*, vol. 2, Paléologue to Doumergue, 18 April 1914, p. 258.

68. G. Buchanan, *My Mission to Russia*, pp. 183–84.

69. Ibid., p. 184.

70. D.C.B. Lieven, *Nicholas II* (New York, 1993), p. 197.

71. Baylen, "The Tsar's 'Lecturer-General,' " p. 54. See also Izvolsky, *Recollections of a Foreign Minister*, pp. 32–33.

72. Bing, *Letters of the Tsar Nicholas and the Empress Marie*, 27 October 1905, pp. 190–191.

73. Baylen, "The Tsar's 'Lecturer-General,' " p. 62.

74. Grant, *The Kaiser's Letters to the Tsar*, p. 229.

75. Izvolsky, *Recollections of a Foreign Minister*, pp. 204–205.

76. Bing, *Letters of the Tsar Nicholas and Empress Marie*, 27 September 1906, p. 219.

77. R.J. Crampton, "The Decline of the Concert of Europe in the Balkans, 1913–1914," *Slavonic and East European Review* 1974, 52 (128), p. 417.

78. Grey, *Twenty-Five Years*, letter from Grey to Nicolson, 14 October 1908, pp. 177–78.

79. *KA*, vol. 5, 1924, Nicholas to Stolypin, 25 April 1909, p. 120.

80. Bing, *Letters of the Tsar Nicholas and Empress Marie*, 12 January 1906, p. 212.

81. A.A. Mossolov, *At the Court of the Last Tsar* (London, 1935), p. 16.

82. Massie, *Nicholas and Alexandra*, p. 65.

83. Mossolov, *At the Court of the Last Tsar*, p. 19.

84. N.V. Tcharykov, "Reminiscences of Nicholas II," *Contemporary Review* 134 (1928), p. 452.

85. Lieven, *Russia and the Origins of the First World War*, p. 70. And A. Verner, *The Crisis of Russian Autocracy* (Princeton, 1990), p. 68. Also see Mossolov, *At the Court of the Last Tsar*, pp. 127–28.

86. For an example of the traditional view, see G. Hosking, *The Russian Constitutional Experiment* (Cambridge, UK, 1973), p. 229.

87. K. Neilson, *Britain and the Last Tsar* (Oxford, 1995), pp. 61–62.

88. Baylen, "The Tsar's 'Lecturer-General,' " p. 35.

89. Ibid., p. 41.

90. Ibid., p. 35.

91. Ibid., pp. 45–46.

92. Bing, *Letters of the Tsar Nicholas and Empress Marie*, 28 February 1907, p. 222.

93. Ibid., p. 232 and pp. 232–33.

94. G. Buchanan, *My Mission to Russia*, p. 175.

95. Frankland, *Crown of Tragedy*, p. 19.

96. Pierre Gilliard, *Thirteen Years at the Russian Court* (London, 1921), p. 47.

97. Bernard Pares, Introduction to *The Nicky-Sunny Letters: Correspondence of the Tsar and the Tsaritsa* (Hattiesburg, Miss., 1970), p. ix.

98. Lieven, *Nicholas II*, p. 48.

99. Dehn, *The Real Tsaritsa*, p. 59. See also, Countess Kleinmichel, *Memories of a Shipwrecked World* (London, 1923), p. 214.

100. Ibid., p. 66.

101. Dehn, *The Real Tsaritsa*, p. 40.

102. Lieven, *Nicholas II*, p. 61.

103. Izvolsky, *Recollections of a Foreign Minister*, p. 294.

104. Massie, *Nicholas and Alexandra*, p. 471.

105. Viroubova, *Memories of the Russian Court,* p. 91.

106. Ibid., p. 57.

107. B. Pares, *The Nicky-Sunny Letters*, p. xii.

108. Massie, *Nicholas and Alexandra*, p. 251.

109. Alexander, Grand Duke of Russia, *Once a Grand Duke* (New York, 1932), p. 149.

110. Bing, *Letters of the Tsar Nicholas and Empress Marie*, 28 September 1895, p. 105.

111. AVPR, f. 133, op. 470, 1912g., d. 176, l. 64, secret telegram, 12/25 September 1912.

112. Lieven, *Russia and the Origins of the First World War*, pp. 70–71.

113. Alexander, *Once a Grand Duke*, pp. 147–48.

114. G. Buchanan, *My Mission to Russia*, p. 177. See also M. Buchanan, *Dissolution of an Empire* (London, 1932), p. 49.

115. Alexander, *Once a Grand Duke*, p. 30.

116. Ibid., p. 68.

117. Ibid., p. 225.

118. Ibid., p. 190.

119. *BD/CP* vol. 5, doc. 4, memorandum by Bernard Pares, June 1907, p. 14.

120. Grey, *Twenty-Five Years*, letter from Nicolson to Grey, 6 November 1906, p. 158.

121. *BD/CP*, vol. 4, doc. 57, Nicolson to Grey, 6 June 1906, pp. 96–97.

122. Ibid., p. 97.

123. A. Verner, *The Crisis of Russian Autocracy*, p. 60.

124. Mossolov, *At the Court of the Last Tsar*, p. 109. See also Lieven, *Russia and the Origins of the First World War*, p. 69.

125. D.C.B. Lieven, "Pro-Germans and Russian Foreign Policy," in *The International History Review* 2, no. 1 (January 1980), p. 44.

126. Ibid., p. 45.

127. Lieven, *Russia and the Origins of the First World War*, p. 75.

128. Dehn, *The Real Tsaritsa*, pp. 44–45.

129. Felix Yusopov, *Gibel Rasputina* (Moscow, 1990), p. 15.

130. Dimitri Shlapentokh, "The French Revolution in Russian Intellectual and Political Life, 1789–1922" (Ph.D. diss., University of Chicago, 1988), p. 290.

131. Kleinmichel, *Memories of a Shipwrecked World*, p. 222.

132. Ibid., p. 101.

133. Ibid., p. 29.

134. Ibid., p. 145.

135. Ibid., pp. 145, 148, and 262–63.

136. Lieven, *Russia and the Origins of the First World War*, p. 67.

Chapter 4

The Vanguard of the Entente Policy: Foreign Ministry Attitudes toward Britain and France

As foreign ministers, A.P. Izvolsky and S.D. Sazonov followed a foreign policy significantly different from those of their predecessors. A consistent policy of maintaining and strengthening the Dual Alliance was buttressed by the, at times, ardent pursuit of friendship and, eventually, alliance with Great Britain, Russia's traditional nineteenth-century foe. From 1906 to the outbreak of World War I, men sympathetic to Britain and France dominated the Russian foreign ministry. Exceptions existed, but contradictory voices were not regularly heeded and their imprint on the overall course of Russian foreign policy was minimal. This "revolution" in foreign policy coincided with the inauguration of the new constitutional regime in Russia and was partly affected by it. Despite the liberal and Western sympathies of several Russian diplomats, however, the Triple Entente policy was pursued primarily as a means of regaining Russian greatness with only passing concern about democratic development. The need to combat German expansionist and hegemonic aspirations and the Austro-Hungarian challenge to Russian power in the Balkans preoccupied Russian diplomats from 1905 to 1914 and drove them to accept, almost overwhelmingly, alignment with the Western constitutional states for reasons of realpolitik, not ideological sympathy.

Russian diplomats and foreign ministry bureaucrats were, arguably, the most Westernized men in Russia, drawn almost exclusively from the upper reaches of the Russian elite and most of them educated at the Imperial Alexander Lycée.[1] Candidates for the foreign service in 1912 were recommended to read *Manuel Historique de la Politique Etrangère* by Emile Bourgeois.[2] The library of the foreign ministry purchased many Western titles, including Albert Sorel's *L'Europe et la révolution française* and J. Morley's *The Life of W.E. Gladstone*.[3] Among Russian diplomats, two tendencies coexisted, not always harmoniously, a European orientation and an Asian one. The Asian Department of the Ministry of Foreign Affairs tended to be very anti-British.[4] The proponents of Asian expansion believed that Russia's mission lay outside European Russia in the development of Siberia and the spread of Russo-European culture in Asia.[5] As a majority under Izvolsky and Sazonov, however, the Europeanists were able to flourish. In general, and not surprisingly given their backgrounds and education, they favored closer relations with Britain and maintenance of the Dual Alliance.[6]

The primary goal of the imperial regime was to maintain Russia's great power status and survive the strains such a policy imposed on the empire. Although there was a close link between foreign and domestic affairs in Russia, particularly the connection between the empire's financial health and its ability to pursue a foreign policy befitting a great power, the domestic ministries were not very involved in the making of foreign policy. Foreign policy was formulated in a void, and Russia's diplomats spent their entire careers abroad in a world of international diplomacy and intrigue, isolated from and with little understanding of the real state of Russia's internal problems and the country's actual needs. A dangerous lack of coordination between military and foreign policy also existed in imperial Russia. Defeat in the Russo-Japanese War was partly the result of this lack of coordination. Consequently, Nicholas II established the Council of State Defense in 1905 to unify military and foreign-policy planning. The council, however, was abolished in 1908. Between 1909 and 1913 Russia's soldiers only rarely advised diplomats about the empire's true military capabilities. Nicholas II's antagonism toward counciliar government aggravated competition between the two ministries. The Fundamental Laws gave the tsar supreme control over foreign policy and military affairs, which meant that these ministers were not accountable to the Duma and therefore not de facto accountable to the other ministers.[7] The end result of this lack of coordination between the military and foreign ministries was that the diplomats were ignorant of Russian military reality, which was quite dismal, while the soldiers were confused about the empire's foreign policy goals, which made strategic planning difficult.

Count V.N. Lamsdorf, foreign minister from 1900 to 1906, haltingly began the new era in Russian foreign policy after the pacification of the 1905 revolution and the conclusion of the Russo-Japanese War with the Treaty of Portsmouth. Since the early 1890s, the Dual Alliance had been the basis of Russian foreign policy, but Lamsdorf did not regard this as tying him in any way. He preferred a policy of retaining "les mains libres."[8] French conduct during the Russo-Japanese War had disappointed Lamsdorf. He believed it necessary, nonetheless, to maintain the alliance "in order to hold restless France in check."[9] Even so, Lamsdorf supported France at the Algeciras Conference partly because he feared that a refusal "might result in a strong nationalist movement" which could "force France into war."[10] Lamsdorf also expressed gratitude to Lord Revelstoke, an influential English banker, and Sir Edward Grey for their part in securing British participation in the 1906 Russian loan.[11] In his cautious fashion, Lamsdorf recognized that a new era in Russian diplomacy had begun.

A.P. Izvolsky, aged fifty, succeeded Lamsdorf in May 1906 and began to chart Russia's new course. Izvolsky belonged to the rural gentry, although his family was not wealthy. In his memoirs he noted with pride a maternal ancestor who took part in the murder of Paul I. He pictured his relative as "an emulator of Brutus. It is more than probable that this contributed to inculcate at an early age the aversion which I have always felt for autocracy, and to turn my mind toward liberal and constitutional ideas."[12] According to D.I. Abrikossov, a Russian diplomat in London, Izvolsky and Count Benck- endorf, Russia's ambassador in London, connected the inauguration of the first Duma with the need to reorient Russian foreign policy radically: "The two diplomats agreed that with the appearance of the Russian Duma with its liberal tendencies, the foreign policy of Russia must be radically changed; and the Minister-to-be declared that he would base his policy on two principles: an understanding with England and a bid for friendship with Japan."[13] Izvolsky worked diligently against serious obstacles for improved relations with Britain and for the maintenance of the Dual Alliance. He hoped to achieve this without alienating Germany, a task that proved impossible to fulfill. As a firm believer in the European traditions of Russian diplomacy, he wanted Russia to accept its exclusion from China, settle with Japan and secure British support in Europe.[14] Izvolsky shared Stolypin's thinking and consequently sought to achieve a relatively long period of quiescence in foreign affairs to enable Stolypin to carry out his policies of "pacification and reform." Izvolsky outlined his program at a meeting of the State Defence Council: "The different questions to which Russia is historically bound and on which its position as a great power depends will be decided not on the shores of the Pacific but in Europe. In the course of the next ten to fifteen years, such questions of world-wide significance as, for example, the Austrian and Turkish, must mature and be resolved, and in these questions Russia must have a strong and weighty voice."[15]

Whatever his intentions of a redirection of Russia toward Europe, Izvolsky inherited a difficult situation. Relations with France and Great Britain were strained as a result of the Russo-Japanese War. Also, those who directed Russian foreign policy viewed "with disquietude and disfavour the advent to office in France of a Government with an advanced Socialistic programme."[16] The British ambassador, Nicolson, also noted that doubts existed "whether the material and moral force of France would at a critical moment render her a valuable ally." Russian sympathy for Britain was also at a low ebb because of its role in the recent war. Many Russians believed, with some justification, that Britain's alliance with Japan had fostered a climate that had encouraged Japan to attack Russia with disastrous consequences.

Izvolsky perceived himself as a minister in a constitutional government. This conceptualization of his role was one of the most striking differences between him and his predecessors. The foreign minister considered public opinion as an important factor and wanted to work with the newly constituted Duma. Izvolsky's support of the Duma, the October Manifesto, and the idea of cabinet government reflected his pro-Western sympathies. Most Duma members and newspapers displayed a keen interest in foreign affairs and were vocal in their criticisms of the ministry and pressed Izvolsky to undertake reforms, which he did try to implement.[17] Ironically, disgruntled public opinion was to be a major factor in his fall from grace during the Bosnian annexation crisis. His appointment as foreign minister had neatly coincided with the opening of the First Duma and was an important symbol of the change in Russian foreign policy. Nicholas II told him that Lamsdorf was "a typical functionary of the old regime, who could not and would not accommodate himself to the new order of things" and inferred that new blood was needed for the new era.[18] Izvolsky welcomed the changes wrought by the October Manifesto.[19] When his colleagues criticized the behavior of the First Duma, Izvolsky defended it, much to the chagrin of the more conservative ministers.[20] The growing conflict between the new parliament and the government worried Izvolsky. He argued at the Council of Ministers for a "Cabinet capable of reconciling the moderate members of the Duma." He also spoke to Nicholas II about this matter.[21] His proposals, however, fell on deaf ears. Izvolsky was concerned about the fate of the First Duma because of his liberal convictions but also because he worried about the impact of the crisis in Europe. He believed that Russia could not aspire to recover its international position until a working arrangement with the Duma was achieved.

Although his attempt to save the First Duma proved futile, Izvolsky continued to work with the Second Duma. One of his first administrative acts was to designate a special ministerial liaison with the Duma.[22] In 1908 and 1909 he received the emperor's permission to report substantively on foreign policy to the Duma during its debate on the foreign ministry estimates.[23] He was the only minister who could appear before the assembly without a storm of protest.[24] In 1908 he outlined the general purposes of the government's foreign policy to the Duma and defended the Anglo-Russian Convention as an aid to peace.[25] In another radical departure from tradition, Izvolsky cultivated contacts with the Russian press, even going so far as to grant off-the-record briefings on current policy. He also established a new press department in the ministry, which compiled, edited, and forwarded to the emperor press reports from foreign and Russian newspapers.[26]

Izvolsky sought to forge a consensus in the government in support of his policy. In this, too, he was unlike his predecessors who, with the emperor's support, had worked in splendid isolation from their colleagues, often not even fully informing them about important matters. This consensus-building approach, however, was as much a result of Izvolsky's limited support as it was of his liberal views. Izvolsky was prepared to act unilaterally without consulting his colleagues if he believed such action was necessary and would succeed. His secret understanding with Aehrentahl over Bosnia-Herzegovina infuriated Kokovtsov and Stolypin when they heard of it. Izvolsky did become actively involved, however, in legislative projects and supported Stolypin's reforms, especially his agrarian ones.[27]

The conclusion of the 1907 Anglo-Russian agreement was a hard fought victory for Izvolsky and in some ways the culmination of his career. George Sanders argues that had it not been for Izvolsky and Sir Arthur Nicolson, the long negotiated accord would not have come to fruition.[28] The Russian foreign minister overcame strong opposition among the General Staff, the council of ministers, and the press to realize his primary goal of an understanding with Britain. Izvolsky promoted the agreement as part of a program to ensure peace "from Kamchatka to Gibraltar for about ten years."[29] In this sense the accord was designed merely to alleviate trouble spots in the Near East, and Izvolsky went to great pains to convince Berlin that the agreement could in "no case" lead "us into a political combination directed against Germany."[30] Izvolsky, however, had other more ambitious designs for the convention. He knew from former negotiations that such an agreement would open the London money market to Russian loans. He also wanted to shift Russian efforts from the Far East to the Balkans and eventually obtain access to the Dardanelles for the Black Sea fleet, thereby gaining the long-coveted entrance to the Mediterranean. To accomplish this goal, Izvolsky realized that he would need diplomatic support against Austria-Hungary. Russian renunciation of any action in the Middle East that would threaten India was the prerequisite for agreement with Britain. As this agreement only acknowledged the reality that Russia no longer had the military capability to face a threat of war from Britain, Izvolsky shrewdly calculated that it was more profitable to negotiate the sacrifice and gain what he could by it. Finally, he realized that, in the light of the 1904 Entente Cordiale between Britain and France, the best means of strengthening the Dual Alliance was improved Anglo-Russian relations.[31]

Thus, the 1907 convention was only the first step in Izvolsky's ambitious program designed to reassert Russia's influence and interests. Nonetheless, the Anglo-Russian Convention was a frail mechanism, one which the British Foreign Office believed had to be nurtured carefully. The only real bond tying the two countries in 1907 was mutual distrust of Germany.[32] Within the Russian government itself conflicting views existed as to the purpose of the accord, and few ministers shared Izvolsky's grandiose vision.[33] Many of his dreams for the accord proved ephemeral, especially his hope of British backing in Russia's quest for access to the Mediterranean.

The 1907 Anglo-Russian Convention on Persia, Afghanistan, and Tibet secured Izvolsky's reputation as an Anglophile both at home and abroad. It was, on the whole, an earned and accurate reputation. The British government was aware of Izvolsky's admiration of Britain and its importance.[34] Under Izvolsky the Russian government cooperated more or less harmoniously with Great Britain in Persia for the first time, a fact frequently and appreciatively noted by British diplomats in Saint Petersburg. In his annual report for 1908, Nicolson praised Russian conduct: "I think that they have shown always a desire to meet the wishes of Great Britain, and when the traditions, habits, and methods of Russian bureaucracy and diplomacy are taken into consideration, it is to my mind remarkable and satisfactory that the cooperation of Russia has been so cordial and of so liberal a character."[35] Nicolson also praised Izvolsky personally for acting "so loyally and straightforwardly with Great Britain" when there was considerable pressure on him to deviate from such a course. Izvolsky's faithful adherence to the 1907 convention regarding such contentious issues as the Baghdad railway, telegraph negotiations, and the dethronement of the shah exemplify his commitment to the accord.

Despite his staunch adherence to the new arrangement with Britain, Izvolsky occasionally became exasperated with British interference in Russian domestic affairs. On these occasions his reactions were typical of all Russian statesmen. In the fall of 1906, for example, a deputation of the British parliament planned to visit Russia, an event viewed with much trepidation by Russian government officials who feared demonstrations and disorder. The proposed visit infuriated the emperor. Izvolsky was also concerned. Consequently, he asked the English ambassador if his government could disavow the deputation, since he realized that it could not be officially stopped. Izvolsky also telegraphed Benckendorf in London to this end and requested him to protest to the British government.[36] On another occasion, he informed Nicolson of his annoyance at British protests on the Jewish question. Izvolsky told Nicolson that "they were being continually reproached for the condition of anarchy in Russia, and when they took steps to suppress the revolutionary movement they were stigmatized as adopting repressive measures."[37] The Russian government considered that when such protests were made by the representatives of foreign governments they were "overstepping somewhat their province in adopting such a course."[38] The British government could also irritate Izvolsky when it acted without informing him of its intentions in Tibet and Japan.[39]

In a similar fashion, certain actions of the French government frustrated Izvolsky. Secret negotiations between Britain, France, and Spain in 1907 and Russian exclusion from Anglo-French negotiations with Japan annoyed him and caused him some trouble with the domestic press, which questioned the solidity of the alliance.[40] When the reactionary newspaper *Grazhdanin* insulted the French ambassador, Maurice Bompard, Izvolsky officially tried to smooth over the incident, but in private he forcibly expressed his exasperation with the erratic behavior of the ambassador, who had abruptly left the capital.[41] Such minor irritations in Izvolsky's relationship with France were just a foreshadowing of what was to be the low point of his career, the Bosnian annexation crisis.

When Izvolsky met the Austrian foreign minister in Buchlau, they struck a secret deal about Russian acceptance of the Austrian-Hungarian annexation of Bosnia-Herzegovina in exchange, so Izvolsky believed, for Austro-Hungarian support for the opening of the Dardanelles to Russian warships, one of the central aims of Russian foreign policy at the beginning of the twentieth century. The Black Sea fleet was now a significant force, yet it was unable to leave the sea, a state of affairs which severely curtailed Russia's ability to defend its interests all over the world. Moreover, the straits were of vital economic importance to Russia as the gateway for grain exports necessary to pay the foreign loans which fueled Russia's military and industrial development. Consequently, Russian statesmen came to regard free use of the straits as vital to Russia's continued existence as a great power. Given Russia's strategic interests in the region, Izvolsky had much to gain from a successful implementation of the Buchlau agreement. When Izvolsky visited Paris in October 1908 and news of the secret agreement was beginning to filter out, he received a cold reception from the French foreign minister and the French press.[42] As the crisis unfolded, he began to doubt, correctly, as events were to prove, whether France would support Russia.[43] Izvolsky's bitterness toward France knew no bounds. He described the French ambassadors at Vienna and Berlin "as advocates of surrender to the Central Powers."[44] In February 1909 the French government's approval of an unofficial Austrian proposal that would have humiliated Serbia "produced an explosion of wrath from M. Isvolsky, who went so far as to declare that France had gone over 'bag and baggage' to Austria, and had practically denounced the alliance with Russia. As he had expressed it at the time France wished Russia to join in a step which she knew Serbia would not accept, and she also suggested that Russia should humiliate herself and hand over defenceless Serbia to the tender mercies of Austria."[45] In retrospect, Izvolsky bemoaned the lack of sincerity which had characterized French behavior in 1909 and the "double role" played by Jules Cambon, the French ambassador in Berlin, "as a channel for Austro-German proposals."[46]

Izvolsky also blamed the British government, which had been unwilling to offer any significant support to Russia. In February 1909 Izvolsky even suspected the British government of secretly reaching an agreement with Germany on the Near East. The British ambassador managed to placate the harried foreign minister and convince him that Britain's feelings toward Russia had not changed.[47] Although the British initially regarded Izvolsky favorably as very intelligent and pro-British, this assessment became more critical over Izvolsky's handling of the Bosnian crisis, resulting in an assessment of the foreign minister as "not a statesman and his tactics have certainly been bad."[48]

Despite his own personal ineptitude and responsibility in the Bosnian annexation crisis, Izvolsky felt humiliated, isolated, and betrayed. The fiasco effectively ended Izvolsky's career as foreign minister. The crisis proved to be a bitter lesson. Prior to the uproar, it had seemed that Russia's diplomatic situation had improved with the acquisition of British friendship in conjunction with the French alliance. The Bosnian crisis "showed that this improvement was more apparent than real"[49] and that collaboration with Austria-Hungary, the basis of Russian Near Eastern policy since 1897, had backfired. As a result, the two powers plunged into "a mortal duel for influence in the peninsula."[50] The clash of Russian and Austro-Hungarian aims in the Near East was a clash of defensive strategies, which is what made it so dangerous. Neither power believed it could allow the other to achieve complete security without fatally damaging its own security.[51] Izvolsky, not unlike other influential Russians, resolved to strengthen the Triple Entente. The major lesson Russia's rulers learned from these unpleasant events "was that if a similar humiliation were to be avoided in the future both the Russian armed forces and the Empire's links with London and Paris would have to be strengthened."[52]

As ambassador from 1910 to 1917 in Paris, the position to which he was exiled in disgrace because of his mishandling of the Bosnian affair, Izvolsky's influence over Russian foreign policy declined. In his letters to

Saint Petersburg, he often criticized French politicians and diplomats and a certain bitterness pervaded the correspondence. Nevertheless, despite his own personal resentments, he worked diligently as ambassador to strengthen the Triple Entente and, if possible, to transform it into a full-fledged alliance. He promoted assiduously the Franco-Russian naval accord of 1912 and while in Paris occupied himself with military matters speculating in his correspondence with Saint Petersburg about German military preparations and intentions.[53]

Izvolsky's reaction to the second Moroccan crisis was typical of the slightly schizophrenic attitude he held toward France throughout the term of his ambassadorship. In general he supported the French government loyally throughout the crisis, but certain French actions and what he considered to be the relative inexperience of the men leading French foreign policy concerned him. In one letter he described the French minister of foreign affairs, C. Cruppi, as "completely sincere," but he worried "that M. Cruppi, who does not have much experience as a diplomat, is abandoning himself to a dangerous and insufficiently founded optimism."[54] In a subsequent letter, however, Izvolsky described the programme of the French government as "without reproach," although he did acknowledge that the problem would lie in carrying it out.[55] In his memoirs Izvolsky used the Agadir episode as a reason to praise France highly: "I was convinced that the French nation, in spite of superficial appearances, had lost nothing of its attachment to the great principles of justice, liberty and progress which had made France the beacon-light of the world."[56] Izvolsky argued that, as a result of the Agadir crisis, the Triple Entente had to be fortified to prepare for the inevitable German aggression. In such an event, Izvolsky felt confident that Russia could rely on French loyalty and "at the supreme hour the French people would arise as one man against the aggressor, regaining in a moment their patriotic 'elan' and their traditional valour."[57] Izvolsky attributed the successful conclusion of the Franco-German dispute over Morocco to the power of the Triple Entente. He maintained that the Entente was a "powerful factor for the maintenance of the peace and the equilibrium in Europe" and had frightened the German chancellor, Bethman-Hollweg, into a retreat.[58]

In his correspondence with Saint Petersburg, Izvolsky stressed frequently his belief that the Dual Alliance formed the immutable base of Russian foreign policy. When French politicians such as Stéphane Pichon or Alexandre Ribot publicly reaffirmed French support of the alliance, Izvolsky's letters would be full of praise and a little relief, betraying his residual anxiety about the reliability of France as an ally.[59] Izvolsky explained realistically to Stolypin that to fail to honor the alliance would discredit Russia in the eyes of its allies and make it impossible for it to contract future alliances, thereby reducing Russia to the ranks of "a second class power if not worse."[60] Izvolsky maintained a genuine enthusiasm for the 1912 Franco-Russian Naval Convention.[61] He also was anxious that the French government pass the law stipulating three years of compulsory military service for young Frenchmen. He believed that the benefits of such a law would be many: "The combat capacity of the army will be considerably enlarged, mobilisation better ensured and the instruction of the army will respond to modern requirements."[62] The fall of the Ribot cabinet, which had planned to repeal the three-year law, thrilled Izvolsky. He told M. Paléologue, the French ambassador to Saint Petersburg, that he had "trembled for our alliance. . . . Never perhaps had the German peril been more menacing."[63] In Izvolsky's opinion, a repeal would have been "a craziness, an abdication, a suicide."[64]

In the beginning of 1914, Izvolsky also worked for the extension of the Triple Entente into an alliance. Izvolsky used the visit of George V to Paris in the spring of 1914 to broach the issue of a closer Anglo-Russian Entente.[65] In June Izvolsky told Paléologue that he saw the only guarantee of European peace in "European equilibrium, that is to say, the equilibrium of alliances, therefore the equilibrium of military forces."[66] Similar views were widely held among the men who directed Russian foreign policy, especially after Germany's attempt to establish its influence at Constantinople during the Liman von Sanders affair.

Although his relationship with Raymond Poincaré did not begin well, Izvolsky eventually became one of Poincaré's many Russian admirers. Izvolsky felt Poincaré was a "passionate character," had too much "self love" and therefore had to be handled carefully so that he would not become offended, something that could harm good Franco-Russian relations.[67] Apparently the suspicion was mutual. Poincaré believed that inadequate diplomatic representation in Paris and Saint Petersburg was partly responsible for the unsatisfactory state of relations between the two allies when he became minister of foreign affairs.[68] Despite his criticisms of Poincaré as minister of foreign affairs, Izvolsky believed that Poincaré as president would best serve Russian interests should war break out, for he was a strong personality and much preferable to some other French politicians who in recent years had led France.[69] In Izvolsky's opinion, a defeat for Poincaré in the presidential election would be a "catastrophe" for Russia because it would be "the debut of an era of Combisme."[70] Izvolsky's fears reflected a feeling prevalent in Russian governing circles toward French radicalism and what this meant for the alliance. Izvolsky regarded Poincaré's election victory as "the decisive triumph of the moderate elements of politics over the extreme radicalism which had always made proof of hostility with regards to Russia and the Franco-Russian alliance."[71] In long conversations, the new president and the new minister of foreign affairs, Charles Jonnart, convinced Izvolsky that France would fulfill her obligations to Russia "with all the necessary sang-froid" and "that the final result of actual complications perhaps for him [meant] the necessity of French participation in a general war."[72] Izvolsky continued to report that if Russia did not act unilaterally, France would support Russia in the Balkans.[73]

Despite all his diligent work as ambassador to increase the effectiveness of the Dual Alliance and his professed liberalism, Izvolsky was a nervous critic of the French domestic scene. The electoral strength of the French left was a regular subject in his reports to Saint Petersburg. Typically, Izvolsky approved of the French government's firm stand against disorder on May Day in 1911.[74] He also noted with pleasure that the Socialist Party was weakened and divided after its annual conference, held at Saint-Quentin in 1911.[75] He kept officials in Saint Petersburg informed about French worker unrest, acts of sabotage, and the French government's reaction to such events.[76] The spring elections of 1914 and their outcome preoccupied Izvolsky. He criticized the outgoing Chamber of Deputies, which had been responsible for a number of measures that he found distasteful, particularly the unsatisfactory state of French finances and the emasculation of the French military because of the introduction of two years' military service.[77] Izvolsky worried that the probable election victory of people like Jaurès, Clemenceau, and Caillaux would lead not only to a repeat "of the sad experiences of the last legislature, but even to their aggravation."[78] Izvolsky believed that the results of these elections were important to Russia, since France's value as an ally was related to its internal stability. Despite all his fears about the specter of socialism and domestic unrest in France, Izvolsky could be moved by a display of French patriotism, such as the one he witnessed during the Bastille Day celebrations of 1913, which he described in detail to Sazonov.[79]

As ambassador, Izvolsky's criticisms of French politicians became an almost tedious refrain in his correspondence with Saint Petersburg. On different occasions the naval minister, the Monis cabinet, C. Cruppi and J. de Selves, ministers of foreign affairs, the foreign ministry itself, George Louis, Paléologue, and Caillaux's ministry came under fire from Izvolsky.[80] The common complaint was these men's lack of experience and judgment. Such constant, almost petty, criticism reflected his dissatisfaction with French support of Russia. He believed a 1911 French loan to Hungary threatened the Alliance. He told the French minister of foreign affairs that every loan given to Austria-Hungary or Hungary alone enfeebled Russia.[81]

Izvolsky's attitude toward France, therefore, was a mixture of admiration, frustration, and deeply rooted distrust. He firmly believed in the value of the Dual Alliance for Russia, but French actions, which he regarded as at best inadequate and at worst disloyal, frequently galled him. Nonetheless, at no point did he consider abandoning the Alliance. His commitment to the Dual Alliance and the Entente with Great Britain was steadfast. It was based on his fear of Germany and his belief that the Entente best allowed Russia to pursue its self-interests. Although Izvolsky professed to believe in constitutional government, this was not the determining factor in his support of the Triple Entente. His country's strategic interests took precedence over his ideological preferences. Fortunately in his case, the two coincided, but there is no doubt as to which was the more influential. Both as foreign minister and as ambassador to Paris, Izvolsky wanted to rebuild Russia's stature and influence in the world after the disaster of the Russo-Japanese War. His alternating satisfaction and dissatisfaction with his Entente partners reflected his assessment of their contribution toward that end.

S.D. Sazonov replaced Izvolsky as Russian foreign minister in 1910. Sazonov maintained the basic contours of his predecessor's foreign policy. Sazonov, however, was more critical of French and British behavior than Izvolsky had been. Nonetheless, Sazonov did nothing significant to disrupt the smooth functioning of the Entente. By 1914, despite a few sobering lessons on the elastic meaning of British "friendship," he even wanted to transform the Triple Entente into a triple alliance. During Sazonov's tenure as foreign minister, Russia began to recover its strength and attempted to pursue a slightly more aggressive policy than had previously been possible.

Saint Petersburg society considered Sazonov inexperienced for such a senior ministerial position. He had been a career diplomat but, like Izvolsky, he had not had stellar postings. It was frequently charged that his main qualification for the job was the fact that he was Stolypin's brother- in-law. Sazonov's appointment did secure for Stolypin a trustworthy colleague who would conduct the empire's foreign policy along lines with which Stolypin agreed. Most importantly, Sazonov shared Stolypin's conviction that it was necessary for several years to avoid any European complications until Russia had perfected its defenses.[82] At this critical juncture, Russian statesmen perceived a close linkage between the empire's internal stability and a successful foreign policy. The nomination also demonstrated the extent of Stolypin's power and influence. Many contemporaries considered Sazonov a weak foreign minister.[83] A lengthy illness early in his tenure compounded the isolation of his being an outsider to the Saint Petersburg bureaucratic scene. While he was foreign minister, a number of Russian diplomats abroad, including Izvolsky in Paris and Hartwig in Belgrade, displayed an alarming independence of action that he was unable to control.[84] Nevertheless, he did have the support of Stolypin and later Kokovtsov in their capacity as chairman of the council of ministers. Central to Sazonov's thinking on foreign policy was his belief that Russia was primarily a European power. In April 1912 he told the Duma: "One must not forget . . . that Russia is a European power, that the state was formed not on the banks of the Black Irtych but on the banks of the Dnieper and of the river Moskva. Increasing Russian possessions in Asia cannot be a goal of our foreign policy; this would lead to an undesirable shift in the state's centre of gravity and consequently to a weakening of our position in Europe and in the Middle East."[85]

Sazonov's foreign policy fit the pattern of Russian diplomacy since the dismal failure of the Far Eastern adventure in 1905. There were three main elements in the post-Bosnian annexation crisis of Russia's foreign policy as conducted by the new minister. First of all, Russia remained firmly committed to Britain and France, despite their recent lack of support over Bosnia-Herzegovina. Secondly, Sazonov sought to repair relations with Berlin and consequently made concessions to Berlin on a range of Middle Eastern economic issues. Finally, Sazonov sought to build up an alliance of Balkan states to oppose any further Austro-Hungarian advances in southeastern Europe. This policy contributed inadvertently to the two Balkan wars, which in turn helped pave the way for the outbreak of a general European war in 1914.

Sazonov gained a reputation as an Anglophile largely as a result of his long posting to London at the beginning of the century, which made him better informed on British affairs than was usually the case for Russian foreign ministers.[86] During these years he acquired the conviction, which he never lost, that Anglo-Russian hostility was only "the result of a long misunderstanding."[87] Sazonov thought that if there were ever "two nations predestined to collaborate it was surely Russia and England." They had no common frontier and different military organizations, one naval, one land, which made attacking each other difficult; yet a conflict existed because neither side "examined 'sine ira et studio' and eliminated the cause of this animosity."[88] Sazonov attached "the highest importance" to the 1907 Anglo-Russian accord partly because it was "in the domain of the great European questions and the first step toward more confident and more normal relations."[89] Sazonov's appointment, initially, did not please the British, especially when his first trip abroad was to Potsdam to meet Bethmann-Hollweg. Gradually, however, the British were reconciled to Sazonov by his helpful attitude toward British policy during the Balkan wars and his own distancing of Russia from Germany.[90]

Before Sazonov was even officially appointed minister of foreign affairs, he accompanied Nicholas II to Potsdam for a visit with Wilhelm II during which they discussed the Baghdad railway and reached a tentative agreement. Sazonov had hoped to improve relations with Germany and thereby induce Germany to restrain Austrian activity in the Balkans and to honor Russian interests in the border regions.[91] Sazonov was anxious to cultivate good relations with Germany while at the same time maintaining the Triple Entente. It would require experience as minister of foreign affairs before Sazonov would realize, as Izvolsky had, that the two goals, given German ambitions and Anglo-German hostility, were not reconcilable. Unintentionally, Sazonov's Potsdam visit created great uneasiness in Paris and London about his intentions toward the Triple Entente. The British embassy reported that Sazonov's actions "all combined to produce the impression that a serious blow had been struck at the stability of the Triple Entente."[92] Once Sazonov realized the seriousness of the situation he sought to placate London and Paris. He eventually mollified the British and convinced them that "M. Sazonoff was at heart a firm advocate of the maintenance" of the Anglo-Russian understanding.[93] As a result of the Potsdam meeting, however, Sazonov acquired in Paris an undeserved reputation as a Germanophile.[94] To counteract this dangerous impression, his first official trip abroad as minister was to France and Great Britain in the fall of 1912 after he had recovered from his long illness. He told the French government that good relations between Russia and Germany should not worry them but rather comfort them. Such relations allowed Russia "to exercise a pacifying influence on the German government to the profit even of France. And that we had done—many times with success—in the most critical moments of Franco-German conflict, from 1875 until the incident at Agadir."[95]

After a shaky start in Anglo-Russian relations Sazonov quickly established an amicable working relationship with the British ambassador, Sir George Buchanan. Buchanan and Sazonov had known each other from Sazonov's London days. According to Buchanan, Sazonov gave him "a most cordial welcome on my paying him my first official visit, and we soon became fast friends. A Russian of the Russians when it was a question of defending his country's interests, he was always a staunch friend of Great Britain; . . . I ever found in him a loyal and zealous collaborator for the maintenance of the Anglo-Russian understanding."[96] The easy relations Sazonov had with Buchanan contrasted sharply with the strained relations between Sazonov and the French ambassador, George Louis. Only the recall of Louis and his replacement by Theodore Delcassé rectified the situation and paved the way for more harmonious Franco-Russian relations.

During Sazonov's tenure, the Anglo-Russian Convention on the whole worked well. Numerous disputes over Persia arose but they were usually settled amicably.[97] Sazonov was willing to make what he perceived to be sacrifices in Persia because he believed in the accord's value. He attributed to it "a political importance which surpassed the limits of the countries which were the object of it."[98] At a difficult point concerning Persia, for example, Sazonov told Buchanan that the Anglo-Russian understanding was "the alpha and omega of his policy, and he only regretted that it had been Iswolsky and not himself, who had put his signature to it. Its maintenance was essential to the vital interests of the two countries, and, were it to break down, German hegemony would at once be established in Europe."[99]

Several days in 1912 spent as the guest of George V and Queen Mary at Balmoral in Scotland—where he had talks with the king, Grey, and Bonar Law, the leader of the opposition—pleased Sazonov and reinforced his confidence in Britain. Years later he looked back fondly on the "amiable hospitality" he received from the royal family.[100] He reported to Nicholas II that the king had deigned to grant him "an excessively cordial welcome" and had stressed his attachment to continued friendship with Russia.[101] While at Balmoral, Sazonov and Grey had the opportunity for "several long and most friendly conversations."[102] The two ministers discussed the possibility of British naval support in the event of a war, as well as Persia, India, Tibet, and the Balkans.[103] These talks laid the foundation for close Anglo-Russian collaboration during the Balkan wars.[104] After his successful visit to Britain, Sazonov traveled to Paris, where he received another warm welcome.[105]

Shortly after this visit the First Balkan War broke out, which was followed quickly by the Second Balkan War. On the whole Russia, France, and Great Britain cooperated well during these tense months, mainly because they all agreed that the fighting could not be allowed to spill over into a general European conflict. Nevertheless, Britain and France frustrated Sazonov because of their occasional reluctance to support wholeheartedly the Russian position. Before the First Balkan War even began, France had expressed to Russia its displeasure at Russia's role in the conclusion of the Serbian-Bulgarian alliance. During Poincaré's August 1912 visit to Saint Petersburg, Sazonov mollified the French foreign minister, but the seeds of discord remained.[106] Poincaré reminded Sazonov that the letter of the alliance treaty called on France to fulfill its obligations toward Russia only if Germany attacked Russia.[107] When the fighting began, Sazonov complained to Buchanan that the Triple Entente was at a disadvantage in the crisis because of its lack of solidarity compared to the Triple Alliance. Specifically, he bemoaned the fact that no one knew what Britain would do in the event of a general European war.[108] Nonetheless, the Triple Entente survived the test of the crisis. The British embassy in Saint Petersburg reported that Sazonov fully appreciated the diplomatic assistance and support that the British government provided.[109]

Like the emperor, Sazonov did not regard France as warmly as he did Britain. He frequently expressed annoyance at French behavior, and minor irritants played a prominent role between the two allies during his stewardship of the ministry of foreign affairs. Most notably during the Agadir crisis of 1911, Russia refused France any real support on the grounds that Russia was unwilling to go to war over a French colonial dispute.[110] The Russian position during the second Moroccan crisis was revenge for the lack of French support during the Bosnian crisis. In 1912 Sazonov was unhappy with the ambassadorship of Georges Louis, and the lukewarm French support of Russian mediation proposals for the Turco-Italian war.[111] During 1913 a misunderstanding over the level of French interest in the Ottoman Conseil de la Régie des Tabacs and French contracts for Turkish railroads marred relations between Paris and Saint Petersburg.[112] Sazonov remarked to Izvolsky that lately it had become "more and more difficult to respond to the doubts and the questions expressed by the representatives of the press and society, which notices a constant disagreement between us and our ally on questions much more essential for us than for them."[113]

The advent of Raymond Poincaré to the French presidency partially calmed Sazonov's apprehensions about the state of the Dual Alliance. Sazonov described Poincaré to the emperor as "an ardent and convinced partisan of a close union between France and Russia." Sazonov believed "a permanent exchange of views between the two allies on all the most important questions of international politics" would be the result of Poincaré's ascension to the presidency.[114] Sazonov feared what he regarded as the German drive to establish Central Power dominance in the Balkans economically and quasi-politically. He was relieved, therefore, that the man at the head of France was one in whom he had "full confidence."[115]

The Liman von Sanders affair of late 1913 and early 1914 became a test of the soundness of the Triple Entente. When the German emperor bade farewell to the von Sanders mission to Constantinople, he called on its officers "to create for me a new strong army which obeys my orders." Wilhelm II also stated that the mission's first priority was "the Germanisation of the Turkish army through [German] leadership and direct control of the organisational activity of the Turkish Ministry of War."[116] Such grandiose and anti-Russian aims alarmed Sazonov and persuaded him that the mission must be thwarted. Angered by German tactics during the Agadir crisis, the French government was prepared to give Russia much greater support in this area than it ever had before.[117] But to Sazonov's mind such support alone was not sufficient to force Germany to remove von Sanders from his new post, which so threatened Russian interests.

British conduct during these months enraged Sazonov. He believed that Germany and Turkey would yield if Russia, France, and Britain took a firm stand. Germany might risk war against Russia and France, he believed, but it could not face the additional danger of a naval war with Britain. The British embassy was aware of Sazonov's discontent: "The Russian government treated this as the first question seriously involving Russian interests in which they had sought for British support, and therefore as one furnishing a test of the value of the Triple Entente; and M. Sazonof declared that the Triple Entente had proved a failure in the present question."[118] The Liman von Sanders crisis marked a double turning point in Russian policies. It seems to have persuaded both Nicholas II and Sazonov of the impossibility of reaching an understanding with Germany. It also prompted Sazonov to seek a proper alliance with Britain, which would serve Russia better during the next crisis than had the Entente during this one.[119] As Izvolsky had from the Bosnian debacle, Sazonov emerged from the Sanders affair embittered and distrustful of Britain, but at the same time resolved to strengthen the Entente to further Russian interests.

By late 1913 there was a sense of urgency in Sazonov's actions that previously had been lacking. His fear of German hegemony and all that that entailed for Russia had increased dramatically. He believed Germany's policy of Weltpolitik threatened the existence of independent states in Europe and was incompatible with the existence of the Russian, French, and British empires.[120] A desire to maintain the status quo in Europe motivated Sazonov as it did Nicholas II. Sazonov believed that Britain had as much reason as Russia to fear a disruption of the balance of power in Europe which war with Germany would cause.[121] Sazonov regarded the Dual Alliance and the Franco-Russian Naval Convention as adequate guarantees of French support in case of a showdown with Germany.[122] He was not as confident of Britain and sought firmer commitments. He began to lobby intensely for an alliance of Russia, France, and Britain to counterbalance the Triple Alliance of Germany, Austria-Hungary, and Italy. In late 1913 Sazonov approached the British ambassador about this matter, saying that the lack of solidarity in the Triple Entente made it a less effective diplomatic instrument, although it was stronger as a fighting combination than the Triple Alliance. Consequently, he argued for "an alliance of a defensive character" that would allow the combination "to impose respect for our wishes without war."[123] To Izvolsky, Sazonov described the conversion of the Triple Entente into a defensive alliance as "an essential problem," which would guarantee Russia's international position.[124]

A naval convention was broached as the first concrete step toward the realization of Sazonov's goal. When the British government in May 1914 agreed to negotiate a convention limited to the Baltic, Sazonov was delighted. He told the French ambassador, Paléologue, that "the accord we are going to conclude with England will ensure the balance and the peace. The tranquillity of Europe will no longer depend on German caprice."[125] Sazonov showed his pleasure by making substantial concessions in Persia, although Grey had agreed reluctantly to the negotiations more to please the French than the Russians.[126] Neither a naval agreement nor an alliance, however, was concluded before the conflict with Germany began in the summer of 1914. Sazonov had worked diligently to achieve an alliance, but traditional British reluctance to become entangled on the continent, British preoccupation with domestic affairs, and a lack of time prevented any firmer agreement before the outbreak of war.

Sazonov's push for an alliance with Britain was partly motivated by his concern about British domestic affairs, which he monitored closely in 1914. He associated Britain's vacillating position in foreign policy with its internal instability. One historian has characterized the years 1910 to 1914 in Britain as a period of "domestic anarchy."[127] A wave of strikes, a militant suffragette movement, and a pitched battle to destroy the House of Lords' legislative veto disturbed the domestic peace. The most serious disturbance, however, arose over the attempt to establish home rule for Ulster. In 1914 this issue completely preoccupied the British government and there was genuine concern that a civil war in Ulster could erupt. To Benckendorf, Sazonov complained bitterly about "the wavering and hollow policy of the English cabinet" which, preoccupied with Home Rule and "other utopias as dangerous," wanted to abstain from any foreign policy initiative.[128] Sazonov also referred to "the strange blindness of Grey." The Triple Entente's existence, he wrote, was as difficult to prove as that of a "sea monster."[129] He informed Buchanan that the Russian government watched anxiously as the crisis over Ulster unfolded. He also expressed his "apprehension lest internal dissensions and disaffection in the army might so weaken England's position as to render her voice of no account in the councils of nations."[130]

A renewal of Anglo-Russian rivalry in Persia and a desire on the part of Britain to revise the 1907 accord also perturbed Sazonov.[131] Despite his frustrations, Sazonov was prepared to work hard to maintain the good relations which had always been a priority in his foreign policy.[132] After enumerating a long list of complaints against Britain, Sazonov reiterated his "promise to remain faithful, to the last limits possible, to my determination to cultivate and to strengthen the ties of friendship with England. This end entails certain sacrifices which we are completely disposed to make. That the English do not demand from us anything too great!"[133]

Given Sazonov's peacetime worries about the value of British friendship, it is not surprising that British actions during the July crisis disappointed him; however, he was gratified by French support, which he described as "particularly precious."[134] Sazonov viewed London's role in the crisis as crucial. He came to believe that a firm commitment by London to the Triple Entente would have prompted Berlin to counsel moderation in Vienna and that the war might have been avoided.[135] British wavering confirmed Sazonov's view that an alliance was the only means of ensuring adequate British support. In the end, Britain did join Russia and France in the war, but Sazonov's main goal in aligning Russia with Britain and France had been to avoid such a devastating and ultimately suicidal conflict for imperial Russia. By this measure Sazonov's Triple Entente policy must ultimately be considered a failure. The creation of the Triple Entente in 1907 did not usher in the decade of peace, desired by Stolypin, the chairman of the council of ministers, and Sazonov's brother-in-law, to build a great Russia. Instead, the Triple Entente drew Russia into a protracted war with both Germany and Austria-Hungary. Despite good intentions, Sazonov was unable to achieve the balancing act of maintaining and even strengthening the Triple Entente while at the same time cultivating cordial relations with Germany and Austria-Hungary.

Count A.K. Benckendorf was the Russian ambassador to London and highly regarded in British circles. The ambassador was thoroughly Westernized, and he and his family moved effortlessly in English society. The "Bencks" were frequent guests of the Asquiths and their circle.[136] Benckendorf consistently used this position and his access to the emperor to improve Anglo-Russian relations. He was a firm supporter of the main lines of Izvolsky's foreign policy.[137] He did not particularly admire, however, the British form of government or wish Russia to emulate it. His desire for Anglo-Russian friendship, although nourished by a fondness for the British monarchy and aristocracy, was fueled primarily by fear of German designs and a belief that the Entente would best serve Russian strategic interests. Like most Russian government officials, Benckendorf was well aware of Russia's need for peace. According to him "nothing was less discussable."[138] The count was a diplomat par excellence, who believed "that in diplomacy there can be no traditional friends or enemies."[139] Consequently, he would not accept the view that Germany was a traditional friend and Britain a traditional enemy. He also thought that many "intelligent men" in Russia misunderstood Britain, not realizing that it merely pursued its own interests, rather than deliberately undermining those of other countries.[140] Like

Izvolsky and Sazonov, Benckendorf also acquired a reputation as an Anglo-phile and was criticized for it.[141] Whether Benckendorf merited the criticism, there is no doubt that the ambassador enjoyed English society and that during his posting he and the Russian embassy occupied a high position in London society.[142]

Benckendorf had a close relationship with Edward VII, which helped to facilitate the rapid improvement in Anglo-Russian relations after 1905. The king often singled out the Russian ambassador for personal attention. Edward VII on various occasions had Benckendorf as a house guest for extended periods at Goodwood, Sandringham, and Balmoral.[143] At Ascot in 1906 the king drove through the crowd three times with Benckendorf seated by his side, an attention Benckendorf especially appreciated as it came after the public furor over the violent pogrom at Bialystok.[144] Benckendorf became genuinely attached to Edward VII, whom he regarded as a sincere friend of Russia.[145] Benckendorf also established a close relationship with George V, although it was not the same as with his father.[146] Benckendorf was attached to British aristocratic society in a sentimental way. When a rumor surfaced that he was to be transferred to another posting, he informed Izvolsky that he felt he could only be ambassador at London and nowhere else.[147] His family became so anglicized during its stay in Britain that his daughter married an Englishman.[148]

Benckendorf was a strong and early advocate of an Anglo-Russian understanding. Even in 1906 he regarded British policy as "pacifist and appeasing," a rare attitude among Russian officials at the time with memories of the British position during the Russo-Japanese War still fresh.[149] Once negotiations were under way, Benckendorf pressed for a speedy conclusion because he feared prolonged talks would cause international nervousness.[150] Benckendorf worried that a failure would lead to an Anglo-German accord.[151] Moreover, he believed that a failure in 1907 would set back Anglo-Russian relations for a generation and all Russian interests would be affected. In the end, failure would lead to a war "for which in every way we will pay the price, and who says war, says revolution." Benckendorf also believed that an Anglo-Russian agreement was necessary to maintain the alliance with France.[152] For his efforts in negotiating the Anglo-Russian convention of 1907, Edward VII awarded Benckendorf the Royal Victorian Order as a personal gift.[153]

As ambassador to London, Benckendorf regularly sympathized with the British point of view on all manner of questions, revealing his belief that Britain should be trusted. While the Anglo-Russian negotiations were under way, a delegation of the First Duma visited London, and the British prime minister, Campbell-Bannerman, made his famous remark: "The

Duma is dead; long live the Duma!" Saint Petersburg did not respond well to this comment and instructed Benckendorf to inform the prime minister that the Russian government found his remark tactless. Benckendorf, however, did not want to jeopardize relations over what he regarded as a trivial incident. Instead of an official note, Benckendorf simply took Campbell-Bannerman aside at a gathering and explained the Russian government's point of view, whereupon the prime minister expressed his regret at having produced such a negative impression in Russia. The prime minister's informal remarks were transmitted to Saint Petersburg as an apology.[154] This small anecdote shows both Benckendorf's sympathy and understanding for British customs and also the gulf between Russian diplomats posted abroad and Russian officialdom in Saint Petersburg.

Benckendorf's sympathetic explanations of British behavior also extended to the British side of Anglo-Russian political or territorial disputes. The ambassador on different occasions argued Britain's case about the detention of a British subject in Russia, the actions of Russian consuls in Persia, and the retention of Russian troops in Persia in 1909.[155] At one point the actions of his government over Persia and their negative effect on Anglo-Russian relations so frustrated Benckendorf that he berated the assistant foreign minister, A.A. Neratov, about the need to have faith in Britain, arguing that it deserved complete trust: "The facts seem clear to me, the two great Powers of the world are tied by a convention, who says convention, says cooperation. . . . In the actual case, it seems to me that we must make more of an effort to conserve the viable, in the sense of a political card on the table."[156]

Despite his deep-seated distrust of Germany, Benckendorf also on occasion defended British actions which could be construed as friendly overtures to Berlin. As a result of the Potsdam meeting between Nicholas II, Wilhelm II, and their foreign ministers in November 1910, Benckendorf believed that Anglo-German negotiations would have to take place but that they were not to be feared because Britain had "a robust faith in Russia's future" and was not contemplating abandoning the Triple Entente.[157] The 1912 Haldane Mission to Berlin, which aimed to halt the Anglo-German naval armaments race, did not perturb Benckendorf, unlike others in the Russian government. The British government informed the Russian ambassador about the trip and the reasons for it. Benckendorf told Grey that he saw "only advantages for the peace that the relations of England with Germany should be as good as her Entente ties with Russia and France permit."[158] Benckendorf acknowledged to Sazonov that it was a problem that Germany and Britain were on such poor terms. Benckendorf believed the Haldane Mission to be necessary to rectify such an undesirable situation, although he did criticize the publicity attached to the visit.[159]

When it came to British domestic politics, Benckendorf was not as tolerant as he was of British diplomacy. The more radical elements of British society repulsed the Russian aristocrat in much the same way that French socialists did Izvolsky. Benckendorf did, however, admire the Liberal Party and particularly Sir Edward Grey.[160] Like many Russian diplomats, Benckendorf attributed British criticism of Russian imperialism to Jewish agitation. He believed that the British opposition to the proposed 1906 British fleet visit to Russia was the result of opposition in the Jewish press and a few Labour members in the House of Commons, which included two Jews.[161] He also held the City in disdain, describing it as "half German, Jews, Americans of whom the nationality is completely vague."[162]

The acerbity of British domestic politics during an election dismayed Benckendorf.[163] He complained to Izvolsky that trying to conduct diplomacy in London while there was an election on was like "drinking sea water."[164] Because of the election, no one was available to see Benckendorf and everything was on hold, a state of affairs Benckendorf found difficult to tolerate.[165] Once the election was over and the Liberals returned to power, diplomacy resumed, much to Benckendorf's relief.[166] The suffragette movement and the struggle for Home Rule also preoccupied Benckendorf.[167] In his opinion, the crisis over Home Rule in 1914 had at least one salutary effect on British foreign policy in that there was less debate about foreign policy in the House of Commons.[168]

When Sazonov first broached the idea of a defensive alliance with Britain, Benckendorf initially supported it, only later to defend British reservations about the plan. In February 1914 Benckendorf told Sazonov that he agreed "entirely and without reserve," although he did caution that the "terrible insular spirit" of Britain was still "too general."[169] Benckendorf was more sanguine about Anglo-Russian relations at the beginning of 1914 and more tolerant than Sazonov of the constraints placed on British foreign policy by the nature of its political system, history, and geography. Benckendorf was well aware that the British government's preoccupation with domestic affairs militated strongly against the possibility of an alliance being concluded soon.[170] By May, Benckendorf was convinced that an alliance was for the moment an impossibility, although he was not worried. He informed Sazonov that he doubted one could "find a stronger guarantee for military cooperation in the case of war than the spirit of this Entente, such as it has revealed itself, reinforced by the military provisions which exist."[171] The decision to begin naval conversations between the two powers pleased Benckendorf.[172] During the July crisis, however, he was forced to acknowledge his error about the reliability of the Entente when he decried "the slow English imagination" as "deplorable." England's preoccupation with Ulster meant that it was "still not awakened enough" to the need to provide Russia appropriate support.[173]

A devoted supporter of the 1907 Anglo-Russian accord, Benckendorf was much more ambivalent toward France. In general, he was critical of Russia's long-standing ally and, in this, he was representative of a general dissatisfaction with the alliance in Russian government circles. Benckendorf did not want Russia to be solely dependent on France. Such an arrangement meant that Russia was "easily and often" put into conflict with Germany. Russian subservience to "French panics and nervousness" was insupportable.[174] Benckendorf recognized Russia's financial reliance on France, since it was the only power that supported Russian credit, without which Russia would go bankrupt. For Benckendorf, bankruptcy meant revolution.[175] Nonetheless, he believed, as did other prominent Russians, that France would only be willing to fight a war for French interests. In such a war Russia would be at a disadvantage, as it would have to fight two powerful enemies, Germany and Austria-Hungary, while France would have only one with which to contend. Consequently, Russia would probably be weaker than France at a peace conference.[176] Nevertheless, despite his serious concerns about France's value as an ally, Benckendorf would still defend France and certainly never contemplated abandoning the Alliance.[177]

Prince Grigorii Nikolayevich Trubetskoy was a diplomat, publicist, and liberal-imperialist. From 1906 to 1912, he was retired from the diplomatic service and wrote frequently on foreign policy. In the summer of 1912, Trubetskoy was appointed head of the Near Eastern Department of the foreign ministry, which covered Balkan and Ottoman affairs. According to B.E. Nolde, Sazonov "felt toward Trubetskoy a very sincere trust and was subject to his undoubted influence."[178] With his brother the philosopher Evgeni Nikolayevich, Grigorii Nikolayevich edited the liberal and Slavophile Moscow weekly, *Moskovskiy Yezhenedel'nik*. G.N. Trubetskoy was a friend of P.B. Struve and was close to Muscovite liberal-imperialist intellectual and business circles. Trubetskoy's appointment as head of the Near Eastern Department has been described as "a remarkable step" that showed "how very close in sympathy were Sazonov and his assistants to the 'responsible Slavophil' elements in public opinion of which Trubetskoy was such a leading and well-known representative."[179]

G.N. Trubetskoy came from one of Russia's oldest aristocratic families, with strong Slavophile connections. Throughout his life he maintained a profound attachment to Orthodox Christianity. Trubetskoy's intense Slavophilism and his belief in the balance of power as the best method to preserve the peace shaped his approach to foreign policy. He believed that Orthodox and Slav ideals should form the basis of Russian foreign policy and that the

Slav idea would aid the development of a unifying patriotism. As a result of his Slavophile views, Trubetskoy believed that Russia's real interests were in the Black Sea and the Balkans as they had been since the reign of Catherine the Great.[180] Trubetskoy regarded the maintenance of Russia's status as a great power as the main goal of Russian foreign policy.

For Trubetskoy, as for Izvolsky and Sazonov, "the threat to European peace came from Germany,"[181] which had grown increasingly powerful since unification in 1870. Because of the German threat, Trubetskoy regarded the Franco-Russian alliance as imperative. His commitment to the French alliance was complete. He criticized the 1907 agreement to preserve the status quo in the Baltic as an effort by Izvolsky to please Berlin, despite Trubetskoy's worry that Germany desired control of the Baltic coastline. Trubetskoy complained that "one cannot close one's eyes to the evident necessity as regards the question of mutual security in Europe to choose between France and Germany. To seek a middle way is equivalent to wanting to sit between two stools. This is scarcely either a profitable or an honourable position."[182] Trubetskoy in 1906 was also a strong advocate of better relations with Great Britain. He accepted the 1907 Anglo-Russian agreement gladly, although he was dissatisfied with some of its terms.[183]

A clear exposition of Trubetskoy's views on foreign policy can be found in the two essays he wrote for *Velikaia Rossiia*, an influential, two-volume work edited by the industrialist P.P. Ryabushinsky and published in 1910 and 1911. Trubetskoy's two essays "Russia as a Great Power" and "Some Thoughts on Russia's Foreign Policy" form a substantial and important part of the work, which Ryabushinsky sponsored in order to bring together the worlds of the liberal intelligentsia and Moscow business.

Trubetskoy's article "Russia as a Great Power," written in October 1910, is a long, thoughtful essay in which he discussed all aspects of Russian foreign policy. Trubetskoy mentioned the alliance with France infrequently in "Russia as a Great Power," creating the impression that he took it for granted. He did describe the Franco-Russian alliance as mutually beneficial, as it provided France security against the German threat while Russia gained "great freedom of action released at the same time from political influence of the Berlin cabinet and economic dependence on the Berlin Exchange."[184] Trubetskoy, however, also recognized inherent dangers in the alliance. He explained that he did not wish to deny the alliance's value and that it was unlikely that France would avoid its obligations in the case of a war. On the other hand, Russia would also have to reciprocate, and in Trubetskoy's opinion the question of war for France was "more serious than for the majority of great powers."[185]

In his harshest criticism, Trubetskoy questioned France's loyalty to Russia during the Bosnian annexation crisis of 1908–9. Trubetskoy, like Izvolsky, objected vehemently to France reaching an agreement with Germany over Morocco while Russia was in a "duel" with Austria-Hungary over Bosnia-Herzegovina.[186] This episode led him to question France's reliability as an ally and to wonder if it seriously envisioned "the possibility of showing us such real support" as Germany did for Austria with its "'friendly' advice in Petersburg," a bitter allusion to the German ultimatum in 1909 during the Bosnian annexation crisis, which forced Russia to capitulate without achieving any of its goals.[187] Trubetskoy's frustration and sense of betrayal ran deep since the international humiliation Russia suffered during 1908–9 struck at both his Slavophilism and his Great Russian patriotism.

In contrast to the scant attention paid to France, Trubetskoy wrote much about Anglo-Russian relations, particularly with regards to Persia. The essay "Russia as a Great Power" reflected Trubetskoy's ambivalence toward Britain. He wanted and valued British friendship, but at the same time he criticized British behavior and was aware of the traditional Anglo-Russian hostility. Trubetskoy enumerated Russia's many long-standing grievances against Great Britain: the Crimean War, the British attitude during the Russo-Turkish War, Anglo-Russian colonial competition in the Near East, and also conflict in the Far East, particularly the Anglo-Japanese alliance, which Trubetskoy felt gave Japan the latitude to wage a humiliating war against Russia.[188] Trubetskoy regarded the 1907 Anglo-Russian Convention, however, as a positive achievement for Russia and as a "further important step" in the formation of a new grouping of powers—France, Britain, and Russia—facing Germany and Austria with Italy floating in between.[189]

Nevertheless, Trubetskoy had serious reservations about friendship with Great Britain, not least because of the specter of British isolationism and the fear that Russia would be forced to pull British chestnuts out of the fire. He wrote, rather caustically, that Britain "probably would prefer that in Europe, as not long ago in Asia, her friends and rivals without her, but for her, settled her scores." Despite his doubts about both Britain and France, instead of rejecting them as partners, he called for strengthened agreements and specific military and naval plans. Trubetskoy's ideas were the same as the policy of the Russian government as it evolved in the immediate prewar years.[190]

Trubetskoy discussed in some detail the usefulness of an actual alliance with Great Britain. He concluded that in the Far East at least such an alliance would be "useless" and "not feasible" because of Russia's improved relations with Japan and the Anglo-Japanese alliance.[191] In Europe his conclusions were not as clear-cut. He believed Russia's next war in Europe would be against Germany and its allies. In such a scenario Britain would probably send one hundred thousand men to aid France, but he questioned the utility of such an expeditionary force for Russia. Although a British expeditionary force struck him as largely irrelevant to Russia's needs, he did conclude that the British fleet could protect Russia from a hostile landing on the Baltic coast and in this respect an alliance with Britain might prove beneficial.[192] Although Trubetskoy acknowledged that an alliance with Britain had some strategic value, the possibility of unnecessarily enraging Germany by such a union troubled him deeply.[193] He feared that Russia could be drawn into an Anglo-German conflict, an event he thought likely given their trading and industrial rivalry. Unprovoked, Trubetskoy argued, Germany would not risk war with Russia since Germany would not wish to lose access to the valuable Russian market. He argued that there was no reason for Germany to wage war against Russia unless Germany "had serious reasons to fear an Anglo-Russian alliance," which would give concrete foundations to the "coalition nightmare." Germany would be forced to strike a blow against the encirclement. He worried that Germany would choose a moment when Britain was occupied elsewhere and then attack Russia.[194]

Having painted such a bleak picture, Trubetskoy concluded that an alliance with Britain would be too destructive to Russo-German relations and therefore not worth the attendant risks.[195] In this respect he differed from his friend Sazonov. Instead, Trubetskoy proposed "an awakening of Pan-Slavic tendencies in Russian foreign policy."[196] He believed that Britain, France, and Italy understood that "assistance to the independent development of Slavic states and people serves as the best protection against the growth of pan-Germanism." He concluded that public opinion and responsible politicians in London, Paris, and Rome were ready to aid Russia in this direction.[197]

In Trubetskoy's contribution to the second volume of *Velikaya Rossiya*, he sounded many of the same themes: pan-Slavism, the need to maintain peace, and ambivalence toward Britain. He discussed Turkey and the Dardanelles, Persia and Britain, and the Far East. Trubetskoy devoted considerable space to Russo-German relations and the November 1910 meeting of Wilhelm II and Nicholas II at Potsdam. He relished British and French alarm over the meeting as revenge for French behavior during the "height of the battle of the Bosnian incident when Russia had greater grounds to count on correct restraint from the Paris cabinet." Trubetskoy regarded the Potsdam meeting as a warning to those "who were inclined to recognize for Russia only responsibility, forgetting about her legitimate rights."[198]

Despite his lingering irritation with the French, Trubetskoy still preferred French over German capital investment in Russia. He criticized the Russian government's August 1911 decision to grant a concession to build a new port on the Black Sea to the National Ottoman Bank, a German concern. The Black Sea was the focal point around which his Slavophile vision of Russian foreign policy revolved, and consequently he regarded German influence there as extremely dangerous and detrimental to Russian interests. He would have preferred the concession to have gone to French interests.[199]

In the 1911 article, Trubetskoy was even more critical of Britain, particularly concerning Persia, than he had been in 1910. The results of the 1907 Anglo-Russian Convention by which Russian "diplomacy completely forfeited" its "independence in this relationship" did not please him. The issue of a constitution for Persia particularly irked Trubetskoy, who resented what he perceived to be Russian dependence on the British cabinet, which in turn was bound by "a democratic and even radical course of public opinion."[200] He believed that Britain did not allow Russia enough freedom of action in Persia and called for the revision of the 1907 agreement, arguing it was necessary to maintain Russian independence.[201] He did add a conciliatory qualification at the end of his diatribe in an apparent attempt to soften the blow. He asserted his belief that Britain and Russia had "so many deep and weighty grounds to maintain a good agreement."[202] Despite his protests of friendship and good will, however, suspicion and mistrust dominated "Some Thoughts on Russian Foreign Policy" and were the leitmotif of Trubetskoy's attitude toward Britain in 1911.

Other members of the Russian diplomatic corps shared the two basic tendencies within the ministry of foreign affairs: reluctant acceptance of the alliance with France and more enthusiastic endorsement of the new relationship with Britain, while maintaining reservations and concerns about British and French domestic affairs. The diplomats at the Russian embassy in Paris represented well the ambivalent acceptance in official Russian circles of the necessity of maintaining the Dual Alliance, despite a clear appreciation of the deficiencies of this arrangement. The Russian ambassador to Paris before Izvolsky, Nelidov, was a faithful adherent to the Dual Alliance. He recognized the important contribution made by Maurice Rouvier, prime minister and minister of foreign affairs, to the successful conclusion of the 1906 loan, which had been so vital to the Russian government's strategy of stabilization and recovery.[203] Nevertheless, Nelidov often criticized the French government's attitude toward socialists and the connection between French socialists and Russian revolutionaries.[204] Near the end of his tenure as ambassador in Paris, Nelidov reached the conclusion that the Triple Entente needed "to be consolidated and developed to oppose a more effective resistance to the aggressive and expansive ambitions of the Triple Alliance."[205] It is no coincidence that Nelidov reached this conclusion shortly after Russia had been forced to accept Berlin's ultimatum in the Bosnian annexation crisis.

The resigned and wary attitude of the counselor of the Russian embassy in Paris, A.V. Nekliudov, was representative of diplomats posted to France and reflected the stable but cool relations between the two countries in 1907.[206] He sent Saint Petersburg lengthy reports on the erratic political situation in France.[207] He recognized that "the conduct of French society and the French government vis-à-vis Russia—from our first serious reverses in the Japanese war—opens them to well founded criticisms, and to very bitter considerations."[208] Nekliudov's list of French offenses included the following: the Entente Cordiale with Britain, a country diplomatically ranged on Japan's side during the recent conflict; the attitude of the French government and its ambassador in Saint Petersburg toward internal events in Russia; the refusal of French credit without Duma approval; acrimonious reproaches addressed to Russia by French capitalists supposedly threatened by the policies of the Russian government; the terms of the Franco-Japanese trade treaty ratified in Paris despite repeated Russian advice.[209] After enumerating this lengthy list of grievances, Nekliudov concluded that Russia's only option was to take stock of the changes that had occurred and to adapt "without useless regrets and dangerous animosities, using well what remains and face bravely our loss of what is no longer."[210] Such a stoical acceptance of a negative situation reveals clearly the difficult diplomatic predicament facing Russia in the years immediately following the defeat against Japan. The alliance with France left much to be desired from a Russian perspective, but Russia had no choice but to accept its inadequacies or be completely without allies.

Franco-Russian relations did not improve quickly, and Nekliudov often complained to Saint Petersburg about French conduct. On one occasion he accused the French of "blackmail" over their attempts to have a large Russian contract awarded to a French firm.[211] French attempts to separate Austria-Hungary from Germany he regarded as futile and naive.[212] He did, however, acknowledge that the radicalism of the French government was nothing to worry about. Once in power, the radical-socialists acted like any other government and were "true bourgeois Frenchmen."[213] Despite his genuine concerns about the effect of militant atheism and radical-socialism on France, Nekliudov concluded that for many years to come "France will be an organism more or less strong and sensible, and conforming to that, her role in international politics will still have significance and force."[214] Clearly, what mattered to Nekliudov was French diplomatic and military strength, and as long as they were intact, imperial Russia could maintain a mutually beneficial alliance with the republic even if he regarded France's political organization with distaste. Another attraction of the Alliance was that France desired a conflict with the Central Powers as little as Russia and regarded the Triple Entente as a means of preserving "the peace and the status quo."[215] Nekliudov concluded that although Franco-Russian friendship no longer existed, France was a faithful ally.[216]

The Anglophiles in the Russian diplomatic corps were more numerous and enthusiastic than any genuine Francophiles. In part, this was the result of the fact that the friendship with Britain was new, and therefore there had been fewer opportunities for disillusionment. Moreover, the conservative monarchical cast of British mainstream political life corresponded more closely to the ideal favored by those in the Russian elite who became diplomats than the more bourgeois French republicanism. The Anglophiles also came from different social groups and different branches of the foreign ministry, signifying the widespread appeal of Britain among Russian diplomats.

N.V. Tcharykov was a prime example of an ardent Anglophile. He came from the landed nobility in the province of Samara, where his father was governor. He entered the diplomatic corps as a young man and became Izvolsky's political assistant in 1908. Later he served as Russian ambassador to Turkey from 1909 to 1912. Tcharykov was one of many Russian nobles who believed in British ideals, having been greatly influenced during his secondary education in Edinburgh.[217] He attributed his admiration for parliamentary government, as practiced in Britain, to an 1881 visit to the House of Commons during which Charles Parnell tried to make the government adopt Home Rule for Ireland.[218] On one occasion Tcharykov, as acting foreign minister, was confronted by Stolypin threatening to resign. During this confrontation Tcharykov kept in mind "the British Parliamentary custom—never to let a Cabinet crisis develop out of a question of foreign policy."[219] Tcharykov's attitudes resembled those of his minister and no doubt had contributed to his appointment.

D.I. Abrikossov was a rarity in the Russian foreign service: a member of the bourgeoisie. He spent almost four years in London as an attaché and developed a strong passion for Edwardian Britain. Abrikossov liked the conservatism of the British people and had "boundless admiration" for the British parliamentary system.[220] He thought the crucial difference between Russia and Britain was that Britain had an intelligent king and a number of clever statesmen, whereas Russia had a weak emperor and practically no statesmen. This difference, he believed, allowed Britain to survive the calamity of World War I, whereas tsarist Russia did not.[221] London, the brilliance of Edwardian society, the beauty and peacefulness of the English countryside and the dignified tranquillity of Oxford all charmed Abrikossov.[222] Implicit in his fulsome praise for Britain was a deep-rooted dissatisfaction with the tumultuous and brutal workings of his own country.

Abrikossov envied the British their stability and prosperity, which contrasted so sharply with the unrest and poverty in Russia.

A final example of a Russian Anglophile in the foreign ministry was A.D. Kalmykov. He was unusual in his admiration for Britain in that he worked for the Asian Department of the ministry of foreign affairs, a department not noted for its sympathy for Britain. Like other Anglophiles, Kalmykov was a "confirmed liberal."[223] In 1906 he told Izvolsky that "there was no major conflict of interests, and the existing friction was groundless and detrimental to both sides [Britain and Russia]" in the Middle East.[224] Kalmykov regarded the Anglo-Russian agreement of 1907 as the crowning achievement of Izvolsky's career.[225] Kalmykov's only criticism of the agreement was that it had not gone far enough and that unfortunately it did not encompass the Balkans.[226] Like Sazonov, Kalmykov believed that a more united Triple Entente could have prevented World War I.[227]

The desire to preserve and enhance Russia's friendship with Great Britain was widespread within the ministry of foreign affairs by 1914. An anonymous ministry memorandum acknowledged that Russian relations with Afghanistan were "abnormal," that to live side by side with a country and have no relations or access was strange, but that relations with Britain had to be considered.[228] To act contrary to the spirit of the 1907 agreement would have a ruinous effect on the friendly relations between Britain and Russia, which were so important.[229] The memorandum also argued that the limited value of trade with Afghanistan was not worth jeopardizing the accord with Britain.[230] Finally, the extent of British influence in Afghanistan was actually not that strong, although the British government did subsidize the Afghan government by 1,800,000 rubles a year. If problems ever arose, the emir would probably look to Russia for help and then Russia could use this to extract some profit for itself.[231] Although the foreign ministry clearly had serious concerns about Afghanistan in terms of access, trade, and military security, it was not willing to jeopardize good relations with Britain, which were regarded as crucial. Consequently, the Russian ministry of foreign affairs was willing to accept an imperfect state of affairs in return for continued Anglo-Russian cooperation. Such a compromise was typical of the entire course of Anglo-Russian relations since 1907 and reveals the deep commitment on the part of Saint Petersburg to make the Entente work.

Support of the Triple Entente was not, however, universal in the Russian foreign ministry. A minority of bureaucrats and diplomats opposed this policy largely because they were suspicious of Britain and worried that Russia would not be able to pursue its own interests in such a combination. Count N.D. Osten-Sacken, the ambassador to Berlin, N.G. Hartwig, the chief of the Middle East section of the Asian department and later minister to Belgrade, Baron R.R. Rosen, the ambassador to Washington, and Baron Taube, an international judge at the Hague, were members of this group. Osten-Sacken, for example, doubted Britain's reliability and blamed Britain for the loss of Port Arthur.[232] Baron Rosen believed Russia's future lay in the east, not the west, and that Russia must disentangle itself from the Entente, which he thought made war inevitable.[233] Such men and their sentiments were, however, in the minority in the Russian foreign ministry, and as they did not share the views of the ministers Izvolsky and Sazonov (Hartwig was the exception), they were unable greatly to influence Russian policy.

A new era in Russian diplomacy had begun with Izvolsky's appointment as foreign minister in 1906. He set Russia firmly on the path of cooperation with Britain and France. His successor, Sazonov, continued Izvolsky's work. Frustrations and resentments were often felt within the ministry of foreign affairs, but overwhelmingly it was believed that the benefits of this policy outweighed the disadvantages. It was recognized, moreover, that Russian options were strictly limited, given its domestic circumstances and its recent military defeat at the hands of Japan. Russia was compelled to defend the status quo in international relations. Russia's diplomats were, on the whole, cognizant of the threat Germany posed and the consequent need to side with Britain and France, the other two status quo powers, to maintain the balance of power in Europe. At the same time there existed a strongly held belief that Russia must maintain its great power status at all costs. The tension inherent in these conflicting goals affected Russian foreign policy and proved to be an extremely difficult balancing act. For many of the men who formulated and carried out the empire's foreign policy, alliance with a secular republic which had beheaded its king, and friendship with the sometimes unruly parliamentary state of Great Britain, were ideologically distasteful. Over and over again, however, Nicholas II's diplomats separated their own political affinities from the practice of Russian diplomacy because their primary goal was the preservation of a great Russian empire which Austro-Hungarian aims, encouraged by Germany, threatened in the Balkans. Within the foreign ministry the Triple Entente was almost universally regarded as the only possible combination that would reestablish and then maintain Russia as a great power. Russian diplomats would often rail about French treachery or British aloofness, but in the final analysis there existed no viable alternative and this they recognized.

NOTES

1. For a succinct account of education at the influential Lycée, see Sinel, *The Classroom and the Chancellery* (Cambridge, Mass., 1973), pp. 37–44.
2. Ibid., p. 88.

3. TsGIA, f. 1278, op. 2, d. 2719, ll. 242–56.

4. A.D. Kalmykov, *Memoirs of a Russian Diplomat* (New Haven, Conn., 1971), p. 26.

5. D.C.B. Lieven, *Russia and the Origins of the First World War* (London, 1983), p. 90.

6. Cecil Spring-Rice, *The Letters and Friendships of Sir Cecil Spring-Rice: A Record* (London, 1924), vol. 2, Spring-Rice to Grey, 2 May 1906, p. 36.

7. W.C. Fuller, "The Russian Empire" in E.R. May, ed., *Knowing One's Enemies* (Princeton, N.J., 1984), pp. 99–102.

8. B.J. Williams, "The Revolution of 1905 and Russian Foreign Policy," in *Essays in Honour of E.H. Carr* (London, 1974), p. 103.

9. Wilhelm von Schoen, *Memoirs of an Ambassador* (London, 1922), p. 29.

10. AVPR, f. 133, 1906g., d. 65, op. 470, l. 64, Spring-Rice to Grey, 24 February 1906.

11. Ibid., d. 97, part 2, ll. 38, 39, ll. 41, 42, correspondence with Benckendorf.

12. A.P. Izvolsky, *Recollections of a Foreign Minister* (Garden City, N.Y., 1921), p. 158.

13. D.I. Abrikossov, *Revelations of a Russian Diplomat* (Seattle, Wash., 1964), p. 128.

14. A.W. Palmer, "The Anglo-Russian Entente" *History Today*, no.11 (1957), p. 752.

15. As quoted in A.V. Ignat'ev, "The Foreign Policy of Russia in the Far East at the Turn of the Nineteenth and Twentieth Centuries," in A. Ragsdale and V.N. Ponomarev, eds., *Imperial Russian Foreign Policy* (New York, 1993), p. 264.

16. *BD/CP*, vol. 4, doc. 187, Report, Nicolson to Grey, 2 January 1907, p. 282.

17. G.H. Bolsover, "Izvolsky and the Reform of the Russian Ministry of Foreign Affairs," *Slavonic and East European Review* 63, 1 (1985), pp. 21–40.

18. Izvolsky, *Recollections of a Foreign Minister*, p. 15.

19. Ibid., pp. 19–20.

20. V.W. Kokovtsov, *Out of My Past* (Stanford, CA, 1935), pp. 165 and 173.

21. Alexander Izvolsky, *Au Service de la Russie: Correspondence diplomatique, 1906–1911* (Paris, 1937), Izvolsky to Nelidov, 22 June/5 July 1906, p. 208.

22. Ibid., p. 299.

23. Geoffrey Hosking, *The Russian Constitutional Experiment* (Cambridge, UK, 1973), p. 228.

24. Kalmykov, *Memoirs of a Russian Diplomat*, p. 175.

25. *Stenografichesky otchet: Gosudarstvennaia Duma*, third convocation, first session (1908), pp. 118–19.

26. D.M. McDonald, *Autocracy, Bureaucracy, and Change in the Formation of Russia's Foreign Policy, 1895–1914* (Ph.D. diss., Columbia University, 1988), p. 388.

27. Izvolsky, *Recollections of a Foreign Minister*, pp. 241 and 244.

28. George Sanders, "Diplomacy and the Anglo-Russian Convention of 1907," *UCLA Historical Journal* 3 (1982), p. 62. See also B.J. Williams, "The Strategic Background to the Anglo-Russian Entente of August 1907," *The Historical Journal* 9, no. 3 (1966), p. 373.

29. As quoted in McDonald, *Autocracy, Bureaucracy, and Change*, p. 360.

30. Izvolsky, *Au Service de la Russie*, vol. 1, Izvolsky to Nekliudov, 26 October/8 November 1906. See also von Schoen, *Memoirs of an Ambassador*, pp. 39–41.

31. John F.V. Keiger, *France and the Origins of the First World War* (London, 1983), p. 23.

32. G. Sanders, "Diplomacy and the Anglo-Russian Convention of 1907," *UCLA History Journal* (1982), p. 69.

33. McDonald, *Autocracy, Bureaucracy, and Change*, pp. 362–363.

34. *BD/CP*, vol. 4, doc. 187, 2 January 1907, Report from Nicolson to Grey, p. 291. Also *BD/CP*, vol. 5, doc. 103, Annual Report on Russia for 1909, p. 370.

35. *BD/CP*, vol. 5, doc. 61, Annual Report for the year 1908, p. 216. Also *BD/CP*, vol. 5, doc. 20, p. 89, doc. 103, pp. 357, 350 and 362.

36. AVPR, f. 133, 1906g., op. 470, d. 97, part 2, l. 147, secret telegram to Benckendorf, 27 September 1906.

37. *BD/CP*, vol. 4, doc. 146, Nicolson to Grey, 20 September 1906, p. 222.

38. Ibid., p. 223.

39. *BD/CP*, vol. 6, doc. 62, Annual Report on Russia for 1910, p. 119 and p. 121.

40. Maurice Bompard, *Mon Ambassade en Russie* (Paris, 1937), p. 267 and p. 273.

41. AVPR, f. 133, op. 470, 1908g., d. 179, l. 3, copy of a letter from Izvolsky to Bompard, 19 January/1 February 1908. Ll. 8–9, telegram from Izvolsky to Nelidov, 22 January 1908. l. 10, draft of a letter from Izvolsky to Panafieu, French chargé d'affaires. Ll. 13–15, draft of a private letter from Izvolsky to Nelidov.

42. TsGIA, f. 560, op. 22, d. 312, ll. 220–23, effront to Kokovtsov, 2/15 October 1908.

43. *BD/CP*, vol. 5, doc. 61, Annual Report on Russia for 1908, p. 205.

44. *BD/CP*, vol. 5, doc. 103, Annual Report on Russia for 1909, p. 336.

45. Ibid., p. 338.

46. *LN*, vol. 1, letter from Izvolsky to Sazonov, 25 October/7 November 1912.

47. *BD/CP*, vol. 5, doc. 103, Annual Report on Russia for 1909, p. 336.

48. Quoted in Keith Neilson, *Britain and the Last Tsar* (Oxford, 1995), p. 68.

49. Rossos, *Russia and the Balkans* (Toronto, 1981), pp. 5–6.

50. Ibid., p. 7.

51. Francis Roy Bridge, "Izvolsky, Aehrenthal, and the End of the Austro-Russian Entente, 1906–1908," *Mitteilungen des osterreichischen Staatsarchivs* 29 (1976), pp. 315–62.

52. Lieven, *Russia and the Origins of the First World War*, p. 37.

53. Fuller, "The Russian Empire," p. 103.

54. *LN*, vol. 1, letter from Izvolsky, 11/24 April 1911, p. 81. Letter from Izvolsky, 28 April/11 May 1911, p. 103.

55. Ibid., letter from Izvolsky, 24 May/6 June 1911, p. 119.

56. Izvolsky, *Recollections of a Foreign Minister*, p. 129.

57. Ibid., p. 130.

58. *LN*, vol. 1, letter from Izvolsky, 24 November/7 December 1911, p. 170.

59. *LN*, vol. 1, letters from Izvolsky, 5/18 January 1911, p. 28, 31 March/13 April 1911, p. 71, 24 November/7 December 1911, p. 170

60. Izvolsky, *Au Service de la Russie*, vol. 2, Izvolsky to Stolypin, 21 July/3 August 1911, p. 300.

61. *LN*, vol. 1, Izvolsky to Neratov, very secret, 5/18 July 1912, p. 298.

62. *LN*, vol. 2, mèmorandum from Izvolsky, 28 February/13 March 1911, p. 43.

63. M. Paléologue, *Au Quai d'Orsay. A la veille de la tourmente* (Paris, 1947), p. 305.

64. Ibid., p. 305.

65. *LN*, vol. 2, Izvolsky to Sazonov, 5/18 March 1914, Izvolsky to Sazonov, pp. 249–251.

66. Paléologue, *Au Quai d'Orsay*, p. 306.

67. *LN*, vol.1, Izvolsky to Sazonov, 1/14 March 1912, p. 216. Izvolsky to Sazonov, 7/20 June 1912, p. 281.

68. Keiger, *France and the Origins of the First World War*, p. 94.

69. *LN*, vol. 1, Izvolsky to Sazonov, 22 November/5 December 1912, p. 364.

70. *LN*, vol. 2, Izvolsky to Sazonov, 3/16 January 1913, p. 9. As French premier from 1902 to 1905, Emile Combes waged a ruthless anticlerical campaign.

71. *LN*, vol. 2, Izvolsky to Sazonov, 17/30 January 1913, p. 19.

72. Ibid., p. 20.

73. Ibid., pp. 19–20.

74. *LN*, vol.1, memorandum from Izvolsky, 28 April/11 May 1911, p. 97.

75. Ibid., pp. 98–101.

76. *LN*, vol. 1, telegram from Izvolsky, 4/17 December 1912, p. 570. Memorandum from Izvolsky, 12/25 April 1911, p. 87.

77. *LN*, vol. 2, memorandum from Izvolsky, 21 November/4 December 1913, p. 247.

78. Ibid., pp. 247–48.

79. AVPR, f. 133, 1913g., op. 470, d. 116, ll. 44–45, Izvolsky to Sazonov, 4/17 July 1913.

80. *LN*, vol. 1, memorandum from Izvolsky, 20 January/2 February 1911, p. 29. Letters from Izvolsky; 17 February/2 March 1911, p. 43. 31 March/13 April 1911, p. 74. 29 September/12 October 1911, p. 147. 13/16 October 1911, p. 152. 26 October/8 November 1911, p. 155. 10/23 November 1911, p. 164. End of December 1911, pp. 174–175. 29 March/11 April 1912, p. 231. 10/23 May 1912, p. 257. 29 March/11 April 1912, p. 231–2. 21 November/4 December 1913, p. 196.

81. *LN*, vol. 1, letter from Izvolsky, 12/25 April 1911, p. 91.

82. S.D. Sazonov, *Les Années Fatales* (Paris, 1927), p. 35.

83. For a contemporary's assessment see Kalmykov, *Memoirs of a Russian Diplomat*, p. 214.

84. McDonald, *Autocracy, Bureaucracy, and Change*, pp. 494–495.

85. As quoted in Lieven, *Russia and the Origins of the First World War*, p. 90.

86. C. de Grunwald, *Le Tsar Nicholas II* (Paris, 1965), p. 283. M. Taube, *La Politique Russe d'avant-Guerre* (Paris, 1928), p. 248. And N.V. Tcharykov, "Sazonoff," *Contemporary Review* 133 (1928), p. 288.

87. Sazonov, *Les Années Fatales*, p. 23.

88. Ibid., p. 24.

89. Ibid., p. 24.

90. Neilson, *Britain and the Last Tsar*, p. 69.

91. Judith A. Head, "Public Opinion and Middle Eastern Railways: The Russo-German Negotiations of 1910–1911," *International History Review* 6, no. 1 (1984), pp. 28–47.

92. *BD/CP*, vol. 6, doc. 92, Annual Report on Russia for 1911, p. 205.

93. Ibid., p. 205.

94. *LN*, vol. 1, Izvolsky to Sazonov, 1/14 March 1912, p. 217.

95. Sazonov, *Les Années Fatales*, p. 43.

96. G. Buchanan, *My Mission to Russia* (Boston, 1923), vol. 1, pp. 92–93.

97. *BD/CP*, vol. 6, doc. 62, Annual Report on Russia for 1910, p. 114. Doc. 92, Annual Report on Russia for 1911, p. 221. Doc. 135, Annual Report on Russia for 1912, pp. 299–300. Doc. 172, Annual Report on Russia for 1913, pp. 359–60.

98. Sazonov, *Les Années Fatales*, p. 64.

99. G. Buchanan, *My Mission to Russia*, p. 111, copy of a letter from Buchanan to Grey.

100. Sazonov, *Les Années Fatales*, p. 61.

101. *LN*, vol. 2, Sazonov's Report to the Tsar, p. 346.

102. GARF, f. 601, op. 1, d. 1219, letter from George V to Nicholas II, 6 October 1912.

103. *LN*, vol. 2, Sazonov's Report to Nicholas II, p. 347.

104. G. Buchanan, *My Mission to Russia*, vol. 1, p. 109.

105. *LN*, vol. 1, Sazonov's Report to Nicholas II, p. 359.

106. Sazonov, *Les Années Fatales*, p. 60.

107. *LN*, vol. 2, Sazonov's Report to Nicholas II, p. 356.

108. G. Buchanan, *My Mission to Russia*, pp. 137–38.

109. *BD/CP*, vol. 6, doc. 135, Annual Report on Russia for 1912, p. 294.

110. J. Keiger, *France and the Origins of the First World War*, p. 89.

111. *BD/CP*, vol. 6, doc. 135, Annual Report on Russia for 1912, p. 295.

112. *LN*, vol. 2, Sazonov to Izvolsky, 8 August 1913, pp. 137–138. Also secret telegram from Sazonov to Izvolsky, 22 July 1912, p. 116.

113. Ibid., p. 116.

114. *LN*, vol. 2, Sazonov to Nicholas II, 24 October 1913, p. 360.

115. Sazonov, *Les Années Fatales*, p. 159.

116. Quoted in Lieven, *Russia and the Origins of the First World War*, p. 46.

117. Ibid., p. 48.

118. *BD/CP*, vol. 6, doc. 172, Annual Report on Russia for 1913, p. 357. See also G. Buchanan, *My Mission to Russia*, p. 149.

119. Sazonov, *Les Années Fatales*, pp. 137–39.

120. Ibid., p. 136.

121. *LN*, vol.2, Sazonov to Benckendorf, 2/15 April 1914, p. 314.

122. Sazonov, *Les Années Fatales*, pp. 61 and 136.

123. *BD/CP*, vol. 6, doc. 172, Annual Report on Russia for 1913, p. 360.

124. *LN*, vol. 2, Sazonov to Izvolsky, 20 March 1914, p. 255.

125. *LN*, vol. 2, Paléologue to Doumergue, 16 May 1914, p. 266.

126. Keiger, *France and the Origins of the First World War*, p. 141.

127. Havighurst, Alfred F., *Britain in Transition: The Twentieth Century* (Chicago, 1979), p. 102.

128. *LN*, vol. 2, private letter from Sazonov to Benckendorf, 6/19 February, 1914, p. 307.

129. Ibid., p. 307.

130. *BD/CP*, vol. 6, doc. 174, Buchanan to Grey, 31 March 1914, p. 380.

131. AVPR, f. 133, op. 470, 1914g., d. 192, ll. 25–26, Sazonov to Benckendorf, 11/24 June 1914.

132. Ibid.

133. Ibid., l. 26.

134. *LN*, vol. 2, secret telegram from Sazonov to Izvolsky, 16/29 July 1914, p. 289.

135. Sazonov, *Les Années Fatales*, pp. 192–193.

136. Neilson, *Britain and the Last Tsar*, pp. 77–78.

137. Izvolsky, *Au Service de la Russie*, vol. 1, Benckendorf to Izvolsky, 28 June/11 July 1906, p. 330.

138. Ibid., Benckendorf to Izvolsky, 8/21 August 1906, p. 352.

139. D.I. Abrikossov, *Revelations of a Russian Diplomat* (Seattle, Wash., 1964), p. 117.

140. Izvolsky, *Au Service de la Russie*, vol. 1, Benckendorf to Izvolsky, 27 July/9 August 1906, p. 349. Also Benckendorf to Izvolsky, 24 June/7 July 1906, p. 324.

141. Taube, *La Politique Russe d'avant-Guerre*, p. 160.

142. Abrikossov, *Revelations of a Russian Diplomat*, pp. 102 and 110.

143. Izvolsky, *Au Service de la Russie*, vol. 1, Benckendorf to Izvolsky, 3/16 July 1906, pp. 332–33. 25 July/7 August 1906, p. 339. Vol. 2, 20 December 1906/2 January 1907, p. 11. 21 July/3 August 1908, p. 187. 10/24 September 1909, p. 242.

144. Ibid., vol. 1, Benckendorf to Izvolsky, 14/27 June 1906, p. 316.

145. Ibid., vol. 2, Benckendorf to Izvolsky, 28 April/11 May 1910, p. 263.

146. AVPR, f. 320, op. 812, d. 10, ll. 96–99, Benckendorf to Sazonov, 6/19 December 1910.

147. Izvolsky, *Au Service de la Russie*, vol. 2, Benckendorf to Izvolsky, 20 July/2 August 1910, p. 288.

148. AVPR, f. 320, op. 812, d. 10, l. 187, Benckendorf to Sazonov, 3/16 January 1911.

149. Izvolsky, *Au Service de la Russie*, vol. 1, Benckendorf to Izvolsky, 25 July/7 August 1906, pp. 339–40.

150. Ibid., vol. 2, Benckendorf to Izvolsky, 2/15 May 1907, p. 39.

151. Ibid., Benckendorf to Izvolsky, 13/24 June 1907, pp. 59–60.

152. Ibid., Benckendorf to Izvolsky, 27 June/10 July 1907, pp. 62–63. See also Abrikossov, *Revelations of a Russian Diplomat*, pp. 112–113.

153. AVPR, FDLCixd, op. 464, d. 295a, l. 6.

154. Abrikossov, *Revelations of a Russian Diplomat*, pp. 137–138. See also Sir E. Grey, *Twenty-Five Years* (Toronto, 1925), pp. 149–150.

155. AVPR, f. 320, op. 812, d. 10, l. 85, Benckendorf to Sazonov, 18/31 August 1909. AVPR, f. 133, 1906g., op. 470, d. 97, part 1, ll. 187–188, memorandum from Benckendorf, 1/14 August 1906. Izvolsky, *Au Service de la Russie*, vol. 2, Benckendorf to Izvolsky, 19 June/2 July 1908, p. 176. Benckendorf to Izvolsky, 21 September/4 October 1909, p. 254.

156. AVPR, f. 320, op. 812, d. 10, ll. 126–129, letter from Benckendorf, 22 November/5 December 1911.

157. AVPR, f.320, op. 812, d.10, ll. 176–179, Benckendorf to A.A. Neratov, 30 March/12 April 1911.

158. AVPR, f. 133, op. 470, 1912g., d. 174, ll. 5–7, confidential letter from Benckendorf to Sazonov, 27 January/9 February 1912.

159. Ibid., ll. 8–12, Benckendorf to Sazonov, 28 January/10 February 1912.

160. Izvolsky, *Au Service de la Russie*, vol. 2, Benckendorf to Izvolsky, 21 July/3 August 1907, pp. 75–76. AVPR, f. 320, op. 812, d. 10, ll. 182–184, Benckendorf to Sazonov, 30 January/12 February 1911. L. 122, Benckendorf to Sazonov, 7/20 December 1911.

161. Izvolsky, *Au Service de la Russie*, vol. 1, Benckendorf to Izvolsky, 28 June/11 July 1906, pp. 327–29.

162. AVPR, f. 320, op. 812, d. 10, ll. 94–95, Benckendorf to Sazonov, 3/16 December 1910.

163. Izvolsky, *Au Service de la Russie*, vol. 2, Benckendorf to Izvolsky, 21 September/4 October 1909, p. 253.

164. Ibid., p. 256.

165. Ibid., Benckendorf to Izvolsky, 23 December 1909/5 January 1910, p. 260.

166. AVPR, f. 320, op. 812, d. 10, ll. 96–99, Benckendorf to Sazonov, 6/19 December 1910.

167. AVPR, f. 133, 1913g., op. 470, d. 20, ll. 4–5, Benckendorf to Sazonov, 16/29 January 1913. Ll. 6–7 Benckendorf to Sazonov, 27 February/12 March 1913. AVPR, f. 320, op. 812, d. 10, ll. 188–90, Benckendorf to Sazonov, December 1910/January 1911. AVPR, f. 133, 1913g., op. 470, d. 20, ll.2–3, Benckendorf to Sazonov, 15/28 January 1913.

168. AVPR, f. 133, op. 470, 1914g., ll. 16–20, Benckendorf to Sazonov.

169. *LN*, vol. 2, Benckendorf to Sazonov, 12/25 February 1912, pp. 308–309.

170. Ibid., Benckendorf to Sazonov, 25 March/7 April 1914, pp. 312–313.

171. Ibid., Benckendorf to Sazonov, 22 April/5 May 1914, p. 316.

172. Ibid., Benckendorf to Sazonov, 7/20 May 1914, p. 324.

173. Ibid., Benckendorf to Sazonov, 13/26 July 1914, p. 330.

174. Izvolsky, *Au Service de la Russie*, vol. 1, Benckendorf to Izvolsky, 23 August/5 September 1906, p. 361.

175. Ibid., vol. 2, Benckendorf to Izvolsky, 17/30 March 1908, p. 147.

176. *LN*, vol. 2, letter from Benckendorf, 12/13 February 1913, p. 306.

177. Izvolsky, *Au Service de la Russie*, vol. 2, Benckendorf to Izvolsky, 9/23 April 1909, p. 223. AVPR, f. 320, op. 812, d. 10, ll. 156–160, Benckendorf to A.A. Neratov, 30 August/12 September 1911.

178. Quoted in Lieven, *Russia and the Origins of the First World War*, p. 91.

179. Ibid., p. 92.

180. G.N. Trubetskoy, "Rossiya kak Velikaya Derzhava," in *Velikaya Rossiya* (Moscow, 1910), p. 31.

181. Lieven, *Russia and the Origins of the First World War*, p. 98.

182. Ibid., p. 98.

183. Ibid., p. 98.

184. Trubetskoy, "Rossiya kak Velikaya Dershava," pp. 29–30.

185. Ibid., p. 89.

186. Ibid., p. 90.

187. Ibid., p. 91.

188. Ibid., pp. 30–31, pp. 21–22, p. 44, pp. 57–58.

189. Ibid., pp. 76–77, 80.

190. Ibid., p. 91.

191. Ibid., p. 94.

192. Ibid., p. 95.

193. Ibid., p. 95.

194. Ibid., pp. 100–101.

195. Ibid., p. 99.

196. Ibid., p. 101.

197. Ibid., p. 104.

198. Trubetskoy, "Nekotorie Itogie Russkoi Vneshnei Politiki," p. 335.

199. Ibid., p. 333.

200. Ibid., p. 346 and p. 349.

201. Ibid., pp. 352–353.

202. Ibid., p. 353.

203. AVPR, f. 133, op. 470, 1906g., d. 107, part 1, ll. 188–89, Nelidov to Lamsdorf, 31 January/13 February 1906. Ll. 190–191, Nelidov to Lamsdorf, 9/22 February 1906.

204. AVPR, f. 133, op. 470, 1907g., d. 104, ll. 33–34, Nelidov to Izvolsky, 25 January/7 February 1907. Izvolsky, *Au Service de la Russie*, vol. 1, Nelidov to Izvolsky, 5/18 January 1908, p. 241.

205. Izvolsky, *Au Service de la Russie*, vol. 1, Nelidov to Izvolsky, 28 May/10 June 1909, p. 252.

206. Similar sentiments toward France were held by Russian diplomats, Sevastopoulo and Demidov. See *LN*, vol. 1, pp. 125–27, 307, and 315–20; vol. 2, pp. 6–7, 11, 158–59. Also AVPR, f. 133, 1913g., op. 470, d. 118, ll. 21–22 and l. 26.

207. AVPR, f. 133, op. 470, 1907g., d. 104, ll. 346–48, Nekliudov to Izvolsky, 14/27 June 1907.

208. AVPR, f. 133, op. 470, 1907g., d. 104, ll. 349–55, confidential letter from Nekliudov to Izvolsky, n.d.

209. Ibid.

210. Ibid.

211. AVPR, f. 133, 1908g., op. 470, d. 195, ll. 16–25, marked "highly secret," Nekliudov to N.V. Charkov, 4/17 September 1908.

212. *LN*, vol. 1, memorandum from Nekliudov, 1/14 December 1910, p. 9.

213. Ibid., p. 3.

214. Ibid., p. 6.

215. Ibid., memorandum from Nekliudov, 1/14 December 1910, p. 16.

216. Ibid., pp. 16–17.

217. N.V. Tcharykov, *Glimpses of High Politics* (London, 1931), pp. 12 and 80.

218. Ibid., p. 247.

219. Ibid., p. 448.

220. Abrikossov, *Revelations of a Russian Diplomat*, pp. 98 and 125.

221. Ibid., p. 140.

222. Ibid., pp. 95, 99, 109, 118, 130, and 142.

223. A.D. Kalmykov, *Memoirs of a Russian Diplomat* (New Haven, Conn.), p. 6.

224. Ibid., p. 177.

225. Ibid., pp. 210–12.

226. Ibid., p. 90.

227. Ibid., p. 22.

228. AVPR, f. 470, 1914g., d. 191, ll. 15–18, undated *spravka*.

229. Ibid., l. 15.

230. Ibid., l. 16.

231. Ibid., ll. 17–18.

232. Izvolsky, *Au Service de la Russie*, vol. 1, Osten-Sacken to Izvolsky, 19 May/1 June 1906, pp. 44–45, 23 March/5 April 1907, p. 85.

233. Lieven, *Russia and the Origins of the First World War*, p. 90.

Chapter 5

Reluctant Partners: Russian Officialdom and the Triple Entente

From 1905 to 1914 the tsarist government's domestic policy of repression and rebuilding was inextricably linked with a cautious foreign policy. All senior officials and members of the imperial government were aware of the imperative need for breathing space, which Izvolsky and Sazonov sought through the Triple Entente. Stolypin's ambitious reform program was the domestic twin to the new foreign policy, both of which were inspired by the desire to retain Russia's status as a great power. In general, most other ministers and important government officials regarded the Entente as a political and financial necessity. Certain high-ranking exceptions, particularly in the military, did exist, but they were unable to alter fundamentally the course on which Izvolsky had set Russia in 1906. Most members of the Russian government and bureaucracy had little sympathy for British and French political ideas, yet they were willing to embrace London and Paris as diplomatic partners and sources of financial support.

The men who ruled Russia formed a bureaucratic ruling elite, derived primarily from the aristocracy and the gentry.[1] The great majority of Nicholas II's ministers and senior officials were aging career civil servants. In 1904 the average age of ministers was sixty-two, whereas members of the State Council averaged over sixty-nine.[2] The top Russian officials of this era were European in their education, their culture, and their values. A small but telling sign of this European orientation was the fact that the English Club was the favored club in Saint Petersburg for the nobility and high officials.[3] Educated Russian society, from which the bureaucrats who administered the empire were drawn, was the most cosmopolitan in Europe. The role of the

English nanny, the French governess, and the German tutor in the upbringing of the Russian nobility was unique to Russia. European literature in the original languages permeated the consciousness of educated society.[4]

Many inefficiencies plagued the tsarist government prior to the 1905 revolution. It lacked clearly defined and generally recognized goals. Each minister sought to implement his own program, counting on the trust of the tsar, and in the process often undercut other ministers.[5] Such a state of affairs clearly did not lead to good government and the fiasco of the Russo-Japanese War, and subsequent revolution made these failings patently obvious. Consequently the government of Nicholas II faced the choice of attempting to reform itself or being swept away by revolution.

In the government discussions that led to the historic October Manifesto, the experience of western Europe was the constant point of reference. The condition for participation in the abortive Bulygin Duma was property ownership, a criterion that transcended to a certain extent the traditional barriers of birth and political rank and thereby confirmed the breakdown of the old estate order. The creators and defenders of this reform justified it as a "social and economic change and a political maturation process not unlike what western Europe had experienced earlier."[6] Opponents of this concept argued that a nonestate-based Duma was "parliamentary, borrowed from Western examples, . . . foreign to the Russian people."[7] An anonymous memorandum submitted to Nicholas II in August 1905 argued that, in light of the anticipated unanimity within the Duma, it would be necessary to form a "uniform ministry or, as it is accepted to call it in the language of political doctrines, a Cabinet."[8] The author compared the gravity of the present situation to the meeting of the Estates General in 1789, when the French government had no program to meet the gathering of representatives.[9]

From this heated debate emerged the October Manifesto of 1905 and the Fundamental State Laws of April 1906, which were to be the basis of the new order in Russia. The provisions on the legislature in Project Number One of the Fundamental Laws "came primarily from the constitutions of western Europe and were liberal in tone."[10] The reforms were bold but they were initiated under threatening circumstances by a weak government that displayed a strong ambivalence toward them and "an almost total lack of consensus about their meaning or their permanence."[11] Moreover, the new political system gave more power to the groups that had the most to lose from reform while underrepresenting the emerging middle classes, which had the most to gain from significant economic and political reforms. The façade of reformed political institutions masked the continued dominance of an established political class that was intent on resisting real change.[12] Rivalries between the new institutions and the autocrat plagued the post-

1905 system. For the chairman of the new council of ministers to function efficiently he needed the tsar's full support. Nicholas II, however, was not prepared to accept any limitations on his authority and undercut his first ministers at critical moments. There was also an inherent conflict between the legislature and the executive as neither laws nor much of the budget could be brought into force without the parliament's consent. Finally there existed antagonism between the appointed State Council, dominated by the land-owning nobility, and the elected Duma. The State Council, like the tsar, had an absolute veto over legislation. Such a situation was a recipe for frustration particularly for the chairman of the council of ministers, who was expected to govern effectively while reconciling all the competing interests of the tsar, the other ministers, and the two legislative chambers.

Despite the serious limitations of the October Manifesto and the Fundamental Laws, they did mark an important turning point in the development of Russian law. Some have even argued that they transformed "the Russian empire from an absolute and unlimited monarchy into a constitutional monarchy."[13] The creation of the council of ministers, the first Western-style cabinet in Russian political life, effectively curtailed the ministerial despotism that had been prevalent until then.[14] Henceforth, all edicts and commands issued by the tsar had to be countersigned either by the chairman of the council or one of the ministers.

The role of the new council of ministers in foreign policy is controversial. Lieven argues that the council's role was limited, but that it could have some influence. Russia in the decade before 1914 "stood somewhere between the old absolutist era and a more modern age in which social forces began to invade the hitherto sacrosanct world of kings and diplomats."[15] D.M. McDonald, on the other hand, argues that the council's role, especially that of the chairman, became increasingly important as domestic concerns remained the government's top priority and no foreign policy imbroglio could be allowed to jeopardize the delicate rebuilding process. While the council's role was strengthened, the emperor retained the final say. Witte's, Stolypin's and Kokovtsov's power all still depended on the continued favor of Nicholas II.[16]

With the Third of June 1907 coup d'état, the Russian government temporarily reestablished its supremacy over society. The Duma and the government settled into a period of uneasy coexistence with the government triumphant for the moment.[17] Stolypin's law increased the predominance of ethnic Russians over minority nationalities and of the center over the outlying territories, ensured the dominance of well-to-do voters over the masses, and institutionalized gerrymandering.[18] The system aimed to produce a cooperative Duma representing the conservatism of its property-owning constituencies. The effect was to grant a virtual political monopoly to the landed nobility, the result of which was a legislative stalemate that "preserved the status quo and eventually allowed the gentry to withdraw into its own cultural, psychological, and political isolation."[19] The implementation of the Third of June system coincided almost exactly with the birth of the Triple Entente. Both were attempts to maintain the empire's status quo, one domestically, the other internationally. Both ultimately were failures.

The revamped Russian government's first foray on the international stage came with the 1906 loan negotiations with France and Great Britain. The French government took advantage of Russia's desperate need of money, demanding and receiving full Russian cooperation at the Algeciras conference.[20] French tactics alienated Russia from Germany and thereby increased Russian reliance on France. Witte and Kokovtsov had wanted Germany to participate in the loan, but Germany refused because of Russian support of France at Algeciras.[21] The intransigent German attitude persuaded the British that they were morally obligated to help the Russians. Cecil Spring-Rice, in charge of the British Embassy in the ambassador's absence, wrote to Grey: "It is therefore of the greatest importance that France and England, who are accomplices in the crime for which Russia is made to suffer, should do their best to help her. It appears to be of the nature of an honourable obligation, which cannot be avoided without serious consequences."[22]

All Russian officials aware of their country's financial condition enthusiastically greeted the final signing of the loan. Witte looked upon the loan as a long, hard-fought battle and a personal victory.[23] Nicholas II regarded the loan as Witte's main accomplishment and as "a great moral success of the government and a guarantee for the future tranquillity and peaceful development of Russia."[24] To show its gratitude, the Russian government decorated various French financiers for their help in securing the loan.[25]

The 1906 loan, the largest international loan ever granted up to that time, had significant ramifications for Russia's position internationally. The loan enabled Russia to maintain the gold standard, ensuring a stable currency, so that in less than ten years the Russian economy was restored. By 1914 the economic situation was more satisfactory than at any previous time.[26] The loan also marked the end of "easy credit" for the Russian government in Paris.[27] German anger over the Algeciras conference and its failure to subscribe to the loan prevented a Russo-German rapprochement. Most importantly, the April 1906 loan transformed the very nature of the Franco-Russian alliance. From the beginning of the alliance until the turn of the century, Russia had been the dominant partner and had exercised caution in formalizing the alliance. From 1901 to 1904 the two countries were more or less evenly matched, each preoccupied with pressing domestic problems.

As a result of Russia's humiliating defeat by Japan and the 1905 revolution, the balance began to shift in favor of France. In April 1906 the French government "used its strong bargaining position as banker to Russia to rearrange the military agreement between the two countries and to subordinate Russia's financial interests to French interests."[28] The two allies agreed that a German defeat would be the primary goal of a European war, and the anti-British elements of the 1901 military protocol were eliminated. The 1906 loan was a powerful symbol of Russian weakness in the international arena, and of French strength.[29] The negotiations for the loan revealed the essential relationships that were to dominate the emerging Triple Entente until 1914. British participation in the loan and the repudiation of the anti-British clause were also the first steps in the Anglo-Russian rapprochement.

S.I. Witte played a preeminent role in both the transformation of Russia from an absolute autocracy to a semiconstitutional state and in the 1906 loan negotiations. In general, as finance minister and then as chairman of the council of ministers, Witte stood for the modernization of Russia. His industrialization policy helped undermine the traditional religious and political loyalties on which the old regime was based and increased the size of the working and middle classes, elements hostile to the autocracy.[30] The results of the rapid industrialization promoted under his leadership led him to advocate political reform. In his memoirs he asserted his belief that Russia would eventually have a constitution "as in other civilized states" and that the principles of civic freedom would take root.[31] The form he favored, however, was something like the Prussian system with himself at the head.[32] His admiration of the Prussian system corresponded with his preferences in foreign policy. During the crisis of 1905, he persuaded Nicholas II to grant the October Manifesto. In a report to the tsar, Witte argued that man's natural striving for personal liberty had become the driving force of historical change. In this sense he linked Russia firmly with its European neighbors.[33] At this time Witte envisioned a Western-style council of ministers, like a cabinet, which would settle its differences internally. Decisions taken in the council would bind ministers, and they would have to resign if they did not accept these decisions. Most significantly, Witte proposed that the chairman of the council would nominate new ministers to the emperor.[34] The emperor accepted the proposals and made Witte the first chairman. Witte, however, did not remain in power long enough to put his stamp on the new government.

While in power, however, Witte did exercise considerable influence on foreign policy, as his role in negotiating the Treaty of Portsmouth and the 1906 loan indicate. In general he distrusted the French and desired some kind of agreement with Germany. When Witte stopped in Paris on his way to Portsmouth, the reception he received insulted him: "In the French capital my feelings as a Russian patriot were hurt at every step. The public treated me, the chief plenipotentiary of the autocrat of all the Russias, as a representative of some political nonentity. Some—a slight minority—sympathised with me, others could not conceal their joy at our misfortune; but the majority treated me with complete indifference. . . . The attitude of the radical press toward the Emperor and our country were insulting."[35] Witte's injured pride was a typical reaction of Russian officials when confronted by Russia's sullied reputation abroad. Witte disliked the Entente Cordiale, referring to it as an "annoying error" and "this sad affair."[36] To his intense chagrin, the French firmly opposed "the idea of the consolidation of the continent."[37] Even after Witte left office, he did not abandon his critical opinions of French diplomacy. Izvolsky recollected that Witte "expressed the conviction that France had lost all remembrance of its ancient warlike virtues; that the immense majority of Frenchmen cared not a whit for the lost provinces, which were only of interest to a handful of chauvinists, possessing little or no influence in the country; and finally that the French nation imbued with the ideas of international socialism and the pacifist propaganda, would always shrink from an armed conflict with Germany, especially if it grew out of oriental affairs."[38]

Witte was a longtime advocate of a continental alliance of Russia, Germany, and France, which would attract all the other European countries. He had approached the German kaiser about this idea as early as 1897. He repeated his ideas to Prince Eulenberg, the kaiser's intermediary, in February 1906, at the height of the Algeciras conference and the loan negotiations: "If we continue mutually to worry each other, we shall only diminish the moral and material forces of Europe. And our elements of weakness will always be put to profit by the maritime powers."[39] Not surprisingly, once out of power, Witte fulminated against the 1907 Anglo-Russian accord and in a March 1914 article in *Novoe Vremia* advocated a Russo-German understanding.[40]

Nonetheless, even Witte was forced to acknowledge Russian financial dependence on its ally in 1905–6 and, despite his worries about French trustworthiness, to shape Russian policy accordingly. Witte pledged Russian government support at the Algeciras conference in return for the French government's promise that a loan would be forthcoming. He worried, however, that once the conference had been completed to French satisfaction, they would not come through with the much-needed funds.[41] To ensure that France fulfilled its part of the bargain, Witte instructed Kokovtsov to warn the French government and banks that if the Russian government should be unable to secure a loan, it would be in no position to protect the interests of foreign holders of Russian securities. He also warned the French chargé d'affaires that if no loan were forthcoming, Russia would be forced to abandon the gold standard, which would adversely affect foreigners as much as Russians.[42] The new French government and in particular the new finance minister, Raymond Poincaré, disturbed Witte. He regarded Poincaré's first official action, his refusal to see E. Noetzlin, the French banker, and A. Rafalovich, Witte's agent in Paris, as a deliberate attempt to postpone the loan indefinitely and as an act of bad faith.[43]

The German refusal to participate in the loan drew a reluctant Witte closer to France and Britain, as their participation became vital to the loan's success.[44] Witte even made informal approaches to the British government, through the British journalist E.J. Dillon, about the possibility of an Anglo-Russian understanding.[45] Witte's proposals came to nought and Spring-Rice was under no illusions as to what motivated Witte in this apparent volte-face: "Witte wants it [an agreement] because he wants money." Nonetheless, Witte's overtures, whatever their motivation, were a marked departure for a man who had made a career of promoting a continental alliance against the maritime powers, especially Britain.[46] In this respect, he was merely coming into line with the new thinking emerging within Russian government circles.

It was, however, too little too late. Witte no longer had the confidence of the emperor. Once the loan was finalized, Nicholas II unceremoniously removed his first minister and replaced him with the aging Goremykin. The emperor rewarded Witte most perfunctorily and never appointed him to another government post. His removal from the chairmanship of the council of ministers was as significant as Lamsdorf's from the foreign ministry, which occurred at almost the same time. Goremykin, however, was only a temporary replacement.

The appointment of Peter Arkadyevich Stolypin as chairman of the council of ministers in July 1906 marked the real change in Russian domestic policy, and it coincided with the beginning of the new foreign policy under Izvolsky. Stolypin's previous appointments as marshall of the Kovno nobilty and then governor of Saratov province meant that he was an outsider to the Saint Petersburg bureaucratic scene, as was Izvolsky. Stolypin was brought to Saint Petersburg in April 1906 as minister of the interior because of his earned reputation for personal bravery in quelling the revolt in Saratov province, where disturbances had been especially severe. The bearded and charming provincial administrator came from an old noble family that had served the tsars since the sixteenth century and had accumulated vast estates in the process. As a child Stolypin had traveled extensively in Europe with his family and spoke English, French, and German fluently. His provincial experience shaped his political outlook and became a dangerous source of friction between him and his rivals. Nevertheless, he quickly exerted his authority and became a dominant force in the Russian government. The absence of Nicholas II from the day-to-day running of government in the years immediately following the 1905 revolution and the emperor's allocation of authority to Stolypin made him an especially powerful figure.

Stolypin used his unique position to attempt to implement his grand design for Russia. He planned to overhaul the administration of government and transform rural society. He wanted foreign relations to become more pacific, public education to be improved, and a national welfare system established for urban workers. In defense of his agrarian program, he explained to the Duma his primary goal: "To you a great cataclysm is necessary, to us a Great Russia!"[47] Stolypin embodied the phenomenon in Russian government of the iron fist and the extended hand. From the outset of his tenure in office a dual policy of force and reform was apparent. Five days after the promulgation of a decree instituting summary field courts martial, Stolypin outlined his program of major reforms. They included more land tenure for the peasants, better state insurance for industrial workers, reforms in local government and the judicial and educational systems, an income tax, and an improved code of civil liberties and equalities. Stolypin's agrarian policy, which actually continued along the path laid down by officials prior to the revolution, was the axis of his general reform policy, calculated to modernize the socioeconomic system of the country. He wrote the provincial governors explaining that the goal was to remove the economic grounds that allowed the revolutionaries to succeed in the countryside.[48] By awakening within the peasantry the instinct of private property and the destruction of the commune, he sought to establish a strong class of Russian peasantry. A new class of prosperous peasant smallholders would provide a bulwark both for the new state system and the Russian nationality. Stolypin had in mind the example of the sturdy conservative French peasantry.[49] Only the landownership and land-consolidation reforms, however, were even partially realized.[50] All of Stolypin's domestic reforms were made under the pressure of extraordinary circumstances, and the goal was the stabilization of the regime. In this respect the conduct of domestic and foreign policy mirrored each other.

Although Stolypin envisioned sweeping changes for Russia, he did not think the Western political path appropriate for Russia. In October 1906 he stated that parliamentarianism "does not and never can" exist in Russia.[51] He told Sir Arthur Nicolson in August 1907 that "political life and parliamentary ideals were enigmas to the vast majority of the nation, ignorant and unlettered as they were, and it was impossible to govern a vast Empire like

Russia on the lines of advanced Western nations."[52] In the Duma, Stolypin explained why Russia could not behave like "most mighty England," which gave broad rights to all because of a superfluity of strength. Rather, he explained: "The Russian Empire owes its origin and development to its Russian roots, and with its growth grew also and developed the autocratic power of the Tsars. To this Russian stem may not be grafted a foreign and alien flower. (Cheers, Centre and Right.) Let our own Russian flower bloom on it."[53] In fact, Stolypin's constitutional model was more Prussian than English. He believed that sovereignty resided with the monarch and his executive and was never to be ceded to a parliament.

From the beginning of Stolypin's tenure as chairman of the council of ministers, he behaved in a highly authoritarian fashion, thus substantiating his public utterances that Russia under his leadership would not follow the Western path. At his direction, papers were closed, editors and journalists arrested and exiled. The ministry of the interior's "special funds" financed an increasing number of right-wing papers. Stolypin earned the unflattering sobriquet "the hangman," and the gallows became known as "Stolypin's necktie" because of the high number of executions.[54]

In spite of a vigorous beginning, his hold on power slowly weakened. Ultimately, even before his August 1911 assassination removed him from the political scene, a lack of support threatened his entire reform program. The left opposed him because of his repression of the revolution and the right, including increasingly the tsar himself, because of his reforms. As T. Shanin has argued, Stolypin attempted a "revolution from above" with virtually no support from below.[55] He sought to transform Russia while using the old Russian method of imposing a solution from the top. One of his tools was the Triple Entente, which he felt would provide Russia with international peace, the most important prerequisite for successful reform.

His belief in the overwhelming need for peace was the leitmotif of Stolypin's attitude toward foreign policy. He expressed his views emphatically, and as it would turn out, prophetically to Izvolsky: "We need peace, war in the next years, especially for reasons which people do not understand, would be fatal for Russia and the dynasty. On the other hand each year of peace fortifies Russia, not only from a military and naval point of view, but again from a financial and economic point of view."[56] He believed that the risks of any foreign policy complication were so great that he, as overseer of Russia's restoration, must be consulted in foreign policy decisions because of their destabilizing potential within the empire.[57] Consequently, he took an active interest in Russian foreign policy. He interpreted the agreement with Britain in purely defensive terms and advocated a policy of inactivity in the Balkans.[58] Until the Bosnian annexation crisis, Izvolsky and Stolypin worked closely together as allies within the council of ministers. They shared a belief in the necessity of a working accommodation between state and society as the basis of the renewal of the empire and a common view on the question of "cabinet solidarity."[59]

Izvolsky's role in the Bosnian crisis and the threat it posed to Stolypin's grand plans effectively ended the close cooperation between the two ministers and strengthened Stolypin's belief that he must keep a close watch on the empire's foreign policy. Stolypin was informed of the Buchlau meeting between the Russian and Austrian foreign ministers only after it occurred. Stolypin was furious that Izvolsky had undertaken concrete agreements in an area of notorious instability and of special Russian strategic interest without informing the council, and had thereby violated the principle of "United Government."[60] Stolypin was not prepared to let the crisis develop into a military conflict. He told his eldest daughter that he would do "everything in the strength of mankind not to allow Russia to go to war because we have not yet accomplished our entire programme of internal recovery. We are unable to match an external enemy while we have not yet humbled the evil internal foes of Russia's greatness, the S.-R.s. . . . And what could create a more propitious atmosphere for revolution than war?"[61] Stolypin's threat to resign led to the abandonment of the attempt to forge a deal with Austria-Hungary over Vienna's annexation of the Ottoman provinces of Bosnia and Herzegovina, even though Nicholas and Izvolsky had already agreed on this policy.[62]

Stolypin's desire for peace made him a strong supporter of the 1907 agreement with Britain. At an August 1907 special conference, he evaluated the benefits of the Anglo-Russian agreement: "The successful conclusion of the agreement with England represents a truly great matter of state. Our internal situation does not allow us to conduct an aggressive foreign policy. The absence of fear from the point of view of international relations is extremely important for us since it will give us the opportunity to dedicate with full tranquillity our strength to repair of matters within the country."[63] After the convention was signed, Stolypin spoke of it in the "warmest terms," saying that Izvolsky "could be well satisfied [with it], even if he never concluded anything else."[64] Stolypin valued British friendship throughout his tenure of office and displayed interest in British domestic matters.[65] He told the influential Professor Bernard Pares that some day he would like to visit Britain and make a serious study of British public life, particularly the administration of the colonies.[66]

The British came to rely on Stolypin as a strong supporter of the Anglo-Russian rapprochement. Professor Pares described Stolypin as "the only real hope of . . . the development of the Anglo-Russian friendship."[67] London regarded Stolypin as the one carrying the reforms through largely by himself.[68] Stolypin was perhaps the only one of Nicholas II's ministers who managed to command the complete respect and trust of the British embassy in Saint Petersburg.[69] So important did the British feel Stolypin to be for their interests that the 1911 ministerial crisis that threatened Stolypin's position deeply concerned them.[70] News of Stolypin's assassination shook the British government. They felt they had lost a "loyal friend whose place it" would be "very difficult to fill."[71] Benckendorf described the shock the news from Kiev produced in London and the "astonishing confidence" Stolypin had inspired in Britain.[72]

Notwithstanding his repeated statements of loyalty to Britain and the British faith in him, Stolypin did have reservations about the trustworthiness of Russia's new partner. Stolypin told Sazonov that if Russia met disaster then all its allies would desert Russia.[73] Just prior to his death, Stolypin believed that Britain was displeased that Russia was regaining its strength: "England fears that its exploitation of such countries as India will someday end and that it not only will be unable to play first violin in the international concert but might become like those great empires of the past which have appeared and declined. England therefore hates Russia above all and will sincerely rejoice if the monarchy in Russia should fall and Russia itself should no longer be a great nation but disintegrate into a number of independent republics."[74] Stolypin also thought France hated monarchical Russia and that the only tie holding the two countries together was French fear of Germany.[75] These notes reveal Stolypin's suspicions toward Britain and France and confirm that for him the Entente was based on pragmatic notions, not ideological sympathy. Although Stolypin embraced the Triple Entente as a foreign policy measure likely to ensure the peace necessary to implement his domestic reforms, he remained ambivalent toward Britain and France, viewing Russia's partnership with them as a utilitarian arrangement, not an ideological union.

Stolypin's successor as chairman of the council of ministers was V.N. Kokovtsov. Before this appointment, Kokovtsov had been the minister of finance, a post he combined with his new responsibilities. In both positions he had important dealings with Britain and France. Unlike Witte and Stolypin, Kokovtsov was a bureaucrat par excellence. He tried without success to uphold the "United Government" approach. He failed in part because he did not have Stolypin's vision of Russia, nor did he have a comparable force of personality. Moreover, he did not have the same personal relationship with Nicholas II that Stolypin had had. Kokovtsov had inherited his ministers, and he had some formidable enemies, including General V.A. Sukhomilov, the minister of war, and Krivoshein, minister of finance. In its annual report on Russia for 1911, the British embassy commented on Kokovtsov's weaknesses but concluded that there was no reason to fear that Stolypin's death would effect any serious change in relations with Britain.[76] Their assessment would prove to be correct.

In October 1911 Nicholas II granted Kokovtsov "the formal authority to intervene in foreign policy formation on a footing equal with that of the minister of foreign affairs."[77] This signified an important departure but was a pyrrhic victory. Kokovtsov was unable to take full advantage of the new powers, as he never secured from Nicholas the same degree of support as had Stolypin. As a sign of Kokovtsov's new role, he addressed the opening session of the Fourth Duma on foreign affairs, the first discussion of such matters in the Duma by a council chairman.[78] After this initial success, how- ever, the council under Kokovtsov became divided and ineffective.

Like Stolypin, Kokovtsov believed that Russia was unprepared for parliamentarianism. Shortly after the inauguration of the First Duma he made this point forcibly in a manner which drew heated criticism from the opposition, exclaiming, "Thank God we have no parliament yet."[79] The experience of republican France frightened Kokovtsov as it did many Russian officials. At a February 1906 conference to revise the Duma statute, he criticized Witte's scheme for two chambers by "referring to the example of republican France, where for half a century there had been an endless struggle to limit the power of the Senate but so far all such attempts had been in vain."[80] In June of the same year, Kokovtsov opposed vehemently the idea of a cabinet drawn from members of the Duma. This, he believed, would pave the way to a system of the English type. Kokovtsov told Nicholas II, "We are not yet mature enough to have a one-chamber constitutional monarchy of a purely parliamentary type, and I believe it my duty to warn you, Sire, not to attempt this new experiment from which there may be no return."[81]

Kokovtsov, as minister of finance and chairman of the council of ministers, however, was well aware of Russia's reliance, especially financial, on Britain and France, and of the need to maintain good relations with them. In 1906, as the Russian government's envoy to Paris, Kokovtsov actively participated in the loan negotiations. French bankers had initially been reluctant to lend Russia money because of the instability plaguing the empire. Kokovtsov credited the French government with applying political pressure on the banks to see that the loan came through. He acknowledged that French support came at the price of Russian acquiescence at the Algeciras conference but, unlike Witte, he seemed to regard the deal as fair.[82] He even described in retrospect his audience with President Loubet as "particularly gracious."[83] Kokovtsov noted approvingly that the French public paid no attention to the Russian press or the Kadet delegation, which was in Paris trying to halt the loan, as they felt it threatened the new Duma's authority.[84] Unlike Witte, Kokovtsov praised Poincaré's role in completing the loan, implying that his efforts had been critical.[85] Kokovtsov also attributed Austria's participation in the loan to the efforts of the French government.[86] Despite his gratitude, however, Kokovtsov acknowledged that the negotiations had been "extremely, extremely difficult."[87] For him the 1906 loan proved to be a lesson in the politics of dependence, and he was quick to appreciate the symbiotic relationship between Russian financial needs and its international position.

With this in mind, Kokovtsov made it a practice to cultivate leading figures in French financial circles. His extensive correspondence with E. Noetzlin, an important French banker, shows that he was an adept flatterer and realized the full value of such friendship for Russia.[88] Kokovtsov confided in Noetzlin on important matters, including the 1907 budget,[89] which Noetzlin described as a "tour de force."[90] The two men also discussed international events including the Bosnian crisis. At the beginning of the crisis, Kokovtsov did not think war likely as Russia was "not isolated" and its "alliance with France and the entente with England" was "one of the factors of high importance" with which Austria must reckon.[91]

Kokovtsov developed similar contacts with de Verneuil, another important French banker, Louis Dorizon of the Société Générale,[92] Jacques Outine, an executive at the Bank of Saint Petersburg, and Louis Dreyfus, head of Louis Dreyfus and Company, which had operated in Russia since 1850.[93] In 1907 the finance minister visited Paris and, according to Effront, a Russian financial agent in Paris, made "the most favourable impression" among government and financial circles. The hesitations and uncertainties that had characterized the attitude of the Paris market toward Russian bonds completely disappeared as a result of Kokovtsov's visit.[94] Kokovtsov regarded the protection of Russia's financial standing in Paris as one of his main functions as minister of finance.

In his effort to repair Russia's image in France, Kokovtsov did not neglect French politicians. He corresponded warmly with the French deputies, Paul Doumer and François Deloncle. In addition, he considered the French ambassador to Saint Petersburg, Maurice Bompard, to be a personal friend.[95] When the French minister of foreign affairs, Pichon, defended the Franco-Russian alliance in the Chamber of Deputies, Kokovtsov was quick to take the opportunity to express his gratitude, linking the matter with his duty to defend Russian credit.[96]

Despite Kokovtsov's awareness of Russian dependence on the French market and his eagerness to please French financiers and politicians, he did occasionally chafe at French dominance in the partnership. In a bitter, confidential letter to A. Rafalovich, his agent in Paris, he complained about the French reaction to the awarding of a contract to a German firm to build Russian ships. The finance minister indicated that only one French firm entered the competition, and that its project was poorly prepared and contained grave faults. Nonetheless it seemed to Kokovtsov that "the knowledge which France has of her wealth and the conviction that Russia can not forgo her gold contributed to create this strange point of view that Russia must not do at home what is most useful and advantageous for her, but that she must inquire at first if such or such measure of a purely interior order is approved by this or that group representing, for the given moment, by its influence, the most important factor in the political life of France."[97] Kokovtsov also expressed the hope that his French colleague would realize that "alliance and friendship are not synonyms for yoke and servitude."[98]

In 1912 the French market and its stand on loans for Russian railroads annoyed Kokovtsov. In a long letter to Poincaré, he outlined his serious concerns.[99] He felt that Russia had been placed in an unreasonable situation not of its own making. In contrast to the situation in 1906, when the Russian government found the Paris market uncooperative, it now turned to London and Berlin, where it had no difficulty meeting its needs. Russia's improved international and financial position meant that the government had greater room to maneuver than it had previously.

In the fall of 1913, Kokovtsov visited Paris, where he received a warm welcome from the French government and held long and frank discussions on all the essential questions between the two allies.[100] In his report to the tsar, he remarked on the conversations' "exclusively amicable character" and the French government's devotion to the alliance.[101] The chairman of the council of ministers, however, did express some serious reservations about Russia's ally. He cast doubt on the "French army's capacity for combat and the talent of its generals."[102] "A strong stagnation of business" alarmed Kokovtsov.[103] After condemning French market insecurity, he offered a damning assessment of France's finances as "far from satisfactory." "Living from day to day the Government will arrive inevitably at the situation . . . of deficit."[104] French pacifism also provoked comment, but he did express gratitude to the French government for its help in securing loans for the construction of Russian railways, revealing that some things in the alliance had not changed.[105] Kokovtsov's report to Nicholas II therefore reflects, paradoxically, both his serious concerns and his belief that Russia could still depend on its ally for financial assistance. He never clearly denounced France or the alliance, but he did cast aspersions on its two main assets, its army, and its financial standing. In the final analysis, however, the chairman of the council of ministers recognized Russia's continued dependence on its ally, whatever France's failings may have been.

Given his financial preoccupations and the preeminence of the Paris market, Kokovtsov expended less energy on Britain than France, but he was a firm supporter of the Entente and believed in the importance of increased trade between the two countries. The British regarded Kokovtsov as a believer in the rapprochement.[106] Kokovtsov told Buchanan that it was "his earnest hope that the two Governments would always keep in close contact and collaborate with each other on all questions of foreign policy."[107] Kokovtsov encouraged British trade in Russia. He maintained cordial relations with the important English banker Lord Revelstoke.[108] In a confidential letter to his agent in Britain, M. V. Rutkovskii, Kokovtsov explained the importance of Britain to Russia, even before the Anglo-Russian accord was concluded in August.[109] Pledging to do everything he could to help British businessmen invest in Russia, Kokovtsov said that he believed that Russia and Britain would "become good friends on the practical basis of mutual economic advantage."[110] He criticized British caution and made it clear that his government wanted British capital to help Russia develop its vast natural resources as quickly as possible.[111]

During his career, Kokovtsov, like Izvolsky and Sazonov, developed a reputation as a pro-Westerner, for which the Russian right criticized him.[112] As minister of finance and chairman of the council of ministers, he sought to maintain good relations with France and Great Britain. He was motivated, however, more by a deep understanding of his country's financial dependence on Western, particularly French, credit than by any ideological sympathy with the Western democracies. For him the Triple Entente was an "unholy alliance" which allowed the Russian empire to recover from the setbacks of war and revolution. He was shrewd enough to realize that even imperial beggars could not afford to be particular about who provided the money. The resentment he occasionally displayed toward French highhandedness was in keeping with the psychology of a dependent relationship in which the weaker partner does not respect or admire the stronger.

The ministry of finance's agents in Paris were suspicious of France and Britain. Arthur Rafalovich, the ministry's agent in Paris, had close dealings with the French banks and press.[113] During the 1906 loan negotiations Rafalovich believed that the French banks were "blackmailing" the Russian government in their attempts to control the government's behavior.[114] Later in the year Rafalovich worried that the French socialists, aided by Russian socialists, would pressure the French government into denying Russia another loan on the French market.[115] Like Kokovtsov, he was well aware of Russian dependence on French loans even if he disliked the radical complexion of the French government. Consequently, when French public reaction to the awarding of a Russian naval contract to a German firm threatened to upset efforts to secure another loan, Rafalovich suggested pragmatically that the contract be awarded to a Russian firm or at least that the results of the contest be delayed.[116] As for the French minister of finance, Joseph Caillaux, Rafalovich described him as a "prisoner of the socialists."[117] The extent of Austrian influence on French banks also worried Rafalovich. He noted in a memorandum that "the principal French groups" were "in a very intimate liaison with those of Austria" and that in this respect it was difficult to decide which of them was "the most subject to Austrian influence."[118]

Rafalovich's colleague in Paris, A. Effront, was even more critical of Britain and France and openly anti-Semitic. In May 1907 he reported to Saint Petersburg that the fall in Russian stocks was due "principally to a pressure made by the Jewish Bank of London. The Israelite financiers of Great Britain, . . . have decided to hinder all upward movement in the market of Russian securities, as long as the Jews of Russia do not obtain civil rights."[119] Effront also believed that "a clandestine, international organisation of Jewish bankers," called l'Oeuvre, had been formed in 1906. The conspirators, according to Effront, were located in New York, Paris and London and included the Rothschilds. Their aim was to spread "systematically tendentious and pessimistic news about the financial and political situation in Russia, and to prevent in this way the rise of our State securities; by sowing trouble in the mind of the French 'rentier' and so rendering impossible the realisation abroad of a new Russian financial operation."[120]

While Effront's anti-Semitism colored his view of the financial world, his distaste for socialism and republicanism affected his judgments of the French government. He described the French cabinet in 1907 as "incoherent" and Clemenceau's Balkan policy as "regrettable" and contrary to Russian interests, even though Russia had supported France at Algeciras.[121] He noted with a certain smugness the difference between Clemenceau's public statements as a journalist and deputy and his actions as leader of the government. In Effront's opinion, Clemenceau had jettisoned his "subversive theories" to become "one of the most despotic chiefs of government."[122] In addition to his harsh criticism of Clemenceau and his cabinet, Effront painted for the Russian minister of finance a devastating portrait of a decrepit French navy. According to Effront the navy was disorganized and lacked discipline, and the ships were poorly maintained.[123] The behavior of the French socialist Jean Jaurès infuriated Effront, who described Jaurès's ideas as "abominable theories of pure anarchy."[124] The anti-Russian campaign led by Jaurès' newspaper, *L'Humanité*, "a quasi-official defender of Russian revolutionaries" particularly offended Effront.[125] The assumption of a link between Jaurès and Russian revolutionaries is telling. Effront's hatred of Jaurès paralleled his deeper aversion toward Russian revolutionaries, who directly threatened his own privileged place in Russian society.

Both Rafalovich and Effront, in their attitudes toward Britain and France, were typical representatives of the Russian government and bureaucracy. Effront tended to be more alarmist than Rafalovich, but suspicion and distrust were a common theme in their reporting from Paris. Despite such negative assessments from his agents in the field, however, Kokovtsov never considered abandoning the alliance with France, primarily because he knew that Russia's financial needs could only be met in Paris.

After the crisis of 1905, when Russia faced bankruptcy, its financial situation gradually improved, but its dependence on foreign credit remained. At the end of 1908 Russia's debt was 8,850,800,000 rubles, 55 percent of which was foreign loans. In 1909, 400,000,000 rubles were needed to pay the interest on the debt. These interest payments swallowed 12 percent of the Russian budget.[126] Substantial alleviation of this burden could come only from national economic recovery. In 1909 Russia entered a period of economic expansion, and in the wake of good harvests state revenues rose accordingly.[127] This economic upswing lasted from 1909 to 1914. Foreign observers thought Russia was a promising giant, stepping boldly into the future. Although the Russian economy expanded rapidly in these years, the preponderant economic influence of other countries over Russia, particularly in the armaments industry, was not reduced. Moreover, the industrial boom did not overcome the basic structural weaknesses of the Russian economy. Since the Western economies grew at a faster rate, attempts to overcome Russia's relative backwardness were completely thwarted.[128]

In this context the Russian government realized foreign trade and investment in Russia were crucial. Foreign trade showed marked growth, with exports rising from 716 million rubles in 1900 to 1,520 million in 1913. Over the same period imports rose from 626 million to 1,374 million rubles.[129] Foreign capital played an important role in the boom.[130] By 1917, 33 percent of the foreign capital in Russia was French, and Britain came second with 23 percent.[131] French investments in Russian government and government-guaranteed loans rose from more than six billion francs in 1900 to ten billion in 1914. By 1914 Frenchmen had invested more than two billion francs in Russian joint-stock companies.[132] Clearly foreign capital was vital to the Russian economy, and the Russian government actively encouraged such investment and entrepreneurs. In October 1907, shortly after the conclusion of the Anglo-Russian Convention, Stolypin told Nicolson that he wanted private enterprise to develop Russia's railway system and that "he would gladly welcome foreign capital to that end."[133] In a study of foreign entrepreneurs operating in Russia, J.P. McKay concluded that, in general, relations between the state and these entrepreneurs were "close and continuous."[134]

If, in the main, the Russian government welcomed foreign capital, in particular it welcomed and received large infusions of French money. By 1917, 731.7 million rubles of French capital had been invested in Russian industry. The largest share, 43 percent, was invested in mining and metallurgy. The second and third largest shares, 21 and 15 percent, were invested in metal processing and machine building and in credit institutions.[135] French concerns had a virtual monopoly in banking. Increased French control of Russian banks after 1907 gave French capitalists a new mechanism to pressure the tsarist government.[136] French interests also played an important role in the textile industry and the infant automobile industry. In 1907, of the 162 automobiles in circulation in Moscow, 72 were French.[137] The interdependence of the French and Russian economies was complementary to political interdependence. Russia became the terrain of choice for French capitalists, and according to Girault this was mutually beneficial. For example, the French helped to complete the network of railways in the Russian empire, which had important strategic significance for mobilization.[138]

French businessmen tried to use this favored status to obtain permission to conduct business in Russia. In 1907 a Franco-American syndicate sought permission to build an Alaskan-Siberian railway. In the letter of application it was pointed out that a large number of the signatories were French; this meant the company could not "have any end but the development of Siberia, in accordance with the views of the Government." Furthermore, their terms would not "impede its foreign policy."[139] Loicq de Lobel, head of the syndicate, came to Saint Petersburg recommended by the French president himself.[140] The chief of the General Staff and the ministers of the imperial court, communications, trade and commerce, justice and foreign affairs all supported the project. The ministers of war, internal affairs, and finance and the state comptroller opposed the project.[141]

The Russian government and French business cooperated closely but some serious problems still existed. The 1905 revolution frightened many French businessmen. Some complained to their consuls that the tsarist government showed no consideration for their problems.[142] Once the country was pacified, relations improved, only to worsen again in 1910–1911. The French began to feel pushed to one side while the Russians asked themselves if they must remain dependent on French finance. Up to 1914 a series of conflicts marred the relationship. A June 1914 drop in the Paris and Saint Petersburg stock markets did not reinforce confidence in the economic relationship between the two countries. On the eve of war, three major problems existed in Franco-Russian economic relations: the role of French capitalists in Russian syndicates, the place of the French in Russia's rearmament effort, and the question of loans for Russian railway construction.[143]

The question of Franco-Russian economic interdependence is contentious. Girault described France as Russia's "golden chain" and argued that a direct connection existed between the economic relationship and the alliance.[144] Soviet historians explicitly drew the connection between economics and diplomacy, describing a bourgeois imperialist conspiracy that drew Britain, France, and Russia together for the advancement of capitalism, making war inevitable.[145] Other historians, however, have downplayed the degree of interdependence and its effect on Russian autonomy.[146] These works, however, ignore the depth of resentment felt within Russian government circles about their situation and the lack of a credible alternative, and seem to equate acceptance of the situation with pleasure over it. The Russian government could not afford to ignore the importance of French capital for its economy. Consequently, it sought to turn a necessity to its advantage.

Russia's economic association with Great Britain differed substantially from its longstanding and complicated relationship with France. When the new friendship with Great Britain began in 1907, trade between the two countries was not significant. From 1907 to the outbreak of World War I, the Russian government actively sought to improve Anglo-Russian trade in an effort to consolidate the diplomatic friendship and to counterbalance its growing rivalry with Germany. Little of the resentment that characterized Franco-Russian economic relations marred Anglo-Russian relations. In both cases, however, trade and finance had diplomatic ramifications.

By 1917 the total British capital invested in Russian industry was 507.5 million rubles. The largest share was in mining, which accounted for 60.7 percent of British investment.[147] The importance of British capital in the Russian mining industry is underlined by the fact that the production of copper by British-financed companies before 1914 and in the first year of the war was more than half of the entire copper production in Russia.[148] In 1914, British-financed companies produced 49.5 percent of the oil from the Grodno region.[149] British businessmen also had interests in textiles, credit institutions, food processing, insurance, chemicals, and real estate, among other things. Britain was Russia's second major creditor in the prewar years. In 1914 Russian debts to Britain were 10.3 percent of Russia's total foreign indebtedness.[150] Britain was second only to Germany in terms of exports to Russia just before the war.[151] From 1906 to 1911, British exports to Russia increased by 47 percent while Russian exports to Britain increased during the same period by 52.5 percent.[152]

In 1908 a new minister of trade and commerce, S. Timiriazev, who favored the development of Anglo-Russian trade, was appointed. Timiriazev was a former bank director who was closely attuned to the wishes of Russian business interests. Shortly after his appointment, Timiriazev was reported to have said "that Anglo-Russian trade for years has been more or less stationary, and that measures must be taken to revive it."[153] In 1910 his ministry issued a report on the importance of Anglo-Russian trade, describing it as having "extremely serious significance."[154] Timiriazev also played an important role in the inauguration of the Russo-British Chamber of Commerce in 1908 and presided over it.[155] He was a member of the Anglo-Russian rapprochement committee, whose object was to give assistance to British visitors to Russia.[156] Probably seeking a British model, Timiriazev, in the winter of 1909, requested information on the British Board of Trade.[157] The equivalent Russian ministry was a recent innovation, having been created in 1905.

On the eve of war, in April 1914, the ministry of trade and commerce submitted a report to the Duma strongly recommending the approval of an Odessa-London cruiser line. The report stressed the importance of British trade for Russia and the advantages of opening "the rich English market" for goods from southern Russia.[158] Significantly, one of the major reasons advanced for supporting the line was Russia's commercial dependence on Germany. The report argued that an Odessa-London cruiser line would reduce that dependence and eliminate the need for Russian exports to Britain to be shipped by rail through Austria-Hungary and Germany. The report concluded that it was in Russia's political and economic interests to support the project, even though it might be unprofitable in the first few years.[159] In addition to Timiriazev and the ministry of trade and commerce, the Russian government as a whole worked to encourage Anglo-Russian trading links. R.J. Barrett, a British journalist and promoter of Russia, reported in 1908 that the Russian government was ready "to do all it fairly" would "to encourage British enterprise." Barrett went so far as to say that "no other country" would "give the capitalist such encouragement."[160] According to Barrett, Russia respected Englishmen and preferred them over Germans.[161] Even the General Staff did not object to the Anglo-Terek Petroleum Company in 1913 increasing its capital from 120,000 to 160,000 pounds sterling.[162]

The Russian government's interest in enhanced Anglo-Russian trade could also be seen in its role in the establishment and functioning of the Russo-British Chamber of Commerce. The chamber received imperial sanction for its statutes in 1908. In addition to the Russian minister of commerce, who was president, an ex-minister of commerce was assistant vice-president. The chamber also received a grant of 2,500 rubles from the ministry of finance and was under the control of the ministry of trade and commerce.[163] Kokovtsov, Izvolsky, and Sazonov were members of the chamber,[164] which suggests that the government regarded it as more than a mere conduit for improved trade. By 1913 the chamber had a membership of over seven hundred.[165] Membership information in 1910 indicates that the majority of members resided in Russia, which seems to suggest that the Russian side had more interest in this venture than the British.[166] To promote its goal of increased Anglo-Russian trade, the chamber established correspondents throughout the Russian empire and in the United Kingdom. The chamber also sponsored lectures, a library, and a journal published in both Russian and English. Furthermore, in 1909 and 1910 branches were opened in Odessa and Warsaw respectively. The chamber served as a source of information and answered 2,300 inquiries from Russian sources in 1910.[167]

By 1912 Anglo-Russian relations had improved to the point that the Russian government warmly welcomed a delegation of British politicians, clergy, businessmen, and academics. The official hospitality extended to this delegation contrasted with the government's dismay in 1906 when a similar visit was proposed. By 1912 the domestic situation had been quieted to the extent that visiting British parliamentarians no longer posed a revolutionary threat. The Russo-British Chamber of Commerce held a dinner honoring the British guests, and the Russian minister of commerce, Timiriazev, the foreign minister, Sazonov, the mayor of Saint Petersburg, and several assistant ministers attended.[168] In an enthusiastic speech Timiriazev stressed the importance of Anglo-Russian economic cooperation. He argued eloquently that Russian and British strengths complemented each other. British capital, enterprise, and technical skill could be used to develop Russia's vast natural resources.[169] Timiriazev praised the guests, whose efforts had "made of your beautiful country an Eden of right and law, and liberty, which are so indispensable and valuable for every human achievement. We realise that the same elements have helped British trade to become so vast and powerful, always guided by principles of high rectitude and honour."[170]

The reformed State Council, the upper house of the post-1905 legislature, also reflected the prevailing official Russian acceptance of the Triple Entente. No less than one third of its members descended from Russia's pre-Petrine social elite.[171] A large number of council members had attended the Western-style Alexander Lycée, as had Izvolsky and Sazonov.[172] Russian educated society, particularly the aristocracy, was highly Westernized, and many liberal Westerners could be found in Nicholas II's State Council.[173] P.P. Semyonov's mother was of Huguenot origin and spoke to her children only in French. The Princes Alexander and Nicholas Dolgoruky were raised by an English tutor. Andrei Saburov was "the embodiment of European Victorianism," and A.N. Schwartz was offered a chair at the Sorbonne and Oxford. A.N. Kulomzin undertook a Grand Tour of Britain as a young man, which made him an admirer of Britain throughout his life.[174] Many members of the State Council maintained close contacts with prominent men in Britain and France.[175] Prince Alexander Obolensky, a member of the State Council, was a vice-president of the Russo-French Chamber of Commerce.[176]

While the majority of the Russian government and bureaucracy welcomed or at least accepted the Triple Entente as beneficial and necessary for Russia, certain elements remained hostile to the idea. Most significantly, the Russian military establishment opposed the rapprochement with Britain and actively campaigned against its establishment. For example, in January 1906, an article offensive to Britain was published with the authorization of the naval minister. The foreign minister, Lamsdorf, was forced to apologize.[177] The General Staff vehemently opposed any agreement with Britain over Persia, which caused Izvolsky great difficulty and delayed the negotiations for the Anglo-Russian Convention.[178]

Not surprisingly, the Russo-Japanese War had caused an upheaval in tsarist military policy. There was unanimous agreement that the Russian empire was dangerously overextended, but there was disagreement as to where Russia should concentrate its efforts. The easterners fought for a total redeployment of the Russian army from Poland to the basin of the Volga. They believed that another war with Japan was the most likely scenario. The westerners, on the other hand, regarded the threat from Germany and Austria-Hungary as the most menacing and therefore believed that Russia should strengthen its French alliance, seek accommodations with Britain and Japan, and fortify its western defenses.[179]

Recovery from the war and revolution would be lengthy, and until the recovery was complete Russia would not be able to defend its position in the world. Well into 1907 the army was being used to quell domestic disturbances, which would have made a complete mobilization difficult in the event of an international crisis. The minister of war wrote: "At the present moment after the war and the current upheaval the condition of our armed forces is such that it is extremely desirable for us to avoid foreign entanglements for some time to come."[180] The majority of the Council for State Defense, founded in 1908 and chaired by Grand Duke Nikolai Nikolaievich, were also realistic in their assessment of Russia's capability to wage war. The council exerted a restraining influence on those prepared to involve

Russia in hostilities with Turkey for the sake of Russian prestige and protection of minority Christians in the Ottoman empire.[181]

In the fall of 1906, General F.F. Palitsyn, the chief of the General Staff, objected to Izvolsky's plans to forego an active policy along Russia's Asian borders. Palitsyn had three major concerns, all of which revealed his distrust of Great Britain. He worried about the German reaction to an Anglo-Russian agreement, Britain's ultimate intentions given the tradition of Anglo-Russian enmity, and Britain's exploitation of temporary Russian weakness.[182] Nicolson regarded Palitsyn as one of "the chief obstacles to an arrangement."[183] In April 1907 Izvolsky presided over a special meeting to discuss Afghanistan, during which he encountered significant opposition. The military group argued that the agreement would be an obstacle to continued Russian expansion in Central Asia.[184] Even Sir Edward Grey acknowledged in his memoirs that it "was no wonder that the Russian Foreign Minister had some difficulty in getting military authorities in Russia to give up something of real potential value to them, while we gave up what was of little or no practical value to us."[185]

Nevertheless, Izvolsky did manage to overcome Russian military opposition and the agreement was concluded in August 1907. The 1907 Anglo-Russian Convention was a victory for the foreign ministry and the military westerners. The lessons of the recent war and revolution and the consequent need to subordinate Russia's goals abroad to domestic pacification and reconstruction were so compelling that General Palitsyn was forced to agree. Such serious opposition meant that while the Russian military leadership accepted the new arrangement with Britain, they were not enamored with it. Once the convention was signed, however, they accepted the new arrangement and participated in British military maneuvers and extended reciprocal invitations.[186]

Influential elements in the Russian military sought to subvert the alliance with France. In late 1908 Sukhomlinov, who was then chief of staff, commissioned a study of the fortress issue by Major General Vitner. Vitner was extremely critical of Russia's western fortresses, and he argued that there was no reason for Russia to go to war with Germany. Vitner advocated a policy of "calm neutrality" for Russia and disengagement from European affairs. After reading the report, Sukhomlinov announced the abolition of the western fortresses.[187] Sukhomlinov continued his eastern strategy with the formulation of mobilization schedule nineteen in 1910. This schedule foresaw a European war beginning with a de facto concession of almost ten provinces of Russia in Poland which would permit the secure mobilization and concentration of Russian troops. Thereafter Russian actions would be dictated by enemy dispositions. If plan nineteen had been implemented as originally envisioned, France's expectations of military assistance from its ally at the beginning of the war could not have been fulfilled. Fuller describes Sukhomlinov's defensist strategy "as a plot against Russia's traditional foreign policy, for the strategy clearly subverted the alliance with Paris."[188] In the end, the 1910 reorientation toward Asia greatly impeded Russian military efforts in 1914.

Despite the efforts of some military men to undermine the alliance with France, the defeat in the Far East caused the Russian army's relationship with France to take on a more dependent cast. The tortuous 1906 loan negotiations forced Russia to revise the Franco-Russian military convention to France's advantage. The amended convention named Germany as the principal enemy of both countries and eliminated the anti-British clause that had been inserted in 1901. Henceforth only German mobilization obliged France and Russia to mobilize immediately, whereas Austrian or Italian mobilization required only that the two allies hold talks to agree to a plan of action. This new arrangement was to Russia's disadvantage, since in 1906 there seemed a far greater chance that Austria-Hungary would attack Russia than that Italy would attack France.[189] Although conversations between the French and Russian General Staffs were held annually after 1910, there was enormous distrust and suspicion between the two sides. France consistently dismissed the idea that Austria-Hungary represented a serious threat to Russia. At the 1911, 1912 and 1913 conferences, Zhilinski, the Russian chief of staff, conceded that Russia recognized the defeat of Germany as the principle goal of the alliance despite the fact that by 1912 Russia had decided on an Austro-centric mobilization plan. France also kept its military plans secret.[190] The July crisis of 1914 made plain that the French General Staff's obsession with rapid Russian mobilization had affected Russian mobilization plans, to Russia's detriment. There were excellent reasons for Russia to delay mobilization until a substantial part of the Austrian forces were entangled in Serbia. At the urging of its ally, however, Russia proceeded with full mobilization, with disastrous consequences.[191]

This unequal situation elicited bitterness and resentment, and the former war minister, General Sukhomlinov, expressed both in his memoirs. Writing in retrospect and exile, he stated that the Dual Alliance had been of greater benefit to France than to Russia. He regarded France's military worth as "extremely insignificant" for Russia, saying that "military matters cannot be based on only platonic speeches,—friendly advice and pretty gestures." He believed that the French valued the Russian people only as "cannon fodder"[192] and that the French bankers used their financial clout to meddle in Russian affairs particularly regarding railroads.[193] Not surprisingly, given his conservatism and patriotism, Sukhomlinov disliked French radicals and socialists, whom he felt favored Russian revolutionaries, Jews, and Poles.[194] He also criticized Kokovtsov's and Izvolsky's policies, which he felt pandered to France and Britain and were not in Russia's interests.[195] Sukhomlinov did not even pay Britain the compliment of an insult. To the Russian military mind, it would seem, British strategic significance was almost nonexistent.

The fact that the most serious opposition to the Triple Entente came from the Russian military and yet essentially was ignored is telling. The Triple Entente evolved into a military alliance even though it was conceived by Russian diplomats who had little understanding of Russia's military capabilities. Moreover, communication between the ministries of foreign affairs and war was poor. Such a lack of coordination between two central ministries was indicative of the serious failings in the late imperial system and produced dire consequences. The Russian generals' foreboding about being drawn into a war they knew they could not win against powerful Germany to further French and British interests proved correct. Not only did Russia fight a war not designed to further its strategic interests, it fought the war to the maximum advantage of France with rapid mobilization to Russia's own disadvantage. Arguably a retreat and consolidation of Russian forces well within Russian territory would have had greater potential for Russian victory than the course adopted in the summer of 1914.

Opposition to the Triple Entente within official Russian circles was not limited to the military. The comptroller of the empire, P.Kh. Schwanebach, held views on France similar to those of Sukhomlinov. In January 1907 Schwanebach denounced the Dual Alliance to Sir Arthur Nicolson in the most violent terms "as having been disastrous to Russia." According to Nicolson, Schwanebach maintained that Russia had no interests in an alliance with France and had been drawn into one "in a moment of pique." The comptroller worried that the alliance would cause an estrangement between Russia and Germany that would not be in Russia's interests. Nicolson summarized Schwanebach's devastating critique this way: "All that was subversive in Russia had been introduced from France, whilst all that was conservative had its origin in Germany. France was in decadence, while Germany had a great future before her, and the alliance with France, from whatever point of view it was regarded, was unnatural and pernicious."[196]

The best-known government critic of the Entente policy was P.N. Durnovo, one-time minister of the interior and member of the State Council. He played a major role in the suppression of the revolution in 1905. In the State Council he led the so-called Right Group from 1907 to his death in 1915. He came from the impoverished gentry and derived his political views from practical experience of Russian society and politics, not from the history of western Europe. As a former officer and policeman, Durnovo believed in the need for stern and resolute political authority, especially in a backward country like Russia. Consequently, he believed that any attempt at democratization would lead only to the disintegration of the empire. In his opinion, only bureaucratic authoritarianism, Russian nationalism, and monolithic discipline could save Russia.[197]

P.N. Durnovo's February 1914 memorandum attacked the course of Russian foreign policy as one that would lead ultimately to revolution. He presented his conservative views to Nicholas II two weeks after the emperor had removed Kokovtsov as chairman of the council of ministers and replaced him with the aged and reactionary Goremykin. Presumably Durnovo hoped to persuade the emperor to introduce a more conservative line in foreign policy as he had recently done in the domestic arena.[198] A loosely knit cabal was formed in February and March 1914 to accomplish Durnovo's goals. It sought to remove Sazonov and replace him with P.S. Botkin, the envoy in Tangiers and an Anglophobe. Sazonov, however, stayed at the foreign ministry, and the Triple Entente remained the mainstay of Russian foreign policy.

Durnovo's memorandum is a prime example of the pro-German view that had always existed in official Russian circles even after 1905.[199] Durnovo believed the rivalry between Britain and Germany to be the central factor in this period, which would eventually lead to war which "in all probability would prove fatal to one of them."[200] Durnovo saw no value and only danger in the arrangement with Britain: "To sum up, the Anglo-Russian accord has brought us nothing of practical value up to this time, while for the future, it threatens us with an inevitable armed clash with Germany."[201] He predicted that in such a war the burden would fall on Russia, since Britain was incapable of playing a major role in a continental war and France would adopt a defensive strategy. Russia would thus be left to act as "a battering-ram, making a breach in the very thick of the German defense."[202] But, he pointed out Russia was unprepared for a European conflict, given its insufficient war supplies, its dependence on foreign industry, and its inadequate network of strategic railways. Most importantly, Durnovo perceived no conflict between German and Russian national interests. He argued that Germany would sooner open the straits to Russian warships than Britain would.[203] Germany and Russia were both "representatives of the conservative principle in the civilized world, as opposed to the democratic principle incarnated in England, and to an infinitely lesser degree, in France." Durnovo's parting shot at Britain was that it would be "the real instigator" of a war, not Germany.[204] Similar to Witte, Durnovo saw Russia's future in a combination with Germany, France, and Japan.

Durnovo had launched a vehement attack on the Triple Entente at the same time Sazonov and Nicholas II were actively lobbying for a defensive alliance with Britain. Durnovo's memorandum was the articulation of the conservative view that the monarchical principle, or a revival of the Dreikaiserbund, could serve as a buttress for the Russian state to impose order within its empire. Although Durnovo in 1914 was a member of the State Council, he was not privy to the discussions of the inner circles of the Russian government and he no longer had the tsar's ear as he once had had. No doubt many conservative Russians shared Durnovo's views, but the emperor and his powerful ministers had set Russia on a different course and they would not be deterred. No matter how prophetic, Durnovo's memorandum proved to be a cry in the wilderness.

From 1905 to the outbreak of war in 1914, the Russian government pursued a policy of continued alliance with France and deepening friendship with Britain. This alignment was designed to ensure that Stolypin's all-important policy of domestic pacification and reform could be accomplished without distractions. Ideological sympathy with the two liberal democracies were not the motivation behind this course in Russian foreign policy. The majority of the Russian government and bureaucracy, like Stolypin and Kokovtsov, accepted the Triple Entente as a necessity for a Russia severely weakened by war and revolution and dependent on loans raised in London and Paris to stay afloat financially. Thus, paradoxically, those of the Russian bureaucratic elite who favored Russia's diplomatic association with the Western democracies saw it as a means of preserving the ancien regime in Russia. The inherent conflict between means and ends in this policy did not escape the notice of the Entente's harsher critics, who found it to be ideologically abhorrent and dangerous for Russia, particularly since it brought Russia into conflict with its powerful neighbor, Germany. Despite serious opposition within the military, the influence of opponents of the Triple Entente was limited, and the Triple Entente remained government policy and never came under serious attack. In general, Russian bureaucratic attitudes toward Britain and France were a mingling of admiration, dependence, and resentment, in almost equal amounts. Such a mixture of emotions indicated a government weak and unsure of itself, trying to maintain an old order through a diplomatic arrangement that ironically, as Durnovo predicted, led to the system's demise.

NOTES

1. D.C.B. Lieven, *Russia's Rulers under the Old Regime* (New Haven, Conn., 1989), pp. 289 and 292. See also G.S. Doctorow, *The Introduction of Par-*

liamentary Institutions in Russia during the Revolution of 1905–1907 (Ph.D. diss., Columbia University, 1976), p. 13.

2. D.C.B. Lieven, "Russian Senior Officialdom under Nicholas II," *Jahrbücher für Geshichte Osteuropas* vol. 32 (1984), pp. 200 and 217.

3. Karl Baedeker, *Russia: A Handbook for Travellers* (A Facsimile of the original 1914 edition) (New York, 1971), p. 93.

4. For a fascinating discussion of imperial Russian society see Alfred J. Rieber, "The Sedimentary Society," in E.W. Clowes et al., eds., *Between Tsar and People: Educated People and the Quest for Identity in Late Imperial Russia* (Princeton, 1991), pp. 367–71.

5. Doctorow, *The Introduction of Parliamentary Institutions in Russia, 1905–1906*, pp. 5–6. See also Andrew Verner, *The Crisis of Russian Autocracy* (Princeton, 1990), pp. 54–55.

6. A.M. Verner, *The Crisis of Russian Autocracy*, pp. 214–215.

7. Ibid., p. 210.

8. D.M. McDonald, *Autocracy, Bureaucracy, and Change* (Ph.D. diss., Columbia University, 1988), p. 277.

9. Ibid., p. 278.

10. G.S. Doctorow, "The Fundamental State Laws of 23 April 1906," *Russian Review* 35, no. 1, (January 1976), pp. 37–38.

11. Ibid., p. 287.

12. Peter Waldron, *Between Two Revolutions: Stolypin and the Politics of Renewal in Russia* (London, 1998), p. 182.

13. Lothar Schultz, "Constitutional Law in Russia," in E. Oberlander, ed., *Russia Enters the Twentieth Century, 1894–1917* (New York, 1971), p. 45.

14. Ibid., p. 50.

15. D.C.B. Lieven, *Russia and the Origins of the First World War* (London, 1983), p. 64.

16. For McDonald's views, see *United Government and Foreign Policy in Russia, 1900–1914*, and "A Lever without a Fulcrum: Domestic Factors and Russian Foreign Policy, 1905–1914" in H. Ragsdale and V.N. Ponomarev, eds., *Imperial Russian Foreign Policy* (New York, 1993), pp. 268–311.

17. V.N. Shanin, *Russia, 1905–07* (London, 1986), p. 58.

18. Doctorow, *The Introduction of Parliamentary Institutions in Russia, 1905–1906*, pp. 602–3.

19. Verner, *The Crisis of Russian Autocracy*, p. 341.

20. R. Girault, *Emprunts russes et investissements français en Russie, 1887–1914* (Paris, 1973), p. 434. See also P. Renouvin, "L'Emprunt russe d'avril 1906 en France," p. 513.

21. *BD/CP*, vol. 4, doc. 25, Spring-Rice to Grey, 11 April 1906, p. 44.

22. Ibid., p. 45. Also doc. 23, Grey to Spring-Rice, 6 April 1906, p. 42.

23. J.W. Long, *The Economics of the Franco-Russian Alliance, 1904–1906* (Ph.D. diss., University of Wisconsin, 1968), p. 191.

24. Quoted in Verner, *The Crisis of Russian Autocracy*, p. 324.

25. TsGIA, f. 560, op. 26, d. 619, l. 2, Rafalovich to the Russian minister of finance, 18 May 1906. Also AVPR, f. 133, op. 470, 1906g., d. 108, l. 472, telegram from Bentrovsky to the Russian ambassador in Paris, 16 May 1906.

26. Long, *The Economics of the Franco-Russian Alliance*, p. 224.

27. Ibid., p. 225.

28. Ibid., p. 181.

29. Girault, *Emprunts russes*, pp. 446–49. See also Olga Crisp, "The Russian Liberals and the 1906 Anglo-French Loan to Russia," *The Slavonic and East European Review* vol. 30 (1961), p. 508.

30. D.C.B. Lieven, "Pro-Germans and Russian Foreign Policy, 1890–1914," *International History Review* 2 (1980), p. 37.

31. S.I. Witte, *The Memoirs of Count Witte* (New York, 1967), p. 399.

32. Verner, *The Crisis of Russian Autocracy*, p. 141.

33. Ibid., p. 232. See also, Doctorow, *The Introduction of Parliamentary Institutions in Russia 1905–1906*, p. 632.

34. Hosking, *The Russian Constitutional Experiment* (Cambridge, UK, 1973), p. 7.

35. Witte, *The Memoirs of Count Witte*, pp. 136–137.

36. BAR, Witte, box 10, d. 17, letter from Witte to Prince Eulenberg, 6 March 1906, pp. 6–7.

37. Ibid., p. 5.

38. A.P. Izvolsky, *Recollections of a Foreign Minister* (Garden City, NY, 1921), pp. 128–29.

39. BAR, Witte, box 10, d.17, letter from Witte to Prince Eulenberg, 6/20 February 1906 and letter from Witte to Eulenberg, 6 March 1906, pp. 1–2.

40. Maurice Bompard, *Mon ambassade en Russie* (Paris, 1937), p. 278. George Buchanan, *My Mission to Russia* (Boston, 1923), pp. 182–183.

41. *KA*, 10 (1925), telegram from Witte to Kokovtsov, 27 December 1905, p. 20. Telegram from Witte to Kokovtsov, 4 January 1906, p. 14. See also B.A. Romanov, *Russkie finansy i evropeiskaia birzha v 1904–1906 gg. Sbornik dokumentov* (Moscow, 1926), doc. 153, telegram from Witte to Rafalovich, 7/20 March 1906, pp. 282–283. AVPR, f. 133, op. 470, 1906g., d. 107, part 1, ll. 196–98, Nelidov to Lamsdorf, 9/2 March 1906.

42. Long, *The Economics of the Franco-Russian Alliance*, p. 148.

43. Ibid., pp. 160–61 and 167–68.

44. Ibid., pp. 143–45 and 173–74. See also Romanov, doc. 176, telegram from Witte to Rafalovich, night 23/24 March, 5/6 April 1906, pp. 296–7. Doc. 179, telegram from Witte to Noetzlin, 24 March/6 April 1906, pp. 297–98.

45. Cecil Spring-Rice, *The Letters and Friendships of Sir Cecil Spring-Rice* (London, 1929), Spring-Rice to Lord Knollys, 3 January 1906, p. 22.

46. Ibid., Spring-Rice to Grey, 29 March 1906, p. 70.

47. M.P. Bock, *Reminiscences of My Father, Peter A. Stolypin* (Metuchen, N.J., 1970), p. 304.

48. Vladimir Lehovich, "Stolypin and the Birth of Modern Counterinsurgency," *Studies in Conflict and Terrorism* 15, no.3 (July-September 1992), p. 194.

49. Hosking, *The Russian Constitutional Experiment*, p. 23.

50. T. Shanin, *Russia, 1905–1907*, p. 237. For two recent assessments of Stolypin's reforms see Avenir P. Korelin, "The Social Problems in Russia, 1906–1914: Stolypin's Agrarian Reform," pp. 139–162 and David A. Macey, "Agricultural Reform and Political Change: The Case of Stolypin," pp. 163–189, both in Theodore Taranovski, ed., *Reform in Modern Russian History: Progress or Cycle?* (New York, 1995). Not as recent but useful is George L. Yaney, "The Concept of the Stolypin Land Reform," *Slavic Review* 103 (June 1964), pp. 275–93.

51. *BD/CP*, vol. 4, doc. 169, "Report by Mr. O'Beirne on the Principal Events which have occurred in Russia during the past fortnight," 25 October 1906, p. 247.

52. *BD/CP*, vol. 5, doc. 6, Nicolson to Grey, 16 August 1907, p. 32.

53. Ibid., doc. 14, "Report by Mr. Bentinck on the proceedings in the Duma during the fortnight ending December 1907. 'Reply of the President of the Council of Ministers in the Duma, 16/29 November 1907,' " p. 53.

54. Shanin, *Russia, 1905–1907*, p. 54.

55. Ibid., p. 249. See also Hosking, *The Russian Constitutional Experiment,* pp. 147, 177–178, 182, and 213–14.

56. A.P. Izvolsky, *Au Service de la Russie* (Paris, 1937), vol. 2, Stolypin to Izvolsky, 28 July 1911, p. 304. See also Bock, *Reminiscences of My Father*, p. 56.

57. McDonald, *Autocracy, Bureaucracy, and Change*, p. 20.

58. Ibid., p. 483.

59. Ibid., p. 330.

60. Ibid., p. 422.

61. Bock, *Reminiscences of My Father*, p. 241.

62. D.C.B. Lieven, *Nicholas II* (New York, 1993), p. 175.

63. Quoted in MacDonald, *Autocracy, Bureaucracy, and Change*, p. 360.

64. *BD/CP*, vol. 5, doc. 23, Nicolson to Grey, 3 March 1908, p. 119. See also doc. 45, Nicolson to Grey, 27 August 1908, p. 148.

65. Ibid., doc. 86, Nicolson to Grey, 12 September 1909, p. 305. Vol. 6, Buchanan to Grey, 18 December 1910, p. 74.

66. *BD/CP*, vol. 6, doc. 85, memorandum by Professor Pares, n.d., p. 184.

67. *BD/CP*, vol. 6, doc. 34, memorandum by Professor Pares, 22 August 1910, pp. 56–57.

68. Keith Nielson, *Britain and the Last Tsar* (Oxford, 1995), p. 74.

69. Michael Hughes, *Inside the Enigma: British Officials in Russia, 1900–1939* (London, 1997) p. 28.

70. AVPR, f. 320, op. 812, d. 10, ll. 180–181, Benckendorf to Neratov, 16/29 March 1911.

71. *BD/CP.*, vol. 6, doc. 81, Buchanan to Grey, 20 September 1911, p. 172.

72. AVPR, f. 320, op. 812, d. 10, ll. 154–155, Benckendorf to Neratov, 14/27 September 1911.

73. Zenkovsky, *Stolypin: Russia's Last Great Reformer* (Princeton, 1986), p. 111.

74. Quoted in McDonald, *Autocracy, Bureaucracy, and Change*, p. 360.

75. Ibid., p. 55.

76. *BD/CP*, vol. 6, doc. 92, Annual Report on Russia for 1911, p. 196.

77. McDonald, *Autocracy, Bureaucracy, and Change*, p. 517.

78. Ibid., p. 537.

79. V.W. Kokovtsov, *Out of My Past* (Stanford, Calif., 1935), p. 205.

80. Ibid., p. 106.

81. Ibid., p. 148

82. *KA*, 10 (1925), p. 14, telegram from Kokovtsov to Witte, 21 December 1905/3 January 1906. Kokovtsov, *Out of My Past*, pp. 91–94.

83. Kokovtsov, *Out of My Past*, p. 95.

84. Romanov, *Russkie finansi*, doc. 213, telegram from Kokovtsov to Witte, 6/19 April 1906, p. 317. Doc. 207, telegram from Kokovtsov to Witte, 4/17 April 1906, p. 314.

85. Kokovtsov, *Out of My Past*, p. 119.

86. Romanov, *Russkie finansi*, doc.190, telegram from Kokovtsov to Witte, 31 March/13 April 1906, p. 304.

87. Ibid., doc. 207, telegram from Kokovtsov to Witte, 4/17 1906, p. 314.

88. TsGIA, f. 560, op. 22, d. 309 contains the Kokovtsov-Noetzlin correspondence. Romanov, *Russkie finansi* also contains some of the letters.

89. TsGIA, f. 560, op. 22, d. 309, ll. 34–39, Kokovtsov to Noetzlin, 14/27 November 1906.

90. Ibid., ll. 40–42, Noetzlin to Kokovtsov, 4 December 1906.

91. Ibid., ll. 190–196, Kokovtsov to Noetzlin, 6 October 1908, marked confidential.

92. Ibid., d. 309, ll. 45–47, Kokovtsov to de Verneuil, 8/21 December 1906. D. 271, l. 177, Kokovtsov to Dorizon, 9/22 September 1908.

93. Ibid., d. 318, l. 177, Kokovtsov to French ambassador, n.d. D. 700, ll. 1, 9, 14, 21–24, 26, and 38.

94. Ibid., d. 312, ll. 77–79, Effront to Kokovtsov, 18/31 October 1907.

95. Ibid., d. 271, l. 142, Kokovtsov to Doumer, June 1908. D. 318, ll. 74–75, Kokovtsov to Deloncle, 11/24 May 1908. D. 318, ll. 150–151, Kokovtsov to Bompard, 9 October 1908.

96. Ibid., d. 271, l. 109, Kokovtsov to Pichon, 26 January/8 February 1907.

97. AVPR, f. 133, 1908g., op. 470, d.195, ll. 8–12, copy of a confidential letter from Kokovtsov to Rafalovich, 31 August/13 September 1908.

98. Ibid., l. 12.

99. TsGIA, f. 560, op. 2, d. 271, ll. 290–294, Kokovtsov to Poincaré, May/June 1912.

100. AVPR, f. 133, 1913g., op. 470, d. 118, ll. 59–60, Izvolsky to Sazonov, 7/20 November 1913. See also *LN*, vol. 2, Izvolsky to Sazonov, 7/20 November 1913, pp. 182–84.

101. *LN*, vol. 2, Kokovtsov's report to Nicholas II, 19 November 1913, p. 393.

102. Ibid., p. 393.

103. Ibid., p. 394.

104. Ibid., pp. 395–96.

105. Ibid., pp. 401–3.

106. *BD/CP*, vol. 4, doc. 187, Nicolson to Grey, 2 January 1907, p. 291. See also Buchanan, *My Mission to Russia*, p. 162.

107. *BD/CP*, vol. 6, doc. 147, Buchanan to Grey, 15 May 1913, p. 317.

108. TsGIA, f. 560, op. 22, d. 271, l. 132, Kokovtsov to Revelstoke, 24 November/17 December 1907.

109. Ibid., d. 271, ll. 145–46, confidential letter from Kokovtsov to Rutkovskii, 5 June 1907.

110. *BD/CP*, vol. 5, doc. 84, report of an interview between the Russian minister of finance with an English journalist, summer 1909, p. 303.

111. Ibid., pp. 302–3.

112. Kokovtsov, *Out of My Past*, pp. 272–74, 307.

113. See chapter six for further information on relations with the French press.

114. Romanov, *Russkie finansi*, doc. 158, Rafalovich to I.P. Shipov, 14/27 March 1906, p. 288.

115. TsGIA, f. 560, op. 22, d. 271, l. 94, secret telegram from Rafalovich, 27 November/10 December 1906.

116. AVPR, f. 133, 1908g., op. 470, d. 195, ll. 13–14, Rafalovich to Kokovtsov, 5 September 1908.

117. Ibid., l. 15, Rafalovich to Kokovtsov, 6 September 1908.

118. *LN*, vol. 2, memorandum from Rafalovich, 14 March 1914, p. 265.

119. TsGIA, f. 560, op. 22, d. 312, ll. 52–53, Effront to Kokovtsov, 2 May 1907.

120. Ibid., d. 271, ll. 127–28, Effront to Kokovtsov, 28 June/11 July 1907.

121. TsGIA, f. 560, op. 22, d. 312, ll. 12–13, Effront to Kokovtsov, 7 February 1907. Ll. 119–20, Effront to Kokovtsov, 15/28 November 1907.

122. TsGIA, f. 560, op. 2, d. 312, ll. 186–88, Effront to Kokovtsov, 17/30 April 1908.

123. Ibid., ll. 26–27, Effront to Kokovtsov, 8/21 March 1907.

124. Ibid., ll. 131–132, Effront to Kokovtsov, 12 December 1907.

125. Ibid.

126. Girault, *Emprunts russes et investissements français*, p. 463.

127. Dietrich Geyer, *Russian Imperialism* (New Haven, Conn., 1987), p. 256.

128. Ibid., pp. 264–71.

129. M.E. Falkus, *The Industrialization of Russia, 1700–1914* (London, 1972), p. 79.

130. Ibid., p. 81.

131. P.V. Ol', *Foreign Capital in Russia* (London, 1983), p. xii.

132. R.E. Cameron, *France and the Economic Development of Europe, 1860–1914* (Chicago, 1965), p. 301.

133. *BD/CP*, vol. 5, doc. 9, 18 October 1907, p. 37.

134. John P. McKay, *Pioneers for Profit: Foreign Entrepreneurship and Russian Industrialization, 1885–1913* (Chicago, 1970), p. 268.

135. Ol', *Foreign Capital in Russia*, p. 10.

136. Girault, *Emprunts russes et investissements français*, pp. 506 and 514.

137. Ibid., p. 528.

138. Ibid., p. 575.

139. TsGIA, f. 1276, op. 1, d. 125, l. 63, letter from Loicq de Lobel to the Russian president of the council, 7/20 March 1907.

140. Ibid., ll. 77–113, untitled/ undated report on the question of the Trans-Siberian railway, l. 78.

141. Ibid., l. 86.

142. Girault, *Emprunts russes et investissements français*, p. 584.

143. Ibid., pp. 553, 575, and 547.

144. Ibid., p. 584.

145. See especially A.V. Ignatiev, *Russko-Angliiskie otnosheniya nakanune pervoi mirovoi voiny 1908–1914* (Moscow, 1962), p. 14.

146. See for example J.P. Sontag, "Tsarist Debt and Tsarist Foreign Policy," *Slavic Review* 27 (December 1968), pp. 529–41. J.P. McKay, *Pioneers for Profit* (Chicago, 1970), p. 275.

147. O', *Foreign Capital in Russia*, p. 55.

148. Ibid., p. 75.

149. Ibid., p. 70.

150. A.V. Ignatiev, *Russko-angliiskie otnosheniya*, p. 26.

151. Karl Baedeker, *Russia: A Handbook for Travellers*, p. lv.

152. *Journal of the Russo-British Chamber of Commerce*, nos. 1–2, 1912, p. 38.

153. *BD/CP* vol. 5, doc. 61, Annual Report on Russia for 1908, p. 254.

154. TsGIA, f. 23, op. 27, d. 836, ll. 99–102, printed report 1910.

155. *BD/CP* vol. 5, doc. 61, Annual Report on Russia 1908, p. 255.

156. H.P. Kennard, *The Russian Yearbook for 1913* (London, 1913), p. 771.

157. TsGIA, f. 23, op. 27, d. 21, ll. 1–2, Rutkovskii to Timiriazev, 23 February/8 March 1909.

158. TsGIA, f. 1278, op. 6, d. 1324, ll. 3–27, Report from the Ministry of Trade and Commerce sent to the Finance Committee of the Duma, 14 April 1914.

159. Ibid., ll. 22–23.

160. R.J. Barrett, *Russia's New Era* (London, 1908), pp. 219 and 211.

161. Ibid., pp. 210 and 236.

162. TsGIA, f. 23, op. 25, d. 296, l. 159, from the General Staff to the Ministry of Trade and Commerce, Trade Department, 13 March 1913.

163. *BD/CP*, vol. 5, doc. 61, Annual Report on Russia for 1908, p. 255.

164. Ignatiev, *Russko-Angliiskie otnoshenie*, p. 19.

165. Kennard, *The Russian Yearbook, 1913*, advertisement section, no page number.

166. *Journal of The Russo-British Chamber of Commerce*, no. 5, May 1911, p. 219.

167. Ibid., pp. 215–217.

168. Ibid., nos. 1–2, 1912, p. 45.

169. Ibid., pp. 37–39.

170. Ibid., p. 40.

171. Lieven, *Russia's Rulers under the Old Regime*, p. 45.

172. Ibid., p. 118.

173. Ibid., pp. 168–69.

174. Ibid., pp. 89–90, 168, 178–80, 201–2, 231.

175. See TsGIA, f. 1642, op. 1, d. 366 for Kulomzin's correspondence with Jules Legras.

176. AVPR, f. 133, 1912g., op. 470, d. 201, l. 101. List of the Executive of the Russo-French Chamber of Commerce.

177. AVPR, f. 133, 1906g., d. 65, l. 4, op. 470, Spring-Rice to Grey, 5 January 1906.

178. Izvolsky, *Au Service de la Russie*, vol. 1, Izvolsky to Benckendorf, strictly personal, 14/27 September 1906, p. 378.

179. See N.C. Fuller, *Strategy and Power in Russia, 1600–1914* (New York, 1992), for an excellent discussion of these issues.

180. Quoted in Fuller, p. 412.

181. Michael Perrins, "The Council for State Defence, 1905–1909: A Study in Russian Bureaucratic Politics," *Slavonic and East European Review* 58, 3 (1980), p. 384.

182. McDonald, *Autocracy, Bureaucracy, and Change*, p. 359.

183. *BD/CP* vol. 4, doc. 187, Report from Nicolson to Grey, 2 January 1907, p. 291.

184. G. Sanders, "Diplomacy and the Anglo-Russian Convention of 1907," *UCLA History Journal* 3 (1982), p. 66.

185. Grey, *Twenty-Five Years*, pp. 154–155.

186. AVPR, f. 133, op. 470, 1913g., d. 91, l. 6, 1911g., d. 203, ll. 4–5, 1909g., d. 191, l. 8, and 1910g., d. 197, l. 4.

187. Fuller, *Strategy and Power in Russia*, pp. 428–430.

188. Ibid., p. 432.

189. Long, *The Economic Aspects of the Franco-Russian Alliance*, pp. 193–197.

190. William Fuller, *The Russian Empire* in Ernest R. May, ed., *Knowing One's Enemies* (Princeton, 1984), p. 104.

191. L.C.F. Turner, "The Russian Mobilisation in 1914," *Journal of Contemporary History* (1968), p. 69. Fuller, *Strategy and Power in Russia*, pp. 396–397 discusses how zigzags in military planning between westerners and easterners had deleterious consequences on Russian military action in 1914.

192. V. Sukhomlinov, *Vospominaniya* (Berlin, 1924), pp. 191–192.

193. Ibid., pp. 192 and 195.

194. Ibid., p. 193.

195. Ibid., pp. 178 and 198.

196. *BD/CP* vol. 4, doc. 193, Nicolson to Grey, 9 January 1907, pp. 323–324.

197. D.C.B. Lieven, "Bureaucratic Authoritarianism in Late Imperial Russia: The Personality, Career and Opinions of P.N. Durnovo," *Historical Journal* 36 (1983) pp. 391–402.

198. D.M. McDonald, "The Durnovo Memorandum in Context: Official Conservatism and the Crisis of Autocracy," *Jahrbücher für Geshichte Osteuropas* 44 (1996), pp. 481–502.

199. The memorandum is reprinted in F.A. Golder, *Documents of Russian History* (Cambridge, Mass., 1964), pp. 3–23.

200. Ibid., p. 4.

201. Ibid., p. 8.

202. Ibid., pp. 9–10.

203. Ibid., pp. 12–13.

204. Ibid., pp. 19 and 22.

Chapter 6

The Tsarist Regime's Manipulation of Public Opinion in Great Britain and France

Russia's humiliating defeats at Mukden and Tsushima at the hands of the Japanese and the brutally repressed revolution of 1905 had produced abroad an unflattering portrait of Nicholas II's Russia. Of Bloody Sunday, the massacre by Russian troops of unarmed civilians demonstrating in Saint Petersburg on 22 January 1905, which precipitated the revolution, *The Times* wrote: "Within the brief space of twenty-four hours Russian autocracy has not only excited the scorn and execration of the whole civilized world but has alienated what little sympathy it retained in the only country in Europe where, up to yesterday, it still counted friends [i.e. France]."[1] *Le Figaro's* editorial about the bloodbath in Saint Petersburg was a mournful lament: "Before such tragedies the gallery, powerless and idle, has but one duty, to fall silent. It keeps however the right to weep. To weep for this noble people, who resembles an old man and a new-born, to whom we owe the greatest joy our soul has known since the loss of 1870: to hear and to shout cries of love."[2] The war against Japan had already severely tested the alliance with France, which had been the cornerstone of Russian foreign policy since 1894.[3] The 1904 Entente Cordiale between Paris and London was causing Saint Petersburg to worry whether France would honor the terms of the alliance, should Britain, Japan's ally, attack Russia. Russian suspicions about France had reached the point that Saint Petersburg believed Paris was revealing Russian military secrets to London.[4] The conflict between Russia and Japan caused Anglo-Russian relations, never good, to deteriorate to the brink of war over the accidental Russian sinking of British boats off Dogger Bank on 21 October 1905.

From 1905 to 1914 the Russian imperial government mounted a full-scale propaganda offensive, unprecedented in its aims and scope, to win public approval from Great Britain and France. The tsarist regime employed subsidies to the press, government pressure, and a wide variety of personal contacts to manipulate public opinion in France and Great Britain. The Russian government had been concerned with its image in western Europe and used similar methods before, but the scale and intensity of the efforts were substantially different from the 1905 revolution on.[5] The Russian government in this period realized that a favorable profile abroad was important in the maintenance of good relations with Russia's two partners in the Triple Entente. Moreover, the need to reestablish political control at home unhampered by foreign policy complications was another significant consideration. The aim of this propaganda offensive was to promote abroad a positive impression of Russian resilience and stability, to counter the damage done to Russia's image as a result of its internal turmoil and its humiliation by Japan. To achieve this end, the Russian government developed a newly found interest in foreign public opinion, particularly British and French. Russian motives in this affair were a combination of financial concerns, considerations about prestige (these had been chronic since the Crimean War but were especially acute after the humiliations of 1904–5), and the belief that people in Britain and France were ignorant about real conditions in Russia and should be educated. This unusual propaganda campaign by the imperial government reveals the unequal relations within the Triple Entente and Russia's desperate attempts to reestablish its standing among the Great Powers of Europe in the critical period from the crushing of the revolution of 1905 to the outbreak of general European war in 1914.

Prior to 1904, the Russian government had subsidized the French press but not for any long period. As minister of finance, S.Yu. Witte and his successors maintained in the ministry of finance a special allocation for bribing French editors.[6] The previously sporadic character of this interference changed when hostilities began in the Far East. From 1904 to 1906 "the tsarist government appropriated over two and one half million francs for the French press."[7] The main reason for these payments was the need to protect Russia's credit rating, which had been badly shaken by the disastrous unfolding of the Russo-Japanese War and the revolution at home.[8] Russia maintained the gold standard and met its financial obligations by securing two billion francs in French loans by 1906.[9] Direct subsidization of the French press continued into 1906. But by October 1906 Kokovtsov, the minister of finance, ordered Arthur Rafalovich, the Russian financial agent in Paris, "to cease all relation of a subsidized order with the press."[10] From 1906 to 1912 the Russian government did not employ subsidies on as large a scale as it had from 1904 to 1906, but it did continue to exert influence on the French press by means of its advertising power.[11] Normally in these years, about twenty French newspapers received Russian advertising money. In 1907, 188,922 francs were paid, 157,854 in 1909, 155,901 in 1910 and 165,297 in 1912.[12] Rafalovich used the stiff competition for imperial contracts as an important bargaining tool. In March 1908 *Le Matin* won a contract for 20,000 francs, making it the best-paid client of the Russian government.[13] In June, however, the paper, alone among French papers, published Tolstoy's famous manifesto, "I Cannot Be Silent," against executions in Russia. The famous writer denounced the Russian government for "destroying the last trace of faith and goodness in men . . . [and for] committing the greatest crimes."[14] Rafalovich suggested that Kokovtsov take the next opportunity to speak to the offending newspaper's correspondent and "to wash his head."[15] Tellingly, Rafalovich described *Le Matin*'s publication of Tolstoy's manifesto as "a breach of contract."[16] In the end, however, no punitive action was taken against *Le Matin*, probably because, as Rafalovich explained in another context, "*Le Matin* is well read: each insertion provides us requests for registration on the list of subscribers [to Russian government loans]."[17]

On occasion, Russian officials would reduce the number of announcements placed, and consequently the sum paid, in an attempt to exercise control over newspaper coverage. In 1910 and 1911 the money paid to *Le Temps* was reduced because Rafalovich felt the newspaper had hurt Russia "by attacks and blunders."[18] For instance, *Le Temps* ran a critical editorial of Nicholas II's friendly November 1910 meeting with Wilhelm II at Potsdam, decrying the fact that the encounter seemed to go beyond "pure courtesy."[19] The Russians found this type of attitude to be most frustrating as it came shortly after France had allowed Germany to humiliate Russia over the Austro-Hungarian empire's annexation of Bosnia-Herzegovina. Yet, when Russia attempted to improve relations with Germany, as the only viable course of action in the circumstances, the French were censorious. The paper's director, Hébard, however, protested the reduction, which caused Rafalovich to rethink his position: "The importance of *Le Temps* is incontestable."[20] By 1912 *Le Temps* was the second best-paid paper after *Le Matin*.[21] In 1913 *Le Temps* informed the ministry of finance that it was creating a "trimonthly 'Russian Numbers,' exclusively devoted to the economic and financial life of the Empire."[22] Presumably the connection between the two events was not entirely fortuitous.[23]

In October 1912, shortly after the outbreak of the First Balkan War and the threatening commencement of military preparations by Russia and Austria-Hungary, the Russian government, on the suggestion of its ambassador in Paris, Izvolsky, decided to resume direct subsidies to the French press. Izvolsky cited three reasons: the unstable situation in the Balkans; the unwelcome change that he detected in the French press's attitude toward Russia; and what he described as the "undeniable role" played by Austrian, German, and Turkish subsidies to the French press.[24] Russian anxiety about their French ally's reluctance to back Russian interests in the Balkans had existed since the formation of the Dual Alliance. As noted earlier, this had recently been sharpened by France's unobliging stance during the Bosnian annexation crisis of 1908–9.

The council of ministers approved Izvolsky's request for three hundred thousand francs to be dispensed over six months to the French press, but not without expressing "the fear that once one engages in this way in the future one has to spend in this end greater and greater sums without sufficient profit." The council indicated that it considered the allocation of three hundred thousand francs as a "unique credit, not susceptible to renewal once it had been spent."[25] Controversy soon erupted, however, between various officials over the best way to administer the money and the most opportune moment to distribute it. This disagreement was indicative of bureaucratic infighting in late imperial Russia and of the lack of a coordinated strategy to shape Russia's image abroad. Despite strong reservations and veiled criticisms of Izvolsky by Kokovtsov, the chairman of the council of ministers at the time, the money was distributed through Alphonse Lenoir,[26] an agent of the French treasury, in conjunction with the French government. This shift in control from Russian to French hands disturbed Rafalovich.[27] The French minister of finance, M. Klotz, wanted to use the money to help ease passage of the French law on three years' compulsory military service. The Russian government, although disturbed by French interference, authorized the second installment. But it stipulated that the money must be used to defend Russian interests. If not, future subsidies of this nature would be suspended.[28] At the end of November 1913 Rafalovich reported that the French government determined who received the money and that the beneficiaries were exclusively organs of the radical-socialist party.[29] The French government had used Russian money to promote its own domestic agenda, rather than to improve Russia's image, much to the chagrin of Russian officials, who felt cheated.[30]

In the course of the First Balkan War in 1912, which the Balkan League of Bulgaria, Serbia, Greece and Montenegro quickly won against Turkey, Izvolsky requested a personal fund of thirty thousand francs "for direct distribution." No one except himself would know the names.[31] Saint Petersburg allocated twenty-five thousand francs to the ambassador for this purpose.[32] In addition to a personal media fund, which he directly controlled, Izvolsky also dictated dispatches, which *Le Temps* printed in its "Dernières Nouvelles" column.[33] When Rafalovich congratulated Izvolsky on this achievement, Izvolsky indicated that he exercised "in effect a certain control on four daily papers, including *L'Eclair*."[34]

In conjunction with the various attempts to influence primarily French newspapers directly by monetary means, the Russian government also monitored the French and British press during these years. It often protested directly to the British and French ambassadors about coverage it found objectionable.[35] For example, when the vicious June 1906 pogrom at Bialystok, instigated by local authorities, received widespread coverage abroad, Izvolsky, then minister of foreign affairs, complained to Sir Arthur Nicolson, the British ambassador to Saint Petersburg, about what he considered "the one-sided reports which many of the correspondents—he especially mentioned *The Times*—sent to their several journals."[36] *The Times* had given the massacre prominent daily coverage, critical of the tsarist government and sympathetic to the Jews. In their view the Duma, which was seeking to end the violence, was "the sole beacon-light of hope." In this vein *The Times* wrote: "The massacre of Jews at Bialystok far eclipses in horror and in dastardly premeditation all the previous outrages which have disgraced Russia under bureaucratic rule."[37] Izvolsky denied to Nicolson that the Russian government had deliberately organized the pogrom, saying it "would, apart from every other consideration, merely bring them [the Russian government] into discredit, and alienate public opinion in Europe."[38] Izvolsky told Nicolson "that he personally, and also his colleagues, attached importance to the British public being fairly and impartially informed, and he could not say that this was at present the case."[39] The British government itself strove to prevent the pogrom (and previous ones before Bialystok) from harming slowly improving Anglo-Russian relations.[40]

The 1906 dissolution of the unruly First Duma in 1906 was a risky venture for a government bent on projecting a moderate, politically stable image. Not surprisingly the government attempted to influence reaction to the move. To this end, Stolypin took the unusual step of responding directly to a telegram from a French journal in order "to calm public opinion and financial circles insufficiently clarified and excited by the attitude of the press."[41] Stolypin's extraordinary action shows that the Russian regime thought it crucial that French coverage of the Duma dissolution be sympathetic. Izvolsky also drew the French ambassador's attention to what Izvolsky regarded as "the frankly malevolent attitude of the French press" toward the Russian government.[42] Izvolsky defended Stolypin's direct correspondence with the French press as a necessary action taken to defend Russian interests and to remedy a situation which the Russian government regarded as out of control.

Other prominent ministers were active in the attempts to manipulate Russia's foreign reputation. For instance, Kokovtsov, in his capacity as minister of finance, was keenly aware of the value of a positive image in Britain and France and took what action he felt necessary to achieve one. He and his ministry actively promoted a favorable account of Russia in both Britain and France. In October 1906, when London and Saint Petersburg were in the midst of the crucial negotiations for the Anglo-Russian Convention, he explained to Izvolsky that he wanted an impartial and conscientious *Times* correspondent in Russia.[43] Dudley Braham, *The Times'* correspondent in Russia from 1901 to 1903, had been expelled because the government found his coverage distasteful. Consequently, *The Times* had adopted a position hostile to the imperial government.[44] Izvolsky instructed Benckendorf to act on this matter "in a completely private fashion."[45] In early December, in terms agreed on between V. Chirol, foreign editor of *The Times* and personal friend of both Hardinge and Nicolson, and Poklevskii-Kozell of the Russian embassy, *The Times* announced that its correspondent in Saint Petersburg, D.D. Braham, had been restored to normal footing and the Russian government had recalled its measures directed against him.[46]

The new arrangement with *The Times* produced immediate results.[47] On Monday 17 December a pro-Russian editorial appeared in *The Times* that maintained that it was Russia's and Britain's duty to promote peace and progress in the Middle East.[48] To that end, trust between the two countries was necessary, and *The Times* hoped that the reestablishment of its correspondent in Saint Petersburg would "promote an intelligent knowledge of Russian affairs in England." The editorial concluded with a strong endorsement of Stolypin's domestic policy: "It seems to have been boldly and wisely conceived, and it has unquestionably been followed with an honesty and a courage which must command the admiration of all honourable men."[49] Such an approving review from the preeminent English newspaper was precisely what the Russian government actively sought. It may have helped prepare British public opinion for acceptance of the forthcoming deal with Russia, not a minor undertaking, since British antipathy toward the tsarist autocracy was strong. Grey recognized that opposition from within the Liberal Party, the government of India, and the British public would make an understanding with Russia difficult to achieve. During the Anglo-Russian negotiations, the Foreign Office was inundated with antitsarist petitions.[50] The Society of Friends of Russian Freedom organized a memorial in an attempt to abort the proposed agreement. Once the convention was concluded, they protested, arguing that the deal would strengthen Russian credit and enable the tsarist government to keep the Russian people in bondage.[51]

Kokovtsov's active involvement in the manipulation of Russia's image abroad continued in his capacity as chairman of the council of ministers. In October 1913, he and Izvolsky used the opportunity provided by his visit to Paris to present official Russian views to the French press. In his report to the tsar on his trip, Kokovtsov described the press as "the force which occupies an important place in the social life of all Western Europe."[52] While in Paris, Kokovtsov received representatives from four newspapers: *Le Temps*, *Le Matin*, *L'Echo de Paris* and *Le Figaro*. Izvolsky singled out these papers for special attention because they had rendered him "important services in supporting the Russian point of view in the diverse phases of Balkan crises and by publishing in their columns a whole series of entirely benevolent articles."[53] Kokovtsov confessed that, although he was initially loath to grant the interviews, the way in which the papers reproduced "with a perfect exactitude the essence" of his explanations pleasantly surprised him.[54]

As minister of foreign affairs, Izvolsky attempted to enlarge the scope of the ministry of foreign affairs chancery newspaper unit and to change it into a genuine press office, in a further attempt to mold Russia's public image. Originally the newspaper unit had been intended to supply the tsar with a daily digest of political articles and news from Russian and foreign newspapers. Izvolsky appointed A. Girs, the head of the Saint Petersburg telegraph agency, to run the newspaper unit and to brief journalists and others on important aspects of Russian foreign policy. He also sent Girs to visit other European foreign ministries to see how their press offices were run. By 1910 the chancery newspaper unit had been expanded considerably to cover more than 150 Russian and foreign newspapers and periodicals. Every day a press review reached Izvolsky's desk by four in the afternoon.[55] In 1910 the council of ministers endorsed a plan to reform the foreign ministry, which included a proposal to turn the existing newspaper unit into a genuine press office responsible to the minister.[56] The proposals finally became law on 7 July 1914, but the outbreak of war prevented their implementation.

In addition to the imperial government's extensive efforts to influence the British and French press, prominent British and French politicians and experts on Russia were also singled out in the quest for a sympathetic profile. Such people secured interviews with important officials, including, on occasion, the tsar himself. Favors, decorations, information, and even money were provided in a massive effort by the tsarist regime to transmit its ideas through unofficial sources that would appear unbiased, and would therefore be more credible.

Jules Hansen, a Dane who became a naturalized Frenchman, was a long-time advocate of the Franco-Russian Alliance and worked for both the Russian embassy in Paris and the French Foreign Office.[57] His two books, *L'Alliance Franco-Russe* (1897) and *Ambassade à Paris du Baron de Mohrenheim, 1884—1898* (1907), promoted the idea of Franco-Russian amity. For several years prior to 1906, Hansen received twelve thousand francs a year from the Russian ministry of finance. In 1906 he indicated that he would be willing to accept six thousand francs a year, apparently because he was no longer working actively for the Russian government. In Rafalovich's opinion, it was necessary to pay him and it "would be hardness not to leave him this pension."[58] As a Conseiller d'Ambassade Honoraire of the Russian embassy in Paris, Hansen sent Nicholas II a copy of his new book, saying his aim had been "especially to show that the author of the Alliance between Russia and France, the Great Emperor Alexander III, had as an end to consolidate and maintain the peace."[59] Hansen's idealized portrait of a peace-loving Russian emperor coincided neatly with the present Russian government's newly found, utilitarian belief in the preservation of peace and maintenance of the status quo as a basis for its foreign policy.

Sir Donald MacKenzie Wallace was a former *Times* correspondent to Saint Petersburg, the author of *Russia* (the standard English-language work on the Russian empire), and a confidant of the British ambassador to Saint Petersburg.[60] Wallace visited Russia in 1906 and 1908, and on both occasions Nicholas II granted him audiences. Wallace had accompanied Nicholas as a political officer on the young tsarevich's Indian tour during the winter of 1890–91. In 1908 the tsar had a long talk with Wallace and sent a letter through him to Edward VII, the tsar's uncle.[61] During the 1906 visit Stolypin also received Wallace at the premier's private home, where they conversed for an hour. Wallace submitted a detailed report of this conversation to the Foreign Office.[62] Such marked attention from the highest levels shows the effort made by the imperial government to propagate its point of view to influential Englishmen, especially after the dissolution of the First Duma, an act which many in Britain had perceived as reprehensible. In the case of MacKenzie Wallace, the effort appears to have borne fruit. He believed that Russia was not ready for parliamentary democracy and that reforms should be implemented gradually to prevent revolution. His opinions caused some to see him as an apologist for tsarism.[63] Wallace stayed at the British embassy while in Russia, and his reports played an important role in keeping the embassy and the Foreign Office informed about the political situation in Russia in the aftermath of the 1905 revolution.[64]

Anatole Leroy-Beaulieu, the director of the Ecole des Sciences Politiques in Paris, a frequent visitor to Russia, and the author of *L'Economiste*

Français, had close connections with the Russian Ministry of Finance, stretching back to 1878. For several years, he had permitted the Russian financial agent in Paris to publish studies on Russia in *L'Economiste Français*.[65] When Leroy-Beaulieu visited Russia in 1907, Stolypin met with him, as did several "of the Tsar's principal ministers."[66] Upon his return to France, Leroy-Beaulieu gave a public lecture on his estimation of the situation in Russia. While not uncritical of the tsarist regime, he was unconditional in his support for the Franco-Russian Alliance and professed sympathy and understanding for the difficult situation that confronted the imperial government. He argued that "Russia, this great country composed in majority by peasants, is not ripe for a representative regime."[67] As these comments preceded the dissolution of the Second Duma and Stolypin's coup d'état of 3 June 1907, they would have proven useful to the imperial government.[68]

Visiting French and British parliamentarians also received official attention. In February 1910 a French deputation visited Russia, and Sazonov attended a banquet in their honor.[69] A similar reception was accorded a British deputation that visited Russia in January 1912. The group was composed of religious leaders, politicians, journalists, and academics, including Sir Donald MacKenzie Wallace, Sir Valentine Chirol of *The Times*, and Bernard Pares, professor of Russian history at the University of Liverpool and secretary of the Anglo-Russian committee, which helped to arrange the visit.[70] Much care had been taken in selecting the delegates in the hope of improving public relations between the two countries. Although this British visit was a private one in return for one by a Russian delegation to Britain in 1909, the Russian government paid it particular attention.[71] Nicholas II and the Ober-Procurator of the Holy Synod both received the guests.[72] At a dinner at the British embassy, Sazonov extended a warm welcome to the British guests on behalf of the tsar's government. No doubt he was sincere when he said that such exchanges established sympathy and friendship between the British and Russians and would "serve better than diplomatic acts to cement the Entente."[73] Buchanan reported that the visit had "served to create a friendly feeling towards England such as has never before existed in this country."[74]

Official Russian efforts to acquire an attractive public profile in Britain and France during the years 1905 to 1914 were extensive and involved the entire Russian government. There were three reasons for this policy: financial considerations; the more intangible matter of Russian pride; and chagrin at what was perceived in Saint Petersburg to be a consistent misrepresentation of Russia because of ignorance. Of critical concern was the regime's extreme dependence on foreign money. In 1905, as a result of the costly war with Japan and the revolution, the Russian government faced bankruptcy. In France, a "société des amis du peuple russe" was formed to protest loans to Russia because such aid would enable the tsar to reestablish absolutism. Members of the society's central committee included Anatole France, Paul Painlevé, and several professors from the Sorbonne.[75] The conclusion of the massive foreign loan in April 1906 saved the autocracy from the brink of insolvency. In his memoirs, Kokovtsov drew the obvious connection between the attitude of the French press and his negotiations for this critical infusion of funds, the largest international loan ever granted up to that time. "During my conferences with the banks I attached great importance to and was greatly worried by the attitude of the Paris newspaper press toward the loan."[76] When a Kadet delegation traveled to Paris in April 1906 to protest and to attempt to halt the upcoming French loan, the Russian embassy followed its movements carefully to assess what effect, if any, its actions would have on French public opinion. Nelidov reported to Lamsdorf that Kadet actions did not pose a serious threat to the Russian government's interests.[77] The loan was successfully concluded before the opening of the First Duma, which ensured the regime's independence from the new parliament and infuriated Russian liberals who had believed they had supporters in the French government.

Even after the successful conclusion of the 1906 loan, however, Russian anxiety about British and French attitudes to their financial standing did not disappear. Not surprisingly, in May 1907, Nicholas II's government greeted with consternation what it perceived to be a French and British press campaign against Russia because it feared damage to Russian securities on the Paris stock market. A. Effront, a Russian financial agent in Paris, believed the campaign, led by the *Daily Telegraph* and *L'Echo de Paris*, hurt Russia's financial interests.[78] On 7 June Kokovtsov sent a letter marked secret to Stolypin informing him that he regarded the recent writings of these two papers as "unfavourable" and as contributing "to the decline of our stocks on foreign markets."[79] In view of the seriousness of the situation Kokovtsov asked Stolypin, who knew E.J. Dillon, a correspondent for the *Daily Telegraph*, to use his personal influence to produce "the correct interpretation" of Russian economic and political affairs.[80]

In June 1907 the Russian government dissolved the Second Duma and illegally rewrote the electoral laws in order to increase the weight of the propertied classes and thereby secure a sympathetic parliament. At the same time, the government took preventive measures to protect its securities on foreign markets. Rutkovskii, from the Russian embassy in London, predicted a drop in government stocks and suggested that the "Council of Ministers [should] publish by telegraph agency in the name of the Government

[the] accusation text of the revolutionary deputies[.] [T]his text would clarify public opinion of the entire civilized world on the fact which obliged the Government to proclaim dissolution."[81] Despite official Russian fears, the French public calmly accepted the dissolution of the Second Duma. According to Effront, the attitude of the Duma itself, especially its unwillingness to accept the law on punishment for political crimes, which had been the pretext for dissolution, prepared the French for the Russian government's action.[82]

Although financial considerations were the primary motive behind the Russian policy to project an image of strength in the West, they were not the only ones. Russia's battered prestige and image as a great power belonging to the family of civilized nations were also of concern. The tsarist regime's claim to legitimacy at home and abroad derived in large part from its ability to maintain Russia's status as a great power and to be regarded as such by the other great powers. A series of devastating setbacks, which included Russia's defeat at the hands of an Asiatic power, the 1905 revolution, and the unilateral annexation of Bosnia-Herzegovina by Austria-Hungary in 1908 without Russian compensation, challenged this position. As a result, the regime's very survival, in the sense of maintaining legitimacy and therefore a mandate to govern, depended in part on a restoration of Russian prestige internationally. A deep concern about Russia's reputation in Europe pervades official Russian correspondence and deliberations during this period. For example, during the spring of 1906, the council of ministers discussed what to do with the First Duma, which had proven to be more recalcitrant than anticipated. Although the difficult introduction of the Duma into Russian politics was a domestic affair, Izvolsky counseled caution against any hasty action because he was concerned about what western Europe would think.[83] In a July 1906, audience he told the tsar that it was necessary to form a government that could work with the Duma. He referred to "the impression produced by our interior crisis upon foreign cabinets and European public opinion."[84] Further, Izvolsky believed that until such a change was accomplished, any steps in foreign relations would be obstructed.[85] Foreign support for the defiant First Duma provoked the Russian government. In particular a British statement of support for the Duma signed by a large number of prominent Englishmen was regarded as interference by foreigners in the domestic affairs of Russia. The Russian embassy in London orchestrated a protest against the memorial. In the end, threats from the Union of Russian Men, Russian government disapproval, criticism in *The Times*, *The Morning Post*, and *The Westminster Gazette* and pressure from the Foreign Office forced the committee to abort the deputation to Russia to present the memorial.[86]

Official Russian sensitivity did not diminish with time despite a marked improvement in the empire's fortunes from the nadir of 1905. In 1914, on the eve of World War I, when the Russian government was advocating a full-fledged alliance with a reluctant Great Britain, a small incident occurred over the London opening of a Bernard Shaw play about Catherine the Great, which illustrates nicely the Russian government's preoccupation with its prestige abroad. The play in question, *Great Catherine*, which Shaw wrote in barely two weeks,[87] ridiculed the empress. He portrayed Catherine as a vain, capricious, amoral, and cruel woman, and stressed her German origins. In a ridiculous scene, she torments an English captain, by tickling him with her big toe after he has insulted her vanity.[88] Shaw depicted Potemkin as an uncouth drunkard, "a violent, brutal barbarian, an upstart despot of the most intolerable and dangerous type, ugly, lazy, and disgusting in his personal habits."[89] The play received lukewarm reviews and ran for only thirty performances.[90] Before it folded, however, Benckendorf engaged in confidential conversations with the Lord Chamberlain's office.[91] The Lord Chamberlain's comptroller recommended to Shaw that Potemkin be portrayed as a teetotaler and Catherine as a monogamist.[92] The imperial embassy in London also suggested to Saint Petersburg that Sir Donald MacKenzie Wallace, the tsar's old traveling companion, be encouraged to write a letter to *The Times* indicating the historical falseness of Shaw's play.[93] The Russian government was so sensitive about the portrayal of Russia that it felt it necessary to protest an unsuccessful bawdy satire, loosely drawn from eighteenth-century Russian history.

The final reason Nicholas II's government went to extraordinary lengths to manipulate and shape its image in Britain and France was the belief, held by several prominent ministers, that ignorance of and malevolence toward tsarist Russia prevailed in the Western liberal democracies and that this had to be actively combatted. In the fall of 1906, following the Bialystok pogrom, an unpleasant incident erupted over an article in the *Jewish Chronicle* concerning the unwillingness of Jewish banking houses to lend money to Russia because of its anti-Semitic policies. Benckendorf and Rutkovskii suspected that the House of Rothschild was behind the article. Benckendorf dictated to Rutkovskii an accusatory letter to be sent to Lord Rothschild.[94] From Rothschild's terse reply it is clear that the letter's allegations had insulted him.[95] In a personal letter to an unknown friend, Benckendorf revealed his hostility to Rothschild and his belief that Russia could not let its prestige and dignity be trampled on by a Jewish banking house. Benckendorf maintained that Rothschild had acted in such a manner because he believed his bank to be indispensable. Benckendorf doubted that it was and pointed out that Russian securities had risen a half point.[96] Benckendorf and

Rutkovskii's actions did not please Kokovtsov, who as a pragmatic man was aware of Russia's dependence on foreign loans, and consequently knew the value of the goodwill of the foreign banking community. Kokovtsov told Izvolsky that Rutkovskii's letter, written "even under the direction of Count Benckendorf," had placed him in a "difficult position."[97]

In 1909, when the recent diplomatic humiliation and isolation of Russia over the annexation of Bosnia-Herzegovina by Austria-Hungary had infuriated both Russian public opinion and the imperial government, a belief gained currency among senior Russian statesmen that a British and French press campaign was being waged against Russia. Stolypin remarked to Kokovtsov on the "disgraceful character" of this campaign taking place just prior to the tsar's important state visit to Britain and France, which was intended to mend relations between the Entente partners, but was strained by the Bosnian debacle.[98] The interior minister also sent Kokovtsov copies of some of the offending articles. One article in *The Star* about conditions in tsarist prisons based on an interview with Prince Kropotkin, the Russian anarchist living in exile in London, concluded: "Let it be understood that he [Nicholas II] will not be welcome. Before English crowds will tolerate the Tsar, the Tsar must learn to tolerate liberty."[99] Stolypin asked Kokovtsov to take what measures he could through his financial agents to halt the negative press coverage of the Russian government. The chairman of the council of ministers worried that the campaign had gone so far as to spill onto the "pages of the solid English papers."[100] Kokovtsov acted almost immediately, instructing Rutkovskii in London to influence the press, using necessary "caution and circumspection" to end the "hostile" campaign against the emperor and his government.[101] In fact, a campaign protesting the tsar's visit was organized by the Society of Friends of Russian Freedom and the *Daily News* and culminated in a 25 July 1909 demonstration in Trafalgar Square.[102]

In addition to malevolence, the tsarist regime felt it had to combat general ignorance about Russia if its government and policies were to be understood. Only a few educated people in France had any real understanding of Russia while most Frenchmen, even politicians, were ignorant of Russia.[103] As ambassador to Paris, Izvolsky wrote to Sazonov that he was "daily struck by the stunning ignorance which political men manifested with regards to Russia and her affairs." To counteract this tendency, Izvolsky told Sazonov that it was "most desirable" that M. Reinach, a French deputy who was to visit Saint Petersburg, should receive "a favourable impression from his voyage to Russia."[104] The cordial 1910 Potsdam meeting between Nicholas II and Wilhelm II had alarmed Paris and London because it seemed to suggest that Russia was moving back into Berlin's orbit. In light of this,

Izvolsky found it difficult to counter the results of a press campaign organized by the Austrian ambassador, A. von Kiderlen-Wächter, which had strongly influenced the French, especially parliamentary circles. Izvolsky told Sazonov: "You would not believe to what point the people even the most serious here are so little informed about Russia and Russian affairs."[105] This was a common complaint among Russian officials.[106]

Arguably on the surface, the Russian government's extraordinary efforts to manipulate public opinion in France and Great Britain and to redeem Russia in the eyes of its Entente partners were at least partly successful. In October 1910 Rafalovich reported to Kokovtsov that in Paris "today, everyone, except the socialists, defends Russian credit."[107] Such was patently not the case in 1906. In 1912 René Marchand, the Saint Petersburg correspondent for *Le Figaro*, one of the papers favored by the Russian government, published a book generally very sympathetic to the imperial government. Marchand argued that Russia was well on the road to recovery after 1905, which was in essence the government's own propaganda line.[108] Yet, in 1912, a half million workers demonstrated on May Day, the highest number since 1905.[109] During the July crisis of 1914, the French press, almost unanimously, supported the Russian position.[110]

Nevertheless, it is impossible to establish a clear correlation between the imperial government's massive propaganda campaign and a positive, enduring change in perception in British and French public opinion.[111] Even the effectiveness of press subsidies in France, a key component of the regime's image-making strategy, was questioned. Some senior members of Russian officialdom doubted their utility. In the fall of 1906, when the first major campaign of subsidies was halted, Kokovtsov indicated his dissatisfaction with the French press's failure to follow through. He admitted that Russia had received satisfactory coverage while he was in Paris in the spring negotiating the loan and that such coverage was important at the time, but "as soon as the money was received, the old attacks accompanied by all sorts of new fantasies, the most incredible noises and tendentious and hostile commentaries began again."[112] Since Russia was not about to negotiate a new loan, Kokovtsov reasoned, subsidies should not be continued. When Nicholas II visited France in 1909, Rafalovich admitted his inability to control the press by financial means.[113] The finance minister was similarly pessimistic about the chances of the new 1912 subsidies achieving the desired result. He told Sazonov that he had drawn Izvolsky's attention to what he regarded as the "sterility . . . of financial pressure and the insignificance of the results attained by us in this order of ideas in 1904 and 1905."[114] In July 1914, just prior to the outbreak of World War I, Rafalovich, who had been largely responsible for the attempts to shape the tsarist regime's image in the French press, expressed to the new finance minister, P.A. Bark, his deeply felt skepticism in general about bribing the press: "I finished by being very skeptical about this type of relation with the press. The public finished also by guessing that it had been paid."[115]

It is worth noting that in February 1917 even the British and French governments, wartime allies of Nicholas II's Russia, which had borne a disproportionate share of the burden of the Great War, let alone the more radical elements of public opinion, did not overly mourn the abdication of the last Russian emperor nor the collapse of the tsarist autocracy. Quite the opposite was true. French and British public opinion welcomed the establishment of the Provisional Government. Many believed it would prosecute the war more effectively. In this vein *The Times* praised the new government's "spirit of liberty, . . . [and] determination to continue the war to the end."[116] *The Times* also reported that in Paris "it has long been recognised that the situation in Russia was impossible, and that although the Tsar never was the accomplice of the pro-German advisers who surrounded him he was nevertheless frequently their dupe, and that something would have to smash." News of the February Revolution created "something like enthusiasm" in the French Chamber of Deputies.[117] *Le Temps* bellicosely hailed the Duma: "In Russia, it's the Duma which means the dismissal of the men and the methods of peace and reclaims for the war a government of war."[118] The fall of the three-hundred-year-old Romanov dynasty and its replacement by a bourgeois, democratic government removed an embarrassing contradiction between the stated allied goal of defeating Prussianism in the name of democracy and, at the same time, being allied with autocratic Russia. If the imperial government did manage at least partly to mold its image in Britain and France before World War I, the effect was not a lasting one.

Russia's crippled status in the international arena caused the Russian government from 1905 to 1914 to regard the question of how Britain and France viewed Russia as a vitally important matter. Moreover, the intensity of Russian propaganda efforts reflected international tensions. Immediately after 1905, a major attempt was made to influence British and French public opinion, which slowed down after 1906. Efforts were revived after the 1908–9 Bosnian annexation crisis and then again during the Balkan Wars of 1912–13 with the resumption of direct money subsidies to the French press. Despite peak periods of activity, however, official concern about Russia's reputation in Britain and France was constant. That a more influential connection with French rather than British sources developed reflects the closer nature of the Franco-Russian alliance, as compared to Russia's ambiguous diplomatic relationship with Great Britain. It is also perhaps indicative of the crasser venality of the French press as compared to the British, although even some of the British media were not above being suborned. The extreme actions taken during these years to manipulate foreign public opinion reveal that Nicholas II's government was not unaware of the power of the press and the role public opinion played in the formation of foreign policy in Britain and France. The tsarist regime calculated that it could use this tool to help achieve its foreign policy goals of good relations with Britain and France. This policy illustrates Russia's dependence on its Entente partners in matters of foreign policy and also indirectly in its conduct of domestic affairs. The Russian government from 1905 on could not act at home with impunity. The British and French public reaction to Russian domestic events—such as the dissolution of the First and Second Dumas and the pogroms—became a matter of serious, high-level consideration. In the final analysis, however, it is clear that the Russian government sought to solve the problem in a superficial way, by extensive but ultimately ineffectual attempts to shape a desired image rather than by fundamentally altering their criticized policies. Not surprisingly, this image of a benign, stable country, which never corresponded with reality, vanished in February 1917 as quickly as the tsarist regime itself.

NOTES

1. *The Times*, 24 January 1905, p. 3. *The Times* provided extensive, detailed coverage of the disturbances in Russia.

2. *Le Figaro*, 25 January 1905, p. 1. *Le Temps* gave the events in Saint Petersburg detailed front-page coverage describing the carnage and decrying the way in which the Russian government had allowed the situation to deteriorate to such brutality. See *Le Temps*, 23 January 1905, p. 1.

3. James W. Long, "Franco-Russian Relations during the Russo-Japanese War," *Slavonic and East European Review* 52 (1974), pp. 213–33.

4. W.C. Fuller, *Strategy and Power in Russia, 1600–1914* (New York, 1992), p. 414.

5. For instance in London, Mme. Olga Novikoff, an influential apologist for the autocracy, campaigned against the Society of Friends of Russian Freedom and carefully vetted Harry de Windt's book, *Siberia as It Is* (1892), which had been commissioned by Alexander III's government to counteract unfavorable publicity generated by George Kennan's revelations in *Siberia and the Exile System*; see Barry Hollingsworth, "The Society of Friends of Russian Freedom: English Liberals and Russian Socialists, 1890–1917," *Oxford Slavonic Papers* 3 (1970), p. 52. There is some information in George Kennan's *The Decline of Bismarck's European Order: Franco-Russian Relations, 1875–1890* (Princeton, 1979) about official Russian concern with its image in France during the years prior to the formation of the Dual Alliance. Dan Morrill suggests that concern about British public opinion was one of the factors which prompted the Russian

government to issue the circular of 24 August 1898, which led to the First Hague Conference; see "Nicholas II and the Call for the First Hague Conference," *Journal of Modern History* 46 (1974), pp. 296–313.

6. S. Iu Witte, "Frantsuzskaia pressa i russkie zaemy," *Krasnyi arkhiv* 3 no. 10 (1925), pp. 36–40.

7. James W. Long, "Russian Manipulation of the French Press," *Slavic Review* 31 (1972), p. 343. See also E.M. Caroll, *French Public Opinion and Foreign Affairs* (New York, 1931), pp. 261–62. According to F. Schuman, responsible ministers in the French government sanctioned and even tacitly encouraged Russian bribery of the French press. See F.L. Schuman, *War and Diplomacy in the French Republic* (New York, 1969), p. 205.

8. Long, "Russian Manipulation of the French Press," p. 345.

9. Ibid., p. 354.

10. Arthur Rafalovich, *L'abominable venalité de la presse* (Paris, 1931), Rafalovich to Kokovtsov, 3 October 1906, p. 146.

11. For examples of the advertisements placed by the Russian government for its foreign loans see *Le Temps*, 17 April 1906, p. 4 and 19 April 1906, p. 3.

12. Rafalovich, *L'abominable venalité*, pp. 184–86, pp. 229–31, pp. 272–73, and pp. 392–93.

13. Ibid., Davidov to Rafalovich, 15 March 1908, p. 196.

14. L.N. Tolstoy, "I Cannot be Silent," in *The Complete Works of L.N. Tolstoy* (Jubilee edition, Moscow, 1928–64) v. 37, p. 83.

15. Rafalovich, *L'abominable venalité*, Rafalovich to Kokovtsov, July 1908, p. 202.

16. Ibid., Rafalovich to Kokovtsov, no date, p. 203.

17. Ibid., Rafalovich to Davidov, 24 December 1908, p. 211

18. Ibid., Rafalovich to Kokovtsov, 16 February 1912, p. 289.

19. *Le Temps*, 6 November 1910, p. 1. For an interesting account of the effect of Russian public opinion on Sazonov during the Russo-German negotiations of 1910–11 see Judith A. Head, "Public Opinion and Middle Eastern Railways: The Russo-German Negotiations of 1910–1911," *International History Review* 6, no. 1 (1984), pp. 28–47.

20. Rafalovich, *L'abominable venalité*, Rafalovich to Kokovtsov, 16 February 1912, p. 289.

21. Ibid., dépenses effectuées en 1912 pour la publication des tirages, p. 392.

22. Ibid., Rivet to Davidov, 23 December 1913, p. 398.

23. On another occasion Rafalovich intervened on behalf of the French journal *La Liberté*, which "had always remained devoted to Russia." Rafalovich requested Kokovtsov's "benevolent protection" for the journal from a reduction in Russian business. Ibid., Rafalovich to Kokovtsov, 26 February 1912, p. 291. In response to two "stupid" articles in *Le Soleil*, Rafalovich proclaimed "*Le Soleil* has never had the advertisements . . . and it never will have them." Ibid., Rafalovich to Davidov, 21 September 1912, p. 319.

24. Rafalovich, *L'abominable venalité*, Izvolsky to Sazonov, 10/23 October 1912, pp. 325–329.

25. Rafalovich, *L'abominable venalité*, Sazonov to Izvolsky, marked "très confidentiel," 17/30 October 1912, pp. 331–332.

26. Long, "Russian Manipulation of the French Press," p. 348. Lenoir acted in this same capacity from 1904 to 1906.

27. Rafalovich, *L'abominable venalité*, Rafalovich to Davidov, 11 December 1912, pp. 345–347.

28. Ibid., Izvolsky to Sazonov, 21 June/4 July 1913, Sazonov to Kokovtsov, 24 June/7 July 1913, and Davidov to Rafalovich, 23 June/6 July 1914, pp. 386–88.

29. Ibid., 6 November 1913, pp. 393–94.

30. The Russian government did not completely cease subsidies to the foreign press after 1913. See ibid., Davidov to Bark, 19 April 1914, pp. 406–407. This letter discusses subsidies to the *Monde Illustré*, *The Times*, and *The Daily Telegraph* and tantalizingly seems to suggest that both *The Times* and *The Daily Telegraph* received Russian government money.

31. Ibid., Rafalovich to Davidov, 30 November/13 December 1912, pp. 349–50.

32. Ibid., Rafalovich to Kokovtsov, "confidentielle," 23 December 1912, p. 355.

33. Ibid., Rafalovich to Kokovtsov, 13 December 1912, pp. 348–349.

34. Ibid., pp. 348–49.

35. For example I.L. Goremykin, chairman of the Council of Ministers, protested to Nicolson as did Stolypin. See *BD/CP* vol. 4, doc. 54, Nicolson to Grey, 14 June 1906, p. 95 and doc. 73, Nicolson to Grey, 2 July 1906, p. 116.

36. *BD/CP*, vol. 4, doc. 70, Nicolson to Grey, 23 June 1906, p. 110.

37. *The Times*, 18 June 1906, p. 5.

38. Ibid.

39. Ibid.

40. Eliyahu Feldman, "British Diplomats and British Diplomacy and the 1905 Pogroms in Russia," *Slavonic and East European Review* 65 no. 4 (1987): pp. 579–608.

41. AVPR, f. 133, 1906g., op. 470, d. 108, ll. 576–77, "Projet d'une lettre à Mr. Nekludow à Paris," 20 July 1906.

42. Ibid., ll. 576–77. For an interesting account of Russian government attempts to manipulate the Russian domestic press see Louise McReynolds, "Autocratic Journalism: The Case of the Saint Petersburg Telegraph Agency," *Slavic Review* 49 no. 1 (1990), pp. 48–57.

43. In the summer Stolypin had complained to D.M. Wallace about *The Times*, as Izvolsky had to Nicolson, about this newspaper's coverage of the pogrom at Bialystok. See *BD/CP*, vol. 4, doc. 70, p. 111, and doc. 108, p. 166. Earlier in 1906 Benckendorf had reported that he had contacts with *The Daily Telegraph*, *The Standard*, *The Morning Post*, *The Westminster* and "extremely in-

termittent and very indirect relations" with *The Times*. See A.P. Izvolsky, *Au Service de la Russie, Alexandre Iswolski, Correspondance diplomatique, 1906–1911* vol. 1 (Paris, 1937), Benckendorf to Izvolsky, 9/22 August 1906, p. 357.

44. Keith Neilson, *Britain and the Last Tsar* (Oxford, 1995), p. 46.

45. AVPR, f. 133, 1906g., op. 470, d. 97, part 1, l. 275, 20 October 1906.

46. Ibid., l. 292, V. Chirol to Poklevskii-Kozell, 3/16 December 1906. See *The Times*, 15 December 1906, p. 11, for the announcement.

47. AVPR, f. 133, 1906g., op. 470, d. 97, part 1, l. 292.

48. *The Times*, 17 December 1906, p. 9.

49. Ibid.

50. Beryl Williams, "Great Britain and Russia, 1905–1907," in F.H. Hinsley, ed., *British Foreign Policy* under Sir Edward Grey (Cambridge, UK, 1977), pp. 138–140.

51. Hollingsworth, "The Society of Friends of Russian Freedom," p. 62.

52. *LN*, vol. 2, Report of V.N. Kokovtsov to Nicholas II, 19 November 1913, p. 390.

53. Ibid., p. 390.

54. Ibid., p. 391. Kokovtsov (Stanford, 1935), also achieved a change in *Le Matin*'s coverage of Russia. See V.N. Kokovtsov, *Out of My Past*, p. 188 and TsGIA, f. 560, op. 22, d. 312, ll. 30–32, Effront to Kokovtsov, 12/25 April 1907. In 1908 Kokovtsov influenced *L'Echo de Paris*; see Rafalovich, *L'abominable venalité*, letter from Kurcz, pp. 179–80. Russian financial agents in Paris, Effront and Rafalovich also worked hard to cultivate French journalists. For examples of this see ibid., pp. 148–49, 246–47 and TsGIA, f. 560, op. 22, d. 312, ll. 150–51, Effront to Kokovtsov, 27 December/9 January 1907.

55. G.H. Bolsover, "Izvolsky and the Reform of the Russian Ministry of Foreign Affairs," *Slavonic and East European Review* 63 no. 1 (1985), p. 26.

56. Ibid., p. 36.

57. Kennan, *The Decline of Bismarck's European Order*, p. 86.

58. TsGIA, f. 560, op. 26, d. 619, l. 5, letter marked "personnelle secrète" from Rafalovich, 29 May 1906.

59. AVPR, f. 133, op. 470, 1907g., d. 104, l. 66, letter from Jules Hansen to Nicholas II, 20 February 1907.

60. Keith Neilson, " 'My Beloved Russians': Sir Arthur Nicolson and Russia, 1906–1916," *The International History Review* 9 no. 4 (1987), pp. 530–31.

61. Nicholas II, *Dnevnik Imperatora Nikolaia II* (Berlin, 1923), p. 248. And GARF, f. 601, op. 1, d. 1388, letter from Edward VII to Nicholas II, 11 December 1908.

62. *BD/CP*, vol. 4, doc. 108, "Report by Sir D.M. Wallace of a conversation with M. Stolypin," 22 July/4 August 1906, p. 166.

63. Neilson, *Britain and the Last Tsar*, p. 95.

64. Michael Hughes, *Inside the Enigma* (London, 1997), p. 32.

65. Rafalovich, *L'abominable venalité*, Rafalovich to Kokovtsov, 10 February 1906, pp. 128–29. Rafalovich had also written anonymously or under a

pseudonym for *Le Journal des Débats, L'Opinion,* and *Le Matin.* Ibid., pp. 117–18, 133–34, 174–75, 194, 215, 236–237, and 288.

66. Anatole Leroy-Beaulieu, "La Crise Russe et L'Alliance Franco-Russe," *La Revue Hebdomadaire* 6 no. 4 (1907): pp. 446 and 452.

67. Ibid., p. 443.

68. The Russian government courted numerous other authors. A close connection was developed between the ministry of finance and H.R. Kennard, the British editor of *The Russian Yearbook.* See TsGIA, f. 23, op. 8, d. 28 for Kennard's correspondence to Kokovtsov. The Comte de Saint-Maurice, the editor of Foreign Affairs at *Gil Blas,* Schelking of *Le Temps,* R.G. Lévy of *Revue des Deux Mondes,* Jules Meulmans, director of *Revue Diplomatique,* and Vicomte d'Avenel, editor of *Revue des Deux Mondes,* all received special attention from officials at the ministry of finance. See Rafalovich, *L'abominable venalité,* pp. 148–49, 158–59, 175, 246–47; TsGIA, f. 560, op. 22, d. 312, ll. 150–51, A. Effront to Kokovtsov, 27 December/9 January 1907; ibid., d. 318, ll. 7, Vicomte d'Avenel to Kokovtsov, 27 January 1908.

69. AVPR, f. 133, 1910g., op. 470, d. 175, ll. 10–11, 7/20 February 1910.

70. AVPR, f. 133, 1912g., op. 470, d. 170, l. 5, Benckendorf to Sazonov, 4/17 January 1912.

71. Ibid., ll. 1–5.

72. Ibid., l. 10, 8 January 1912, and l. 14, 10 January 1912.

73. Ibid., l.22.

74. Quoted in Neilson, *Britain and the Last Tsar,* p. 323.

75. Pierre Renouvin, "Les relations franco-russes à la fin du XIXe siècle et au début du XXe siècle. Bilan des recherches," *Cahiers du monde russe et soviétique* 1 (1959), p. 145.

76. Kokovtsov, *Out of My Past,* p. 120.

77. AVPR, f. 133, 1906g., op. 470, d. 107, part 1, ll. 199–200, Nelidov to Lamsdorf, 6/19 April 1906.

78. TsGIA, f. 560, op. 22, d. 312, ll. 56-57, Effront to Kokovtsov, 3/16 May 1907.

79. Ibid., d. 271, l. 126, Kokovtsov to Stolypin, 7 June 1907, marked "secret."

80. Ibid., Dillon had also been used by Witte. See Hosking, *The Russian Constitutional Experiment, Government, and Duma, 1907–1914,* p. 93.

81. TsGIA, f. 560, op. 22, d. 275, l. 131, telegram from Rutkovskii, 3/16 June 1907.

82. Ibid., d. 312, ll. 63–64, Effront to Kokovtsov, 14/27 June 1907.

83. Kokovtsov, *Out of My Past,* p. 141.

84. Izvolsky, *Recollections of a Foreign Minister,* p. 191.

85. In a 1912 letter Izvolsky explicitly drew the direct connection he saw between foreign press coverage of Russian affairs and Russian foreign policy. See Rafalovich, *L'abominable venalité,* Izvolsky to Neratov, 31 October/13 November 1912, p. 337.

86. B. Hollingsworth, "The British Memorial to the Russian Duma, 1906," *Slavonic and East European Review* 53 (1975), pp. 539–57.

87. Michael Holroyd, *Bernard Shaw: Volume 2, 1898–1918: The Pursuit of Power* (London, 1989), p. 273.

88. Bernard Shaw, "Great Catherine," in *Bernard Shaw: Complete Plays with Prefaces*, vol. 4 (New York, 1963), p. 600.

89. Ibid., p. 569.

90. For a review of the play see *The Times*, 19 November 1913, p. 11.

91. AVPR, f. 133, 1914g., op. 470, d. 191, l. 8, secret telegram from Benckendorf, 4/17 February 1914.

92. Holroyd, *Bernard Shaw*, p. 174.

93. AVPR, f. 133, 1913g., op. 470, d. 22, l. 22, telegram, London to Saint Petersburg, 5/18 November 1913.

94. AVPR, f. 133, 1906g., op. 470, d. 97, part 1, ll. 243–45, letter from Benckendorf, 26 October/8 November 1906. In this letter Benckendorf acknowledges that he dictated the letter to Lord Rothschild. See l. 262 for the letter from Rutkovskii to Lord Rothschild.

95. Ibid., l. 263, Lord Rothschild to Rutkovskii, 23 October/5 November 1906.

96. Ibid., ll. 243–45, Benckendorf letter, 26 October/8 November 1906. It is not clear to whom this letter was addressed.

97. Ibid., l. 267, secret letter from Kokovtsov to Izvolsky, 10 November 1906. Effront, a Russian financial agent in Paris, also believed Jewish publishers were responsible for the anti-Russian tendencies of two French periodicals. TsGIA, f. 560, op. 22, d. 312, ll. 192–96, Effront to Kokovtsov, 1/14 May 1908.

98. TsGIA, f. 560, op. 22, d. 271, l. 200, letter marked "very secret" from Stolypin to Kokovtsov, 7 June 1909.

99. Ibid., *The Star*, 3 June 1909, p. 2.

100. Ibid., l. 200, "very secret" letter from Stolypin to Kokovtsov, 7 June 1909.

101. Ibid., l. 203, Kokovtsov to Rutkovskii, 12 June 1909. In 1912 on the occasion of Raymond Poincaré's visit to Russia, Rafalovich referred to the "systematic disparagement of which we have been the victims." Rafalovich, *L'abominable venalité*, Rafalovich to Kokovtsov, 10 August 1912, p. 308.

102. Hollingsworth, "The Society of Friends of Russian Freedom," p. 62.

103. See Paul Gerbod, "Image de la Russie en France de 1890 à 1917," *Information historique* (May-June 1979), p. 120.

104. *LN*, vol. 2, Izvolsky to Sazonov, 26 January/8 February 1911, p. 471.

105. *LN*, vol. 1, Izvolsky to Sazonov, 2/15 February 1911, p. 35. For similar comments see *LN*, vol. 2, Izvolsky to Sazonov, 26 January/8 February 1911, p. 471.

106. For further examples of official Russian concern about ignorance and misrepresentation abroad, see Wilhelm von Schoen, *Memoirs of an Ambassador* (London, 1922), p. 31. Maurice Bompard, *Mon ambassade en Russie, 1903–1908*

(Paris, 1937), p. 228. *BD/CP*, vol. 4, doc. 135, Nicolson to Grey, 7 September 1906, p. 210; doc. 187, Nicolson to Grey, 2 January 1907, p. 290; doc. 232, Nicolson to Grey, 29 May 1907, p. 378. Izvolsky, *Au service de la Russie*, vol. 2, Benckendorf to Izvolsky 2/15 May 1907, p. 41. AVPR, f. 320, personal file S.D. Sazonov, op. 812, d. 10, l. 88, Benckendorf to Sazonov, 1 November 1910.

107. Rafalovich, *L'abominable venalité*, Rafalovich to Kokovtsov, 3 October 1910, p. 267. According to Rafalovich by 1912 the improved state of Russia's finances had prevented the French press from publishing any negative commentaries about a loan: Rafalovich to Kokovtsov, 10 August 1912, p. 308. Both *Le Temps* and *Investor's Review* commented favorably on the Russian budget: Rafalovich to Kokovtsov, 24 October 1911, pp. 276–279.

108. René Marchand, *Les Grands problèmes de la politique intérieure de la Russie* (Paris, 1912). Another example of a positive contemporary French assessment of the Russian situation is Edmond Thèry, *La Transformation economique de la Russie* (Paris, 1914).

109. Haimson, "The Problem of Social Stability in Urban Russia, 1905–1907, Part I," *Slavic Review* 23 no. 4 (1964), p. 626.

110. Schuman, *War and Diplomacy in the French Republic*, p. 221.

111. In the only monograph on French public opinion before WWI, E.M. Caroll discounts the effect Russian subsidies had on the press. See Caroll, *French Public Opinion*, p. 276.

112. Rafalovich, *L'abominable venalité*, Kokovtsov to de Verneuil, 29 September/12 October 1906, pp. 149–50. In 1912, when subsidies were resumed on Izvolsky's initiative, Kokovtsov authorized the funds but made clear to Sazonov his belief in the futility of the project with a pointed reference to the earlier subsidy effort. Ibid., Kokovtsov to Sazonov, 3 December 1912, p. 351.

113. Ibid., Rafalovich to Kokovtsov, 28 June 1909, pp. 223–224.

114. Ibid., Kokovtsov to Sazonov, 3 December 1912, marked "tout à fait confidentiel," pp. 350–354.

115. Ibid., Rafalovich to Bark, 4 July 1914, p. 407.

116. *The Times*, 17 March 1917, p. 7.

117. Ibid., p. 8.

118. *Le Temps*, 17 March 1917, p. 1. In *Le Figaro* Alfred Capus of the Academie française also argued that the new Provisional Government would wage war more effectively than the tsarist regime and help France win the war, the only consideration that seemed to concern the French. See *Le Figaro*, 17 March 1917, p. 1.

Conclusion

Russia was not a passive adherent to the Triple Entente but an active architect of it and a full partner in the alignment. The policy of the Triple Entente was one of two pillars of the Russian government's approach to the dual crisis, domestic and international, which confronted the autocracy in 1905. The Triple Entente was the imperial government's foreign policy solution to the aftermath of the Russo-Japanese War and the revolution, and as such went hand in hand with Stolypin's domestic reform plan. Together these two planks were meant to preserve the autocracy and Russia's status as a great power. Ironically, the diplomatic union of Russia, Great Britain and France, by frightening Germany with the prospect of encirclement and furthering the entrenchment of the alliance system in Europe, contributed to the outbreak of World War I and ultimately the destruction of imperial Russia.

Official Russian attitudes toward Britain and France from 1905 to 1914 spanned the spectrum from admiration to condemnation. Despite this wide range, considerations of realpolitik led to a surprising consensus within Russian governing circles about the necessity for and value of the Triple Entente. This broadly based support of the Entente as an important diplomatic strategy, however, was not paralleled by any widespread desire to emulate within Russian governing circles the practices of the Western democracies. The country's rulers believed that Russia needed the economic, diplomatic and military benefits of harmonious relations with Britain and France, but they did not want to adopt the liberal customs of Western political systems. The Russian government viewed attempts by British and French liberals to support their Russian counterparts with active hostility and measures were taken to stop what was regarded as unwarranted interference in Russia's domestic affairs.

In 1905 the revolution and the humiliating military defeat at the hands of Japan had severely weakened Russia. The government recognized its financial dependence on France and its need to improve relations with Britain. The insurrection in the countryside and armed rebellion in the major cities forced the autocracy to seek breathing space in the international arena. These dire domestic circumstances were the crucial factors influencing Saint Petersburg in the formation of the Entente. In the immediate pre–World War I period there existed among Russia's rulers a keen awareness of the real constraints on Russian power. Most Russian statesmen, diplomats and bureaucrats realized that another disastrous military foray such as the Russo-Japanese War could well foment another revolution and so end the ancien regime in Russia. This awareness drove Russia's cautious foreign policy and shaped its dependent relationships with Britain and France. Saint Petersburg's inability to pursue Russian interests independently, in particular the opening of the straits to its warships, proved most frustrating. Kokovtsov had remarked bitterly to Rafalovich that he hoped his French colleague would realize that "alliance and friendship are not synonyms for yoke and servitude."[1] This lack of autonomy produced strong feelings of resentment toward Britain and France, which colored the relationship but did not fundamentally alter the structure of the Entente.

In the beginning, official Russia was wary in its approach to the new diplomatic alignment between Russia, Great Britain, and France, especially after the Entente appeared to fail its first test during the Bosnian annexation crisis of 1908. As Russia slowly recovered from the trauma of 1905, it began to make greater demands on its two partners because it felt its prestige could not withstand further diplomatic setbacks. This new assertion of Russian interests was evident in Russia's detached stance during the 1911 Agadir crisis and during the Liman von Sanders affair in the winter of 1913–1914. By the spring of 1914 both the emperor and Sazonov were seeking a defensive alliance with Britain to transform the Entente into a more effective instrument against the Triple Alliance of Germany, Austria-Hungary, and Italy.

The push in 1914 to form an alliance reflected the government's uneasiness about the ambiguous relationship it had with Britain and a desire to ensure British military support in the event of a conflict with the Triple Alliance. Strongest support for the Entente had always existed in the Foreign Ministry, particularly when it was led by Izvolsky from 1906 to 1910. This pro-British and French sentiment, however, continued unabated within the

Foreign Ministry after Izvolsky's dismissal and the appointment of Sazonov. Support for the Triple Entente also existed at the Ministry of Finance, the Ministry of Trade and Commerce, and within the emperor's family and the court. Stolypin, as the powerful chairman of the new Council of Ministers, backed the new policy. But there were a few notable exceptions. Opponents of the association with Britain and France were strongest within military circles. Anti-Entente sentiment, although sometimes vehemently articulated by influential individuals like Sukhomilov and Durnovo, was never sufficiently powerful to alter the course embarked upon by Izvolsky and Nicholas II.

In the summer of 1914 Russia stumbled into a major European conflict, having spent the better part of a decade trying to avoid just such a catastrophe. In 1913 Lenin had said to Gorky that "a war between Russia and Austria would be a very useful thing for a revolution, but the chances are small that Franz Joseph and Nicky will give us such a treat."[2] The imperative felt by the Russian autocracy to conduct an imperialistic foreign policy however—as the regime's raison-d'être—created the circumstances of which Lenin had only dreamed. The Russian government's conception of honor would not allow it, yet again, to capitulate in the face of an Austrian ultimatum backed by Germany. Ultimately, the regime's foreign policy of alignment with the other two status quo powers—in order to maintain its position as a great power and to contain Germany and Austria-Hungary—was as unsuccessful as its domestic reform policy. Nicholas II and his government had pursued the policy of the Triple Entente in the hopes of preserving peace in Europe and Russia's position in Europe. Yet, tsarist Russia's uneasy partnership with Britain and France led to a war that ended with the Bolshevik government's complete rejection of both the imperial system and bourgeois western Europe. The tsarist autocracy gambled on the Triple Entente as the best means of preserving European peace and, by this, its system of rule and privilege. In the end, its Faustian alignment with the liberal democracies led it instead into a war quite beyond its strength, which resulted in the collapse of the imperial system. Instead of maintaining a Great Russia as envisioned by the architects of the Triple Entente, Nicholas II's foreign and domestic policies inadvertently established the preconditions for a Bolshevik Russia.

NOTES

1. AVPR, f. 133, 1908g., op. 470, d. 95, l. 12.

2. Quoted in Orlando Figes, *A People's Tragedy: The Russian Revolution, 1891–1924* (London, 1996), p. 249.

Selected Bibliography

ARCHIVAL SOURCES

Arkhiv Vneshnei Politiki Rossii (AVPR) (Moscow)

fond 133	Kanstelyariya MID 1906–1914
fond 320	Lichnii arkhiv Sazonova, S.D.
fond	Departamenta Lichnogo Sostava i Khozyaistvennikh del

Gosudarstvennyi Arkhiv Rossiiskoi Federatsii (GARF) (Moscow)

fond 559	A.P. Izvolskii
fond 579	P.N. Miliukov
fond 601	Nikolai II

Tsentral'nyi Gosudarstvennyi Istoricheskii Arkhiv (TsGIA) (Saint Petersburg)

fond 23	Ministerstvo Torgovli i Promyshlennosti
fond 560	Obshchaya Kanstelyariya Ministerstva Finansov
fond 727	E. Yu. Nolde
fond 934	P.N. Durnovo
fond 966	V.N. Kokovtsov
fond 1276	Sovet Ministrov
fond 1278	Gosudarstvennaya Duma
fond 1672	A.N. Kulomzin

Bakmeteff Archive (New York)

Manuscript Collection S.I. Witte Box 10

PUBLISHED PRIMARY SOURCES

Document Collections

Documents Diplomatiques Français, 2e serie. Paris, 1930–35: 3e serie Paris, 1929–36. (Referred to as *DDF*)

Golder, F.A. *Documents of Russian History*. Cambridge, Mass., 1964.

Gooch, G.P. and Temperley, H., eds. *British Documents on the Origins of the War, 1898–1914*. London, 1927–38. (Referred to as *BD*)

Krasnyi Arkhiv, "Anglo-russkaia konventsiia 1907 g. i razdel Afganistana," vol. 10, pp. 55–66.

————. "Iz perepiski Nikolaia i Marii Romanovykh v 1907–1910 gg.," vols. 50–51, pp. 161–93.

————. "Iz perepiski Nikolai Romanova s V.A. Romanovym," vol. 17, pp. 219–22.

————. "K istorii anglo - russkogo soglasheniia 1907g.," vols. 69–70, pp. 3–39.

————. "K peregovoram Kokovtsova o zaime v 1905–1906gg.," vol. 10, pp. 3–37.

————. "Nikolai Romanov o anglo-burskoi voine," vol. 63, pp. 124–126.

————. "Perepiska Nikolaia II i Marii Fedorovny," vol. 22, pp. 153–209.

————. "Perepiska Nikolaia II i Stolypina v 1906–1911gg.," vol. 5, pp. 102–128 and vol. 30, pp. 80–88.

Lieven, Dominic, ed. *British Documents on Foreign Affairs: Reports and Papers from the Foreign Office Confidential Print*. Series A Russia, 1859–1914, vols. 4, 5, 6. University Publications of America, 1983. (Referred to as *BD/CP*)

Marchand, R., ed. *Un Livre Noir: Diplomatie d'Avant-Guerre d'après les Documents des Archives Russes*. 2 vols. Paris, 1923. (Referred to as *LN*)

Rafalovich, Arthur. *L'abominable vénalité de la presse*. Paris, 1931.

Romanov, B.A., ed. *Russkie finansi evropeiskaia birzha v 1904–1906 gg. Sbornik dokumentov*. Moscow-Leningrad, 1926.

Newspapers and Journals

Ezhegodnik Gazety Riech'
Le Figaro
Journal de Saint Petersbourg
Novoe Vremia
Riech'
Le Temps
The Times
Vestnik Russko-Angliiskoi Torgovoi Palati, 1911–1914

Diaries, Memoirs, and Other Contemporary Works

Abrikossov, Dmitri I. *Revelations of a Russian Diplomat.* Seattle, Wash., 1964.

Alexander, Grand Duke of Russia. *Once a Grand Duke.* NewYork, 1932.

Baedeker, Karl. *Russia: A Handbook for Travelers.* A facsimile of the original 1914 edition. Reprint, New York, 1971.

Bark, Peter. "Glava iz vospominanii." *Vozrozhdenie,* no. 43 (July 1955), pp. 5–27.

Basily, de Nicolas. *Memoirs: Diplomat of Imperial Russia, 1903–1917.* Stanford, Calif., 1973.

Baylen, Joseph O. "The Tsar's 'Lecturer-General.' W.T. Stead and the Russian Revolution of 1905 with Two Unpublished Memoranda of Audiences with the Dowager Empress Maria Fedorovna & Nicholas II." *Georgia State College School of Arts & Science Research Papers,* no. 23 (July 1969).

Bock, M.P. *Reminiscences of My Father, Peter A. Stolypin.* Metuchen, N.J., 1970.

Bompard, Maurice. *Mon Ambassade en Russie, 1903–1908.* Paris, 1937.

Buchanan, George William. *My Mission to Russia and Other Diplomatic Memories.* 2 vols. Boston, 1923.

Buchanan, Meriel. *The Dissolution of an Empire.* London, 1932.

Chirol, Sir V. *Fifty Years in a Changing World.* London, 1927.

Danilov, Yu N. *Velikii Kniaz Nikolai Nikolaievich.* Paris, 1930.

Dehn, Madame "Lili." *The Real Tsaritza.* Boston, 1922.

Gilliard, Pierre. *Thirteen Years at the Russian Court.* London, 1921.

Grant, N.F., ed. *The Kaiser's Letters to the Tsar.* London, 1920.

Grey of Fallodon, Viscount. *Twenty-Five Years, 1892–1916.* Toronto, 1925.

Gurko, V.I. *Features and Figures of the Past: Government and Opinion in the Reign of Nicholas II.* Stanford and London, 1939.

Hansen, Jules. *Ambassade à Paris du Baron de Mohrenheim, 1884–1898.* Paris, 1907.

Izvolsky, A.P. *Recollections of a Foreign Minister: Memoirs of Alexander Iswolsky.* Garden City, N.Y., and Toronto, 1921.

———. *Au service de la Russie, Alexandre Iswolski, Correspondance diplomatique, 1906–1911.* 2 vols. Paris, 1937.

Kalmykov, A.D. *Memoirs of a Russian Diplomat: Outposts of the Empire, 1893–1917.* New Haven, Conn., 1971.

Kennard, Howard P., ed. *The Russian Yearbook for 1912.* London, 1912.

———. *The Russian Yearbook for 1913.* London, 1913.

Kleinmichel, Countess. *Memories of a Shipwrecked World.* London, 1923.

Kokovtsev, V.N. *Out of My Past.* Stanford, 1935.

Korff, Baron, S.A. *Russia's Foreign Relations during the Last Half Century.* New York, 1922.

Leroy-Beaulieu, Anatole. "La crise russe et l'alliance franco-russe." *La Revue Hebdomadaire.* 6, no. 4 (22 June 1907), pp. 436–57.

———. *Un homme d'état russe d'après sa correspondence inédite. Etude sur la Russie et la Pologne pendant le règne d'Alexandre II.* Paris, 1884.

————. "La Russie devant la Troisième Douma." *La Revue des deux mondes* 41 (1907), pp. 383–86.

Lichnovsky, N., trans. *Lettres des Grands-Ducs à Nicholas II*. Paris, 1926.

Marchand, René. *Les grands problèmes de la politique intérieure de la Russie*. Paris, 1912.

Marie, Grand Duchess of Russia. *Education of a Princess: A Memoir*. New York, 1931.

Memorial France et Russie et les Allies . . . Des idées, des faits, des actes 1890 à 1918. Paris, 1919.

Meshcherskaya, Ekaterina. *A Russian Princess Remembers: The Journey from Tsars to Glasnost*. New York, 1989.

Miliukov, P. "The Case of the Second Duma." *Contemporary Review* 92 (October 1907) pp. 457–67.

————. *Constitutional Government for Russia*. New York, 1908.

————. *La Crise Russe: Ses Origines—son Evolution ses Conséquences*. Paris, 1907.

————. *Political Memoirs, 1905–1917*. Ann Arbor, Mich., 1967.

————. "Present Tendencies of Russian Liberalism." *Atlantic Monthly* (March 1905), pp. 404–14.

Mossolov, General A.A. *At the Court of the Last Tsar*. London, 1935.

Narishkin-Kurakin, E. *Under Three Tsars*. New York, 1931.

Nicholas II. *Dnevnik Imperatora Nikolaia II*. Berlin, 1923.

————. *Letters of Tsar Nicholas and the Empress Marie*. Edited by Edward J. Bing. London, 1937.

————. *The Nicky-Sunny Letters: Correspondence of the Tsar & Tsaritsa, 1914–1917*. Hattiesburg, Miss., 1970.

Nekliudov, A.V. *Diplomatic Reminiscences before and during the World War, 1912–1917*. London, 1920.

Oudendyk, William J. *Ways and By-Ways of Diplomacy*. London, 1939.

Paléologue, M. *Au Quai d'Orsay à la veille de la tourmente*. (Journal 1913–1914). Paris, 1947.

Poincaré, Raymond. *Au Service de la France: Neuf années de souvenirs*. 10 vols. Paris, 1926–33.

Pokrovsky, M.N., ed. *Perepiska Nikolaia i Aleksandry Romanovykh*. Moscow, 1923.

Rosen, Baron R.R. *Forty Years of Diplomacy*. 2 vols. London, 1922.

Ryabushinsky, P.P. ed. *Velikaya Rossiya*. 2 vols. Moscow, 1910–11.

Sazonov, S.D. *Les Années Fatales*. Paris, 1927.

de Schelking, E. *Recollections of a Russian Diplomat: The Suicide of Monarchies*. New York, 1918.

Schoen, Wilhelm von. *Memoirs of an Ambassador*. London, 1922.

Semennikov, Vladimir Petrovich. *Nikolai II i velikie kniazia*. Leningrad, 1925.

Shulgin, V.V. *The Years: Memoirs of a Member of the Russian Duma, 1906–1917*. New York, 1984.

Spring-Rice, Cecil. *The Letters and Friendships of Sir Cecil Spring-Rice: A Record*. Edited by Stephen Gwynn. 2 vols. London, 1929.

Struve, Peter. "A Great Russia." *The Russian Review* 2, no. 4 (1913), pp. 11–30.

Sukhomlinov, V. *Vospominaniya*. Berlin, 1924.

Suvorin, A.S. *Dnevnik A.S. Suvorina*. Moscow, 1923.

Taube, Baron M. *La Politique Russe d'avant-Guerre*. Paris, 1928.

Tcharykov, N.V. *Glimpses of High Politics through War and Peace, 1855–1929*. London, 1931.

———. "Reminiscences of Nicholas II." *Contemporary Review* 134 (1928).

———. "Sazonoff." *Contemporary Review* 133 (1928).

Thèry, Edmond. *La Transformation économique de la Russie*. Paris, 1914.

Vinogradoff, Igor. "Some Russian Imperial Letters to Prince V.P. Meshchersky (1839–1914)." *Oxford Slavonic Papers* 10 (1962), pp. 105–58.

Viroubova, Anna. *Memories of the Russian Court*. New York, 1923.

Viviani, René. *As We See It*. New York, 1923.

Witte, S.I. *The Memoirs of Count Witte*. New York, 1967.

Yusopov, F. *Gibel Rasputina. Vospominaniya*. Moscow, 1990.

Zenkovsky, Alexander. *Stolypin: Russia's Last Great Reformer*. Princeton, 1986.

Zvegintsev, A.I. "The Duma and Imperial Defence." *Russian Review* 1 (1912), pp. 49–63.

SECONDARY SOURCES

Acton, E. *Russia: The Tsarist and Soviet Legacy*. London, 1995.

Adams, A.E. "Pobedonostsev and the Rule of Firmness." *Slavonic and East European Review* 32 (December 1953), pp. 132–39.

Albertini, L. *The Origins of the War of 1914*. London, 1965.

Allain, J.C. *Agadir 1911, une crise impérialiste en Europe pour la conquête du Maroc*. Paris, 1976.

Anderson, E.N. *The First Moroccan Crisis, 1904–1906*. Chicago, 1930.

Andrew, C. "German World Policy and the Reshaping of the Dual Alliance." *Journal of Contemporary History* 1, no. 3 (1966), pp. 132–51.

———. *Théophile Délcassé and the Making of the Entente Cordiale, 1898–1905*. London, 1968.

Andrew, C., and Neilson, K. "Tsarist Codebreakers and British Codes." *Intelligence and National Security* 1 (1986), pp. 6–12.

Askew, W.C. and Wallace, L.P., eds. *Power, Public Opinion, and Diplomacy: Essays in Honour of E.M. Carroll*. Durham, N.C., 1959.

Avdeev, V.A. "Posle Mukdena i Tushimy." *Voenno-Istoricheskii Zhurnal* 8 (1992), pp. 2–9.

Barlow, I.C. *The Agadir Crisis*. Durham, N.C., 1940.

Baykov, A. "The Economic Development of Russia." *Economic History Review*, Vol. 7 (December 1954), pp. 137–149.

Berghahn, V.R. *Germany and the Approach of War in 1914*. London, 1973.

Bestuzhev, I.V. *Bor'ba v Rossi po Voprosam Vneshnei Politiki, 1906–1910gg.* Moscow, 1961.

———. "Russian Foreign Policy February–July 1914." *Journal of Contemporary History* 1, no. 3 (1966), pp. 93–112.

Billington, James H. *The Icon and the Axe.* New York, 1967.

Black, Cyril E. "The Nature of Imperial Russian Society." *Slavic Review* (1961), pp. 562–582.

Bobroff, Ronald, *Roads to Glory? Sergei D. Sazonov, the Turkish Straits, and Russian Foreign Policy, 1910–1916.* Ph.D. diss., Duke University, 2000.

Bolsover, G.H. "Izvolsky and the Reform of the Russian Ministry of Foreign Affairs." *Slavonic and East European Review* 63, no. 1 (1985), pp. 21–40.

Bovykin, V.I. "The Franco-Russian Alliance." *History* 64 (1979), pp. 20–35.

———. *Iz Istorii Vozniknoveniya Pervoi Mirovoi Voiny: Otnosheniia Rossii i Frantsii v 1912–1914gg.* Moscow, 1961.

Bridge, F.R. "Izvolsky, Aehrenthal, and the End of the Austro-Russian Entente, 1906–1908." *Mitteilungen des osterreichischen Staatsarchivs* 29 (1976), pp. 315–62.

Byrnes, Robert F. "Russia and the West: The Views of Pobedonostsev." *Journal of Modern History* 40 (June 1968), pp. 234–56.

Cameron, R.E. *France and the Economic Development of Europe, 1860–1914.* Chicago, 1965.

Caroll, E.M. *French Public Opinion and Foreign Affairs, 1870–1914.* New York, 1931.

Carrère d'Encausse, Hélène. "L'agitation révolutionaire en Russie de 1898 à 1904 vue par les réprésentants de la France." *Revue d'histoire moderne et contemporaine* 27 (1980), pp. 408–42.

Christian, David. *Imperial and Soviet Russia: Power, Privilege, and the Challenge of Modernity.* New York, 1997.

Churchill, R.P. *The Anglo-Russian Convention of 1907.* Freeport, N.Y., 1972.

Clowes, E., Kassow, S.D., and West, J.L., eds. *Between Tsar and People: Educated Society and the Quest for Public Identity in Late Imperial Russia.* Princeton, 1991.

Cohen, Stuart A. "Sir Arthur Nicolson and the Case of the Baghdad Railway." *The Historical Journal* 18, no. 4 (1975), pp. 863–72.

Cooper, M.B. "British Policy in the Balkans, 1908–9." *Historical Journal* (1965).

Corbet, Charles. *L'Opinion française face à l'inconnu russe (1799–1844).* Paris, 1967.

Corp, Edward T. "Sir William Tyrell: The 'Eminence Grise' of the British Foreign Office, 1912–1915." *The Historical Journal* 25, no. 3 (1982), pp. 697–708.

Cosgrove, R.A. "A Note on Lloyd George's Speech at the Mansion House on 21 July 1906." *Historical Journal* 12, no. 4 (1969).

Costello, D.R. "*Novoe Vremia* and the Conservative Dilemma, 1911–1914." *Russian Review* 37 (1978), pp. 30–50.

Crampton, R.J. "The Decline of the Concert of Europe in the Balkans, 1913–1914." *Slavonic and East European Review* 52, no. 128 (1974), pp. 393–419.

Crisp, Olga. "The Russian Liberals and the 1906 Anglo-French Loan to Russia." *The Slavonic and East European Review* 39 (1961), pp. 497–511.

Cronin, Vincent. *Paris on the Eve, 1900–1914*. Paris, 1989.

Curtiss, J.S., ed. *Essays in Russian and Soviet History*. New York, 1963.

Daly, Jonathan W. "On the Significance of Emergency Legislation in Late Imperial Russia." *Slavic Review* 54, no. 3 (1995), pp. 602–29.

Dilks, David, ed. *Retreat from Power: Vol. One, 1906–1939*. London, 1981.

Doctorow, G.S. "The Fundamental State Laws of 23 April 1906." *Russian Review*, 35, no. 1 (January 1976), pp. 33–52.

———. "The Introduction of Parliamentary Institutions in Russia during the Revolution of 1905–1906." Ph.D. diss., Columbia University, 1976.

Drimaracci, Jacques. "La Politique de Délcassé et la Triple Entente (1898–1907)." *Information Historique* 29, no. 4 (1967), pp. 181–89.

Eksteins, Modris. *Rites of Spring, the Great War, and the Birth of the Modern Age*. Toronto, 1989.

Esthus, R.A. "Nicholas II and the Russo-Japanese War." *Russian Review* 40 (1981), pp. 396–411.

Falkus, M.E. *The Industrialization of Russia, 1700–1914*. London, 1972.

Fay, Sidney Bradshaw. *The Origins of the World War*. NewYork, 1928.

Feldman, Eliyahu. "British Diplomats and British Diplomacy and the 1905 Pogroms in Russia." *Slavonic and East European Review* 65, no. 4 (1987), pp. 579–608.

Ferro, Marc. *Nicholas II: The Last of the Tsars*. London, 1991.

Figes, Orlando. *A People's Tragedy: The Russian Revolution, 1891–1924*. London, 1996.

Fischer, Fritz. *Germany's Aims in the First World War*. New York, 1967.

Frankland, Noble. *Crown of Tragedy: Nicholas II*. London, 1960.

Fuller, W.C. *Strategy and Power in Russia, 1600–1914*. New York, 1992.

Georgiev, A.V. "Tsarizm i Rossiskaia Diplomatiia Nakanune Pervoi Mirovoi Voiny." *Voprosy Istorii* 3 (1988), pp. 58–73.

Georgiev, A.V. et al. *Vostochnyi vopros vo vneshnei politiki Rossii*. Moscow, 1978.

Gerbod, Paul. "D'une révolution à l'autre: les français en Russie de 1789 à 1917." *Revue des études slaves* 57, no. 4 (1985), pp. 605–20.

———. "Image de la Russie en France de 1890 à 1917." *Information historique* (1979) pp. 115–22.

Geyer, Dietrich. *Russian Imperialism: The Interaction of Domestic and Foreign Policy, 1860–1914*. New Haven, 1987.

Gillard, D. *The Struggle for Asia, 1828–1914*. New York, 1977.

Girault, René. *Emprunts russes et investissements français en Russie, 1887–1914.* Paris, 1973.

Gordon, M. "Domestic Conflict and the Origins of the First World War." *Journal of Modern History* 64 (1974), pp. 191–226.

Greaves, R.L. "Some Aspects of the Anglo-Russian Convention and Its Workings in Persia, 1907–1914." *Bulletin of School of Oriental and African Studies* 31 (1968).

———. "Themes in British Policy towards Persia in Its Relation to Indian Frontier Defence, 1798–1914." *Asian Affairs* 22, no.1 (1991), pp. 35–45.

Grunwald, Constantin de. *Le Tsar Nicholas II.* Paris, 1965.

Guthrie, C.R. "The *Revue des Deux Mondes* and Imperial Russia, 1855–1917." *Revue des études slaves* 57, no.4 (1985), pp. 605–20.

Haimson, Leopold. "The Problem of Political and Social Stability in Urban Russia on the Eve of War and Revolution Revisited." *Slavic Review* 59, no. 4 (2000), pp. 848–75.

———. "The Problem of Social Stability in Urban Russia, 1905–1917, Part One." *Slavic Review* 23, no. 4 (1964), pp. 619–42.

———. "The Problem of Social Stability in Urban Russia, 1905–1917, Part Two." *Slavic Review* 24, no.1 (1965), pp. 1–22.

Hamburg, G.M. "The London Emigration and the Russian Liberation Movement: The Problem of Unity, 1889–1897." *Jahrbücher für Geshichte Osteuropas* 25 (1977), pp. 321–39.

Haumant, Emile. *La Culture française en Russie (1700–1900).* Paris, 1913.

———. "Le roman français en Russie." *Journal des Débats,* 20 May 1896.

———. "La Sorbonne et la Russie." *Revue internationale de l'enseignement supérieur* (1903), pp. 385–93.

Head, Judith A. "Public Opinions and the Middle Eastern Railways: The Russo-German Negotiations of 1910–1911." *International History Review* 6, no. 1 (1984), pp. 28–47.

Helmreich, E.C. *The Diplomacy of the Balkan Wars.* Cambridge, Mass., 1938.

Hinsley, F.H., ed. *British Foreign Policy under Sir Edward Grey.* Cambridge, 1977.

Hobsbawn, E.J. *The Age of Empire, 1875–1914.* London, 1987.

Hogenhuis-Seliverstoff, *Une Alliance Franco-Russe.* Brussels, 1997.

Hollingsworth, Barry. "The British Memorial to the Russian Duma, 1906." *Slavonic and East European Review* 53 (1975), pp. 539–557.

———. "The Society of Friends of Russian Freedom: English Liberals and Russian Socialists, 1890–1917." *Oxford Slavonic Papers* 3 (1970), pp. 45–64.

Hosking, Geoffrey A. *The Russian Constitutional Experiment, Government, and Duma, 1907–1914.* Cambridge, UK, 1973.

Hughes, Michael. *Diplomacy before the Russian Revolution: Britain, Russia, and the Old Diplomacy, 1894–1917.* New York, 2000.

———. *Inside the Enigma: British Officials in Russia, 1900—1939.* London, 1997.

Hutchinson, J.F. "The Octobrists and the Future of Russia as a Great Power." *Slavonic and East European Review* 50, no. 119 (1972), pp. 220–37.

Ignatiev, A.V. *Russko Angliiskie otnosheniya nakanune pervoi mirovoi voiny (1908–14)*. Moscow, 1962.

———. *Soiuz s Frantsii vo vneshnei politike Rossii v kontse XIX v*. Moscow, 1993.

Ingram, E. "A Strategic Dilemma: The Defence of India, 1874–1914." *Militargeschichtliche Mitteilungen* 14 (1974), pp. 216–24.

Ito, Takayuki, ed. *Facing up to the Past: Soviet Historiography under Perestroika*. Sapporo, Japan, 1989.

Jelavich, B. *Century of Russian Foreign Policy, 1814–1914*. Philadelphia and New York, 1964.

———. *Russia's Balkan Entanglements, 1806–1914*. New York, 1991.

Joll, James. *The Unspoken Assumptions*. London, 1968.

Judge, E.H., and Simms, J.Y., eds., *Modernization and Revolution: Dilemmas of Progress in Late Imperial Russia*. New York, 1992.

Kaylani, Nabil M. "Liberal Politics and the British Foreign Office, 1906–1912: An Overview." *International Review of History and Political Science* 12, no. 3 (1975), pp. 17–48.

Kayser, Jacques. *De Kronstadt à Khrouchtchev: Voyages franco-russes, 1891–1960*. Paris, 1962.

Kazemzadeh, F. *Russia and Great Britain in Persia, 1864–1914*. New Haven, Conn., 1968.

Keiger, John F.V. *France and the Origins of the First World War*. London, 1983.

Kennan, George. *The Decline of Bismarck's European Order: Franco-Russian Relations, 1875–1890*. Princeton, 1979.

———. *The Fateful Alliance: France, Russia, and the Coming of the First World War*. New York, 1984.

Kennedy, Paul. *The Realities behind Diplomacy: Background Influences in British External Policy, 1865–1980*. Glasgow, 1981.

———. *The Rise and Fall of the Great Powers*. London, 1988.

———, ed. *The War Plans of the Great Powers, 1880–1914*. London, 1985.

Kent, H.W. *Oil and Empire: British Policy and Mesopotamian Oil, 1900–1920*. London, 1976.

Kingston-Mann, Esther. "In Search of the True West: Western Economic Models and Russian Rural Development." *Journal of Historical Sociology* 3, no.1 (1990), pp. 23–49.

Klein, I. "The Anglo-Russian Convention and the Problem of Central Asia, 1907–1914." *Journal of British Studies* 11, no. 1 (1971), pp. 126–147.

Koch, H.N., ed. *The Origins of the First World War*. London, 1984.

Kohn, H. *Panslavism*. New York, 1960.

Lafore, Laurence. *The Long Fuse*. New York, 1971.

Langer, William Leonard. *The Franco-Russian Alliance, 1890–1894*. London, 1929. Reprint New York, 1967.

Langhorne, R. *The Collapse of the Concert of Europe*. London, 1981.

LeDonne, John P. *The Russian Empire and the World, 1700–1917*. Oxford, 1997.

Lehovich, Vladimir. "Stolypin and the Birth of Modern Counterinsurgency." *Studies in Conflict and Terrorism* 15, no.3 (1992), pp. 185–199.

Lieven, D.C.B. "Bureaucratic Authoritarianism in Late Imperial Russia: The Personality, Career, and Opinions of P.N. Durnovo." *Historical Journal* 26 (1983), pp. 391–402.

———. "Bureaucratic Liberalism in Late Imperial Russia: The Personality, Career and Opinions of A.N. Kulomzin." *Slavonic and East European Review* 60 (1982), pp. 413–32.

———. *Empire: The Russian Empire and Its Rivals*. London, 2000.

———. *Nicholas II: Twilight of the Empire*. New York, 1993.

———. "Pro-Germans and Russian Foreign Policy, 1890–1914." *International History Review* 2 (January 1980), pp. 35–54.

———. *Russia and the Origins of the First World War*. London, 1983.

———. "Russian Senior Officialdom under Nicholas II: Careers and Mentalities." *Jahrbücher für Geschichte Osteuropas* 32 (1984), pp. 199–223.

———. *Russia's Rulers under the Old Regime*. New Haven, Conn., 1989.

Lincoln, W. Bruce. *In the Vanguard of Reform: Russia's Enlightened Bureaucrats, 1825–1861*. DeKalb, Illinois, 1986.

———. *In War's Dark Shadow: The Russians before the Great War*. New York, 1986.

Long, J.W. *The Economics of the Franco-Russian Alliance, 1904–1906*. Ph.D. diss., University of Wisconsin, 1968.

———. "Franco-Russian Relations during the Russo-Japanese War." *Slavonic and East European Review* 52 (1974), pp. 213–33.

———. "French Attempts at Constitutional Reform in Russia." *Jahrbücher für Geschichte Osteuropas* 23, no. 4 (1975), pp. 496–503.

———. "Organized Protest against the 1906 Russian Loan." *Cahiers du Monde russe et soviétique* 13 (1972), pp. 24–39.

———. "Russian Manipulation of French Press." *Slavic Review* 31 (1972), pp. 343–54.

Malcolm, Neil, et al. *Internal Factors in Russian Foreign Policy*. Oxford, 1996.

Manfred, A.Z. "Quelle fut la cause de l'alliance franco-russe?" *Cahiers du monde russe et soviétique* 1 (1959), pp. 148–64.

Martin, Vanessa. "Hartwig and Russian Policy in Iran, 1906–1908." *Middle Eastern Studies* 29, no. 1 (1993), pp. 1–21.

Massie, Robert K. *Nicholas and Alexandra*. New York, 1967.

May, Ernest R., ed. *Knowing One's Enemies: Intelligence Assessment before the Two World Wars*. Princeton, 1984.

Mayer, A.J. "Internal Causes and Purposes of War in Europe, 1870–1956." *Journal of Modern History* 41 (1969), pp. 291–303.

McCullough, Edward E. *How the First World War Began*. Montreal, 1999.

McDonald, D.M. "The Durnovo Memorandum in Context: Official Conservatism and the Crisis of Autocracy." *Jahrbücher für Geshichte Osteuropas* 44 (1996), pp. 481–502.

———. *United Government and Foreign Policy in Russia, 1900–1914.* Cambridge, Mass., 1992.

McKay, John P. *Pioneers for Profit: Foreign Entrepreneurship and Russian Industrialization, 1885–1913.* Chicago, 1970.

McKercher, B.J.C. "Diplomatic Equipoise: The Lansdowne Foreign Office, the Russo-Japanese War of 1904–1905, and the Global Balance of Power." *Canadian Journal of History* 24, no. 3 (1989) pp. 299–339.

McKercher, B.J.C. and Moss, D.J., eds. *Shadow and Substance in British Foreign Policy, 1895–1939.* Edmonton, Alberta, 1984.

McLean, D. "English Radicals, Russia, and the Fate of Persia, 1907–1913." *English Historical Review* 93 (1978), pp. 338–352.

McReynolds, Louise. "Autocratic Journalism: The Case of the Saint Petersburg Telegraph Agency." *Slavic Review* 50, no. 1 (1991), pp. 48–57.

———. "Imperial Russia's Newspaper Reporter: Profile of a Society in Transition, 1865–1914." *Slavonic and East European Review* 68, no. 2 (April 1990), pp. 277–293.

———. "Newspaper Journalism in Prerevolutionary Russia." *Soviet Studies in History* (summer 1986), pp. 3–9.

Menashe, L. "'A Liberal with Spurs': Alexander Guchkov, a Russian Bourgeois in Politics." *Russian Review* 26 (1967), pp. 38–53.

Mendel, Arthur. "Peasant and Worker on the Eve of the First World War." *Slavic Review* 24, no. 1 (1965), pp. 23–33.

Michon, Georges. *The Franco-Russian Alliance.* New York, 1969.

Morrill, Dan L. "Nicholas II and the Call for the First Hague Conference." *Journal of Modern History* 46 (1974), pp. 296–313.

Mosse, W.E. "Imperial Favourite: V.P. Meschersky and the *Grazhdanin.*" *Slavonic and East European Review* 59 (1981), pp. 529–47.

Narotchnitzky, P. "Deux tendences dans l'histoire des relations franco-russes." *Revue Historique* 237, no. 1 (1967), pp. 99–124.

Neilson, Keith. *Britain and the Last Tsar: British Policy and Russia, 1894–1917.* Oxford, 1995.

———. "A Dangerous Game of American Poker: The Russo-Japanese War and British Policy." *Journal of Strategic Studies* 12, no. 1 (1989), pp. 63–87.

———. " 'Greatly Exaggerated': The Myth of the Decline of Great Britain before 1914." *International History Review* 13, no. 4 (1991), pp. 695–725.

———. " 'My Beloved Russians': Sir Arthur Nicolson and Russia, 1906–1916." *International History Review* 9 (1987), pp. 521–54.

Neiman, L.A. "Franko-russkie otnosheniya vo vremya marokkanskogo krizisa 1911g." *Frantsuzskii Ezhegodnik* (1969), pp. 65–91.

Nicolson, Harold. *The First Lord Carnock: A Study in the Old Diplomacy.* London, 1930.

Nish, Ian. "Politics, Trade and Communications in East Asia: Thoughts on Anglo-Russian Relations, 1861–1907." *Modern Asian Studies* 21, no. 4 (1987), pp. 667–78.

Nolde, Boris. *L'Alliance franco-russe: Les Origines du système diplomatique d'avant guerre*. Paris, 1936.

Oberländer, Erwin, et al. *Russia Enters the Twentieth Century 1894–1917*. New York, 1971.

Ol', P.V. *Foreign Capital in Russia*. 1922. Reprint, London, 1983.

Oldenburg, S.S. *The Last Tsar: Nicholas II, His Reign and His Russia*. 4 vols. Gulf Breeze, Fla., 1975.

Papayoanou, Paul A. *Power Ties: Economic Interdependence, Balancing, and War*. Ann Arbor, Mich., 1999.

Perrins, Michael. "The Council for State Defence, 1905–1909: A Study in Russian Bureaucratic Politics." *Slavonic and East European Review* 58, no. 3 (1980), pp. 370–98.

Petrovich, M.B. *A History of Modern Serbia*. New York, 1976.

Pipes, Richard. *Russia under the Old Regime*. London, 1995.

Pisarev, I.A. "Rossia i Mezdunarodnyi krizis v period pervoi Balkanskoi voiny." *Istoria SSSR* 4 (1986) pp. 56–67.

———. "Russkii Diplomat Kniaz' G.N. Trubetskoi o Nachale Pervoi Mirovoi Voiny." *Novaia i Noveishaia Istoriia* 5 (1990), pp. 132–44.

Raeff, Marc. "Russia's Perception of Her Relationship with the West." *Slavic Review* 23 (1964), pp. 13–19.

———. *Understanding Imperial Russia*. New York, 1984.

———. "Un Empire comme les Autres?" *Cahiers du Monde Russe et Soviétique* 30, nos. 3–4 (1989), pp. 321–27.

Ragsdale, Hugh, *The Russian Tragedy: The Burden of History*. New York, 1996.

Ragsdale, Hugh, and Ponomarev, V.N., eds. *Imperial Russian Foreign Policy*. New York, 1993.

Rawson, Don C. *Russian Rightists and the Revolution of 1905*. Cambridge, U.K., 1995.

Remak, J., ed. *The Origins of World War One*. New York, 1967.

Renouvin, P. "L'emprunt russe d'avril 1906 en France." *Études suisses d'Histoire générale* 1 (1960), pp. 507–15.

———. "Les relations franco-russes à la fin du XIXe siècle et au début du XXe siècle: Bilan des recherches." *Cahiers du monde russe et soviétique* 1 (1959), pp. 128–47.

Renzi, William A. "Who Composed 'Sazonov's Thirteen Points'?: A Re-examination of Russia's War Aims of 1914." *American Historical Review* 88, no. 2 (1983), pp. 347–57.

Riha, Thomas. "*Riech* 'A Portrait of a Russian Newspaper." *Slavic Review* 22 (1963), pp. 663–82.

———. *A Russian European: Paul Miliukov in Russian Politics*. Notre Dame, Ind., 1969.

Roberts, Henry L. "Russia and the West: A Comparison and Contrast." *Slavic Review* 23 (1964), pp. 1–12.

Rogger, Hans. "Russia in 1914." *Journal of Contemporary History* 1, no. 3 (1966), pp. 95–119.

———. *Russia in the Age of Modernization and Revolution, 1881–1917.* London, 1983.

Rolo, P.J.V. *Entente Cordiale: The Origins and Negotiation of the Anglo-French Agreements of 8 April 1904.* London, 1969.

Rossos, A. *Russia and the Balkans, Inter-Balkan Rivalries and Russian Foreign Policy, 1908–1914.* Toronto, 1981.

Rozental, E.M. *Diplomaticheskaia istoriia russko-frantsuzskogo soiuza v nachale xx veka.* Moscow, 1960.

Rukalski, Zygmunt. "Fin-de-Siècle in France and Russia." *Études Slaves et Est-Européens* 12 (1967), pp. 124–27.

Rywkin, Michael, ed. *Russian Colonial Expansion to 1917.* New York, 1988.

Sabrosky, Alan Ned. "From Bosnia to Sarajevo: A Comparative Discussion of Interstate Crises." *Journal of Conflict Resolution* 19, no. 1 (1975), pp. 3–24.

Sakhorov, A.N. et al., eds. *Istoriia vneshnei politikii Rossii.* Moscow, 1997.

Sanders, George. "Diplomacy and the Anglo-Russian Convention of 1907." *UCLA History Journal* (1982), pp. 61–72.

Schaeffer Conroy, Mary. *Peter Arkad'evich Stolypin—Practical Politics in Late Tsarist Russia.* Boulder, Colo., 1976.

Schmitt, B.E. *The Annexation of Bosnia, 1908–1909.* Cambridge, Mass., 1937.

———. *The Triple Alliance and the Triple Entente.* New York, 1947.

Schuman, Frederick Louis. *War and Diplomacy in the French Republic.* 1931 Reprint, New York, 1969.

Seton-Watson, Hugh. *The Decline of Imperial Russia, 1855–1914.* London, 1985.

Seton-Watson, Robert William. "Bernard Pares." *Slavonic and East European Review* 28 (1949–50), pp. 28–31.

Shanin, Teodor. *Russia as a Developing Society. The Roots of Otherness: Russia's Turn of the Century.* London, 1985.

———. *Russia, 1905–07: Revolution as a Moment of Truth.* London, 1986.

Shlapentokh, Dimitri. "The French Revolution in Russian Intellectual and Political Life, 1789–1922." Ph.D diss., University of Chicago, 1988.

———. "The French Revolution in Russian Political Life: The Case of Interaction between History and Politics." *Revue des Études Slaves* 61 (1989), pp. 131–42.

———. "The Images of the French Revolution in the February and Bolshevik Revolutions." *Russian History* 16, no. 1 (Spring 1989), pp. 31–54.

Simmons, E. *Continuity and Change in Russian and Soviet Thought.* Cambridge, Mass., 1955.

Sinel, A. *The Classroom and the Chancellery: State Educational Reform in Russia under Count Dmitry Tolstoi.* Cambridge, Mass., 1973.

Snyder, Glenn H. *Alliance Politics*, Ithaca, N.Y., 1997.

Sontag, J.P. "Tsarist Debt and Tsarist Foreign Policy." *Slavic Review* 27 (December 1968), pp. 529–41.

Spring, D.W. "The Trans-Persian Railway Project and Anglo-Russian Relations, 1909–1914." *Slavonic and East European Review* 54 (1976), pp. 60–82.

Stavrou, T.G., ed. *Russia under the Last Tsar*. Minneapolis, Minn., 1969.

Steiner, Z.S. *Britain and the Origins of the First World War*. London, 1977.

Sternheimer, Stephen. "Administering Development and Developing Administration: Organizational Conflict in Tsarist Bureaucracy, 1906–1914." *Canadian-American Slavic Studies* 9, no. 3 (fall 1975), pp. 277–301.

Taranovski, Theodore, ed., *Reform in Modern Russian History: Progress or Cycle?* New York, 1995.

Tarle, E.V., ed. *Problemy istorii mezhdunarodnykh otnoshenii*. Leningrad, 1972.

Thaden, E.C. *Russia and the Balkan Alliance of 1912*. University Park, Pennsylvania, 1965.

Trachtenberg, Marc. "The Meaning of Mobilization in 1914," *International Security* 15, no. 3 (1990–1991), pp. 120–50.

Treadgold, Donald W. *The Development of the USSR*. Seattle, Wash., 1964.

Trumpener, U. "Liman von Sanders and the German-Ottoman Alliance." *Journal of Contemporary History* 1 (1966).

Turnbull, David. "The Defeat of Popular Representation, December 1904: Prince Mirskii, Witte, and the Imperial Family." *Slavic Review* 48, no. 1 (Spring 1989), pp. 54–70.

Turner, L.C.F. "The Russian Mobilisation in 1914." *Journal of Contemporary History* 3 (1968), pp. 65–88.

Verner, Andrew M. *The Crisis of Russian Autocracy: Nicholas II and the 1905 Revolution*. Princeton, 1990.

Viatkin, M.P., ed., *Monopolii i inostrannyi kapital v Rossi*. Moscow and Leningrad, 1962.

von Laue, Theodore H., "The Chances for Liberal Constitutionalism." *Slavic Review* 24, no. 1 (1965), pp. 34–46.

Vucinich, Wayne. *Serbia between East and West, 1903–1908*. Stanford, Calif., 1954.

Waldron, Peter. *Between Two Revolutions: Stolypin and the Politics of Renewal in Russia*. London, 1998.

Warth, D.C. "Before Rasputin: Piety and the Occult at the Court of Nicholas II." *Historian* 47 (1985), pp. 323–37.

Wcislo, Francis W. "Bureaucratic Reform before World War One." *Russian History* 16, nos. 2–4 (1989), pp. 377–87.

Weber, Eugen. *France Fin de Siècle*. Cambridge, Mass., 1986.

Weeks, Theodore R., "Polish-Jewish Relations, 1903–1914: The View from the Chancellery." *Canadian Slavonic Papers* 60, nos. 3–4 (1998), pp. 233–249.

White, J.A. *The Diplomacy of the Russo-Japanese War*. Princeton, 1974.

Williams, Beryl J. "The Revolution of 1905 and Russian Foreign Policy." In *Essays in Honour of E.H. Carr*. London, 1974.

—————. "The Strategic Background to the Anglo-Russian Entente of August 1907." *The Historical Journal* 9, no. 3 (1966), pp. 360–73.

Wilson, K. "The Agadir Crisis: The Mansion House Speech and the Double-Edgedness of Agreements." *Historical Journal* 15, no. 3 (1972).

—————. "The British Demarche of 3 and 4 December 1912: H.A. Gwynne's Note on Britain, Russia and the First Balkan War." *Slavonic and East European Review* 62, no. 4 (1984), pp. 552–59.

—————. *The Policy of the Entente: Essays on the Determinants of British Foreign Policy, 1904–1914*. Cambridge, U.K., 1985.

Wortman, Richard. "Invisible Threads: The Historical Imagery of the Romanov Tercentary." *Russian History* 16, nos. 2–4 (1989), pp. 389–408.

Yaney, George L. "The Concept of the Stolypin Land Reform." *Slavic Review* 23 (1964), pp. 275–93.

—————. *The Systematization of Russian Government*. Urbana, Ill., 1973.

Yapp, M.A. "British Perceptions of the Russian Threat to India." *Modern Asian Studies* 21, no. 4, (1987), pp. 647–65.

Index

About the Author

FIONA K. TOMASZEWSKI is Professor of History at John Abbott College in Sainte Anne de Bellevue Quebec.